Christmas '96

Dear Olly,.

MERRY

CHRISTMAS

Love

Francis

ONE-MAN COMMITTEE

The controversial reign of the England cricket supremo

Ray Illingworth and Jack Bannister

HEADLINE

First published in 1996 by
HEADLINE BOOK PUBLISHING

10 9 8 7 6 5 4 3 2 1

British Library Cataloguing in Publication Data

Illingworth, Ray
  One-man committee: the controversial reign
  of England's cricket supremo
  1. Illingworth, Ray
  2. Cricket managers – England – Biography
  3. Cricket – England
  I.Title II. Bannister, Jack
  796.3'58'092

  ISBN 0 7472 1515 4

Typeset by Avon Dataset Ltd, Bidford-on-Avon, Warks

Printed and bound in Great Britain by
Mackays of Chatham PLC, Chatham, Kent

HEADLINE BOOK PUBLISHING
A division of Hodder Headline PLC
338 Euston Road
London NW1 3BH

CONTENTS

INTRODUCTION

Few roots penetrate deeper than those of the Yorkshireman, especially one like Raymond Illingworth. Now in his 64th year, he has lived in only six houses since his birth on 8 June 1932, and all six are within three miles of each other. Pudsey and Farsley are his dominion, and one of which he becomes ever more proud. Pudsey St Lawrence, whisper it quietly, would provide the perfect setting for a White Rose *Coronation Street*, with buildings and people still to be overtaken by the march of time. Cobblestones and tram cars are no more, but the modern architect has still to make a big impression around Pudsey and Farsley.

Pudsey's cricketing roll of honour is small but select, and includes Leonard Hutton, Herbert Sutcliffe and son Bill, Long John Tunnicliffe, Major Booth and Harry Halliday. The combined 133 England caps of Hutton and Sutcliffe were subsequently supplemented by Illingworth's 61. Sutcliffe's son Bill captained Yorkshire and also became an England selector, while Tunnicliffe and Booth were county stalwarts before the First World War, in which the latter was killed. 'Major' was not a military rank but a no-nonsense christened first name.

Illingworth shares one other thing with Hutton, Halliday and Tunnicliffe – the absence of a second forename. Somehow it seems fitting that having, presumably, thought long and hard about names, their respective parents decided that one was enough – and a no-nonsense one, of course. Choices such as Wayne, Gary, Shane, Dean and Kirk are quite rare in the West Ridings.

I have known Illingworth since 1955, when we played our one and only game together for MCC against Gloucestershire at Lord's.

1

My Warwickshire captain, the late 'Tom' Dollery, was so impressed with Illingworth's all-round abilities – five for 60 from 29 overs in the match, and 39 out of a partnership of 106 in 70 minutes with Dollery – that he organised an official approach to Yorkshire for the services of the then uncapped all-rounder.

In those times before the advent of the specially registered overseas cricketer, Yorkshire provided a steady stream of exports to other counties, few of which were without a Tyke, but any official approach for a player usually concentrated the mind of chairman Brian Sellers, as it did with Illingworth, who was awarded his county cap a few weeks later.

I played against him regularly until the late 1960s, and watched with interest how the modern game's most astute cricketing brain took tactical appraisal to depths unique in English postwar cricket. Dollery became the first full-time professional county captain, and was easily the shrewdest cricketer I played with, but Illingworth had the advantage of being able to think like both a batsman and a bowler. Add to that an early appreciation of the golden rule that a sportsman should always try to do what the opposition likes least, his understanding of turf and its behaviour under different climatic conditions, and the best of all postwar chairmen of selectors was beginning a successful course in the hardest subject of all – how to outwit county and international opponents, some of whom might have possessed superior cricketing skills.

Illingworth's approach to cricket reflects his attitude to life. No frills. Be honest and straightforward, even to the point of a bluntness that some regard as unnecessary. He has never made a secret of the fact that he is not one of nature's altruists, but a refusal to suffer fools at any price can be unfairly interpreted as something akin to selfishness. Certainly he rarely embarks on anything without careful consideration of personal consequences, but he wears that attitude as a badge of pride. In his local vernacular, 'If you can get the penny and the bun, you've done well.'

He enjoys the story concerning himself and Brian Close, when a friend of both was asked how he would have reacted to serving in the trenches with each in turn as his commanding officer. The considered verdict was this: 'Closey, without a single glance to see whether anyone was following, would leap over the top and charge at the enemy regardless of odds, the disposition of the troops and guns, without a thought about whether there was cover. Illy would call for a full intelligence report on the enemy's strength and positions, a detailed survey of the terrain between us, an up-to-date report from the Met Office, a final check on the men and weapons of his own forces, and then would probably be against going because the odds were wrong.'

Critics maintain that Illingworth was a fine cricketer and a good captain, but little more. They quote his return to Yorkshire as manager in 1979 as proof of a misjudgement which they say was carried into man management. Certainly, his simple approach to life – 'nowt for nowt', and always speak your mind – was never likely to succeed in a turbulent political maelstrom, the like of which even one of Pudsey's most famous sons had never seen before.

His path to the Test selection chair has been interesting, and one down which he had no great wish to go after several brushes with the Establishment as England captain. As captain of his country, he did not suffer the first of only five defeats in 31 Tests until the 20th, and successfully defended the Ashes after becoming only the fourth England captain in the 20th century to regain the Ashes in Australia – 'Plum' Warner (1903–04), Johnny Douglas (1911–12) and Douglas Jardine (1932–33) were the others before, uniquely since the Second World War, Illingworth won them back in 1970–71. Michael Atherton was the 13th man to lead his country in Australia since 1946, of whom only Illingworth, Hutton, Mike Brearley and Mike Gatting were successful.

Even that triumph 25 years ago was marred by a breakdown in the relationship between Illingworth and the tour manager, David Clark. Such a captaincy–managerial marriage was made a long way from heaven, and it was inevitable that two men from such widely differing backgrounds would approach touring problems from viewpoints that proved to be incompatible. At least that incompatibility led to a more enlightened method of choosing the manager, with the captain now usually chosen first, and then his views taken into account. It seems that Clark was chosen before the people concerned knew that Illingworth would be captain. This curious situation probably arose because the Board had been in existence for only two years, and many lines of procedure were still blurred with the MCC, who had always traditionally been responsible for England overseas touring parties.

Illingworth has this to say of his manager.

Illingworth
I started off the tour with an open mind but by the end of it I was forced to tell him that I honestly believed he was more of an asset to the Australians than to us. I told him he was there

as team manager, not as an ambassador of goodwill on behalf of MCC. We wanted all the help we could get. For instance, when the Australians wanted an extra Test to compensate for the rain-ruined one at Melbourne, we discovered that their players were being paid an extra fee. The manager refused, and it was getting to the stage of a mutiny, because we had one or two militants in the side and, anyway, I agreed with them. We didn't want to play the extra match – that meant five Tests in six weeks – and eventually Mr Clark agreed to ring Lord's and came back with an offer of £25, which was much less than the 200 dollars a man the Aussies were getting.

I know we made a stand on money, but it was the principle as well. The extra Test at Melbourne was drawing over 50,000 a day and the third day produced world record receipts of £25,070, so why should the players be short-changed out of a decent fee for an extra match which produced so much cash?

I knew we were not on the same wavelength when, earlier in the tour, he publicly stated that he would rather Australia win the series than have all the matches drawn. And then there was his reaction during the bottle-throwing incident in the Sydney Test when I took the players off the field because of the crowd's behaviour. He was adamant we had to go back on, and I was equally determined we would not until things were sorted out.

It was a tour in which the results were good, but the relationship between the manager, and me and the rest of the players was not.

Those differences of opinion with Clark, together with Illingworth's decision not to tour India and Pakistan three years later, were perceived by him to have precipitated his removal from the England captaincy, following a 2–0 defeat in the home three-match series against West Indies in 1973.

His next involvement at England level was so short – a few minutes when he was spoken to about the new England post of coach which was eventually filled by Micky Stewart in 1985 – that it seemed he would quietly play out his working life with BBC television and the *Daily Express*.

How and why he got the call to the colours is fascinating, as is an analysis of his hands-on approach to the post of chairman of selectors, which has been held by only six other men in the last 40 years – 'Gubby' Allen, Walter Robins, Doug Insole, Alec Bedser, Peter May and Ted Dexter.

Typically, Illingworth laid down his pre-conditions which, also typically, included a bottom-line executive responsibility which was denied him when he was interviewed for the post awarded to Stewart nine years earlier.

His first two years as chairman were to be littered with controversial brushes with the media, culminating with the blow-up with Devon Malcolm at the end of the tour to South Africa. Illingworth is not the sort of man to court favourable publicity, yet is often upset at the methods used by the media to denigrate him. They accuse him of double dealing, in that he is quick to take the credit for success, but equally quick to deflect criticism to other people regarding adverse results.

At the end of his first year as chairman, he could point to a good home summer against New Zealand and South Africa, followed by a poor tour of Australia in which he ruffled many feathers by his willingness to go into print from 12,000 miles away. His short trip to Australia in the middle of the Ashes tour was to inflame further the section of the media that was determined to propagate so-called evidence of a bitter feud between Illingworth and Michael Atherton.

Such a theory did not square remotely with the facts, yet it was consistently written from as early as his first weeks in office between the end of the tour of West Indies and the beginning of the 1994 English season. Even when Illingworth's action to save Atherton from the probable loss of the captaincy after the Lord's Test against South Africa made clear his wish to keep him as captain, the theory was repeated so often that he could have been forgiven for thinking there was a campaign to bring him down.

The journalists now know they had the wrong man. In his first two years, he was faced with two major issues of a magnitude rarely, if ever, faced by a chairman of selectors. He killed the Atherton dirt-in-pocket affair within hours as far as the authorities were concerned by swift and decisive action.

A year later, also at Lord's, he took the unprecedented action of re-selecting the England side against West Indies by dropping wicket-keeper Steve Rhodes from the XIII to allow Alec Stewart to keep wicket. The easy thing would have been to have left the original selection unaltered but, once he discovered the original information conveyed to him was, unwittingly, wrong, he had the strength of mind to act.

No one man has had so much power in English cricket at selection and managerial level. According to the media, no one man has ever been at such odds with his captain, but history will tell a different story.

The Illingworth–Atherton axis survived the traumas of the Australian tour, on and off the field. It then forged a spirited attitude among players, senior and junior alike, which earned a drawn series against the West Indies, and followed with a tour of South Africa which, but for one mad hour in which a tenth-wicket partnership turned the series upside down, might have been crowned with success.

The swift disintegration of the last 17 days of that tour should not cloud a general picture of a fighting England side which drew Tests at The Wanderers and Port Elizabeth that would probably have been lost in the pre-Illingworth era. Such determination had also been displayed against the West Indies at Old Trafford, Trent Bridge and The Oval.

Illingworth's second year in office also tells much about the man. There is his mental hardness. He has a stubborn streak which borders on the intransigent. He also has a tendency – maybe an eagerness – to shoot from the lip which would often be turned against him by journalists, and would therefore upset players.

Illingworth is a man who will not be deflected once he has made a decision. Unsubtle he might be, abrasive also. Dogmatic and single-minded to the point of being blinkered are other appraisals of his character that, at times, are near the mark.

Critics see those traits as faults. Illingworth sees them as strengths which earned him a job in which he has taken great pride. Pride. One dictionary definition says 'a proper sense of what is becoming to oneself and scorn of what is unworthy.'

That is Raymond Illingworth's philosophy on life: scorn of what is unworthy. And that is what drives the man on, regardless of the consequences. He did not ask for the job. He did not need it, financially, or from any other angle, except for a pride in cricket and his country. He accepted it because he thought he could do a job. And he has.

This book was not written as a diary, but neither was it written from hindsight. The original idea was that it would cover Illingworth's first year as chairman but, at his request, publication was delayed for a year which would therefore allow a second home series, followed by the tour of South Africa, to be included. Judgements made at the time in his first year have not been altered, and the result is an account from England's first supremo of events as he saw them at the time.

Part I
INTO THE FRAY

1
THE APPROACH

Ted Dexter resigned as chairman of the selectors in early August 1993, during the fifth Test against Australia at Edgbaston, six months before the end of his five-year appointment, yet Illingworth was not approached for a further four months, and then only after a curious procedural tug-of-war involving a number of county chairmen who sought to dilute the influence of the Test and County Cricket Board's executive committee.

Their intention to appoint M.J.K. Smith as Dexter's immediate successor before the end of the season was sufficiently advanced for them to seek and receive an agreement from Smith that an announcement could be made, only for the block to be put on by those chairmen who believed the time had come to review the position of the England committee.

Also, during Dexter's time as chairman of the committee, several county chairmen were unhappy at the appointment of Keith Fletcher as Stewart's successor for five years, without what they saw as proper discussions by the full Board. A body such as the TCCB is unwieldy, and only through a small executive committee can the day-to-day running of English cricket be successfully accomplished.

Nevertheless, the poor results of the national team, together with an increasing feeling of dissatisfaction about relations with the media, and a growing feeling among the official club delegates that they were being bypassed too often in important decisions, led to an instruction to chief executive Alan Smith to defer any announcement until the full Board had met. Dexter's appointment in March 1989 had caused similar misgivings, mainly because he held his first press conference before his appointment had been rubber-stamped by the

March Board meeting. The then chairman, Raman Subba Row, played a leading part in that appointment, together with the formation of the new England committee, and the county chairmen were determined that those procedural mistakes should not be repeated.

Illingworth

The first approach I got was a phone call from the Yorkshire president, Sir Lawrence Byford. It was in December 1993, and he asked me if I was interested in Yorkshire putting my name forward. At that stage, I never really thought anything would come of it, because I knew that Mike Smith was a front-runner, and I thought the clubs would go for him. Of course I was pleased to be asked, but I honestly thought my time had come and gone when I refused to take things any further with the England coach's job a few years before.

Sometimes, I find it hard to understand why the authorities want to employ someone, yet won't give him the power and responsibility to carry his ideas through. I have always been my own man, and I think my track record shows that I can do a good job. I have never been any different, and now I never will. If I believe in something, I will fight for it all the way. Also I have never believed in going behind people's backs. Sometimes you have to persuade people, and I know you can't deal with everyone on the same basis. But that does not alter my basic philosophy. Be straight, and at least everyone knows where they stand.

I got to know Illingworth well during the period between 1986 and 1992, when neither of us missed a televised Test match in England, and also commentated for the BBC on their only overseas commitment, the World Cup in India and Pakistan in 1987. Each Test match is a week out of your life, and with most commentary boxes on the small side, an eight-hour day, for five successive days, provides a wall-to-wall cosy environment in which it is easy for the odd difference of opinion to fester.

That it never did during those seven English seasons says much for the personnel in the box, which included three Test captains in Illingworth, Richie Benaud and Tony Lewis – and a fourth in Geoffrey Boycott, who led England four times. Having played against Illingworth about two dozen times, I soon realised I hardly knew him until we shared a microphone. There can be no easier man to work with. No need to think how to phrase a question. No need to explain what you, as commentator, want from him as an expert.

He is not a natural broadcaster, but that is a strength, not a weakness as some critics say, because if he has nothing worth saying he will not waffle. Like Lester Piggott, he goes straight to the heart of the matter, and does not believe in wasting words. Like Boycott, his content is flawless but, unlike his former county and Test colleague – whose parents also tested the memory of the vicar at his christening with only one forename – he does not hammer his point home. Let your attention wander and you miss him whereas, with Geoffrey, you can often go off and make a cup of tea and still get the message.

It is worth expanding upon his television involvement, because it played a big part in his nomination for the vacant chairmanship of the England selectors. Those administrators with the ear of the players were well aware of the respect he commanded from cricketers young enough to be his son – even grandson, at least as far as John Crawley is concerned.

It was a rare home Test match in which at least one England player did not approach him for advice. Similarly with umpires who, at the pleasant after-match drinks get-together organised by Cornhill Insurance, would take without umbrage any Illingworth view about a decision he thought they had got wrong. Umpires like David Shepherd, Dickie Bird, Kenny Palmer, Jack Hampshire *et al.* trusted him because they spoke the same language. Also, they knew that he fully appreciated the demands of their job, and would offer a view only when asked.

He was a regular, welcome visitor in every committee room on the Test match circuit – all of which must have helped when his hat was finally slipped into the ring.

The process of organising the hat-tossing competition began a month after Dexter announced his departure. A special meeting of clubs was held at Edgbaston in October, and it was agreed to review the role of the England committee. The delegates met again at the winter Board meeting in December and decided to split the duties of the England committee into two. An old-style selection committee would be chaired by the new man, and to recommend that man, a working party would be set up to consider candidates. Additionally, a new development committee would be established and the England committee disbanded.

The Board's chairman, Frank Chamberlain, would preside over a four-man working party comprising chief executive Alan Smith, former cricket chairman Ossie Wheatley, and two county chairmen. It was left to the first three officials to appoint the other two, and Worcestershire's Duncan Fearnley and David Acfield of Essex were chosen in early January 1994.

As for the development committee, that was finalised and confirmed at the March Board meeting that year, and would include M.J.K. Smith as chairman, the England captain, manager and chairman of selectors, the chairman of cricket – now Acfield – Alan Smith, and the Board's new chairman, Dennis Silk. This group was to develop cricket throughout the country.

The choice of Fearnley and Acfield was significant, and reflected the need to call on as much former playing and current administrative experience as possible.

Fearnley was one of the main driving forces behind his county's emergence in the mid-1980s as a big-money club, following the signing of Ian Botham and Graham Dilley. The new chairman of Essex, David Acfield, was, at the age of 47, the youngest member of the working party by several years, and had played regular county cricket until well into the 1980s.

The two men provided a nice contrast in character. Both were former players, Acfield with more success, and both possessed an enthusiasm for the game which, coupled with keen cricketing brains, made them ideal as members of a brains trust whose task was to put the England cricket train back on track after several shapeless years. Alan Smith and Wheatley, both of whom were educated at King Edward's High School in Birmingham, were members of the former England committee, while Chamberlain was the successor as Board chairman to Subba Row, who was the prime force behind Dexter's appointment.

The Dexter vision extended much further than picking a few teams, but several factors conspired against him. He got off to the worst possible start when Wheatley vetoed his first choice as captain in March 1989 – Mike Gatting.

Wheatley acted upon what he saw as a matter of principle regarding the Shakoor Rana affair in Pakistan in 1987, but an even bigger principle surely was the one in which a new overlord of selection was denied his first choice for the most important appointment of all. Not only would the veto be made public at a later date, it would also do little for the next man in line – in this case David Gower – to know he had got the job by default.

It is to the eternal credit of Gatting that, having quickly found out about the veto, he kept it to himself throughout a summer in which he finally became so disenchanted with the authorities that he was more vulnerable than most to an offer from South Africa. Within a couple of weeks of discovery of what he saw as unfair retrospective action concerning his tour of Pakistan in 1987, he tackled Alan Smith in public about the existence of a veto on selection.

It happened at an annual general meeting of the Cricketers' Association at Edgbaston in April of that year. Smith agreed to attend to explain his Board's policy on several issues. When Gatting asked about a veto, virtually everyone among the 100 people present assumed he was talking about the possibility of cricketers being vetoed from selection for England, even after serving their time for any unauthorised cricketing visit to South Africa.

I listened to the game of verbal ping-pong between Gatting and Smith, in which the latter would insist that, while the veto was in existence, he was sure it would never be used. Gatting then asked why there was a veto, if it would not be implemented. Smith said that it was there because the counties wanted it, but repeated that it would never be used. 'In which case, why have it?' 'Because the counties want it.' And so on, with none of us aware that Gatting had a primed hand grenade in his pocket although, to his credit, he did not pull the pin. Such an action would have embarrassed the Board and would have brought the heavy guns of the national press to bear on a situation which, as far as Dexter was concerned, must have bordered on the untenable.

The news dribbled out several months later – not from Gatting, but because of a leak of Dexter's first report to the board after his first season in charge – and so started a feeling of disquiet among those county officials who did not see the England committee as the panacea envisaged by its original supporters. It was a mistake to include selection among a much wider and praiseworthy range of duties, as was recognised by the decision to revert after five home summers.

The counties forced a switch of the veto from Wheatley to the chairman of the Board, now Chamberlain, and Gatting led the ill-fated trip to South Africa.

It would have taken an imaginative mind to forecast a scenario, five years later, in which an appointee presumably approved by Wheatley – namely Illingworth – would restore Gatting into the England touring party.

So how did such an apparent official volte-face come about? The input of Fearnley and Acfield must have been crucial, representing, as they believed, a strand of opinion among the counties that the national side and its selection needed a change of direction. In particular, the all-powerful cabal of captain and manager needed to be split. There is a fine balance between these two men having considerable input into selection and carrying all before them. Get it right, and a healthy set-up follows. Get it wrong, as Graham Gooch later admitted he did with David Gower, and it is a recipe for disaster. An effective selection committee must have checks and balances, simply because no one man has infallible judgement.

The working party drew up its list of runners, headed by the then favourite, M.J.K. Smith, now on duty as manager on the tour of the West Indies. They could approach anyone, and even Tony Greig was considered among at least 20 names who were discussed.

Had Greig been appointed, the wheel would have completed a bigger circle than any other in history, following what most people at Lord's thought in 1977 was a betrayal of the highest playing office in English cricket, the captaincy, when Greig acted as agent for Kerry Packer.

The preliminary talk with Greig amounted to nothing more once he was told that he would have to give up his varied media work, but it says much for the determination of the working party to consider all possible candidates that the former England captain was not excluded. Hampshire's Mark Nicholas was also mentioned in despatches, as were Mike Brearley, Bob Willis and three Yorkshiremen – Illingworth, Boycott and Brian Close.

Brearley felt he could not spare the time and, anyway, thought he was out of touch with the modern game. Boycott, like Greig, could hardly be expected to cut short a flourishing media career and, after three meetings at Lord's in February, the shortlist contained two names – Mike Smith and Illingworth. The lines were hot between NW8 and Torremolinos where the Yorkshireman has wintered for many years. He was already contracted to the *Daily Express* and could expect more BBC television work, although not so much as in previous years. He had already been told by executive producer Keith Mackenzie that he would not be used for the three Tests against South Africa, which meant he would miss his first-ever Test in the commentary box since he started in 1984. He commented: 'Keith did not give me a specific reason why he offered me less work, but I assume it was because of the decision to employ Geoff Boycott and David Gower.'

His media fees were discussed and it was agreed that, should he be successful in the postal vote held before the March 1994 Board meeting, a sum of £25,000 would be paid to him for each of two years. Talk of a higher figure was wrong, as was a literal interpretation of the word 'compensation'.

What the TCCB did was to agree to match his media earnings. Put another way, they were prepared to employ Illingworth at an annual salary of £25,000, plus expenses for travel and hotels on what turned out to be over 100 days' work in his first summer.

Illingworth

The next contact I had after Sir Lawrence Byford sounded me out in December was a call from Lord's in late January. By now, the idea appealed to me for several reasons. Like everyone else, I felt we had not made the most of our talent in recent years, and I did not agree with some of the selections and policies. For instance, too much time was spent in what I saw as the wrong sort of training. It would have been acceptable if the cricketing fitness improved, but the reverse seemed to be true. Hardly a quick bowler stayed fit, and I was sure that a lot of races were being left on the gallops.

Take the bowlers. Bowling for a living is an unnatural exercise which calls for muscles to be used in a different way from other sports. The quicks need a strong back and legs – a good arse, we say in Yorkshire – and their fitness has to have a strong element of endurance. Fred Trueman was the perfect example. I know he sometimes goes on a bit about what he did and how he did it, but the point is that he actually did most of what he says. He had a magnificent action and hardly ever missed a match because of injury. That is why he bowled over 1000 overs in most seasons. He played over 600 first-class games in 20 years, and took 2304 wickets from 16,643 overs, so he must have done something right. That's a strike rate of a wicket every 43 balls, and he took one every 49 balls for England – that's better than every other England bowler since the war, and better than every other Test bowler in the same period, except for Waqar Younis and Malcolm Marshall.

The point is that bowling fitness is like no other, and that is what I want to try to get back into our cricket.

I spoke over the phone to the working party, and I told them how I would operate. I asked for – and got – an assurance I would have the final say, and that was the most important thing of all to me. If I do a job, I want to do it well, and it is vital that I am in charge. It is not a matter of an ego trip – rather that I

15

have always been keen for responsibility, and everyone then knows where the buck stops. I don't hide from anything or anybody, and I told the working party that I was quite prepared to be judged on results, and therefore I would be accountable.

Once Illingworth agreed to be nominated, the work of Messrs Chamberlain, Smith, Wheatley, Fearnley and Acfield was done. Their shortlist comprised two men, Mike Smith and Illingworth, who offered the counties the perfect choice of contrasts, with common denominators of age and career experience that included distinguished captaincy of county and country. Illingworth is a year older, and played 11 more times for his country, and captained in six more Tests. Both men played county cricket from the early 1950s until the mid-1970s, with Illingworth's subsequent return to Yorkshire bringing him the captaincy at the age of 51.

The main cricketing contrast was in their records as captain of England. Illingworth won 12 matches, drew 14 and lost five, while Smith won five and lost three of his 25 games in charge, with 17 drawn. Both men were innately cautious, but Illingworth possibly had a more flexible tactical approach because of his bowling ability.

The real contrasts were in background. Frances Street School and Wesley Street School in Farsley do not have quite the same ring as Stamford and St Edmund Hall, Oxford, and both men played on opposite sides in the traditional Gentlemen v. Players game fixture at Lord's, which ended in 1963 when cricket dispensed with the twin tags of amateur and professional and went open.

After playing, Smith graduated naturally to administration, both at Edgbaston, where he is now chairman, and at Lord's, where he sits on several key committees, including development and registration. It is an over-simplification to say that Smith is an Establishment man and Illingworth is not, but typical Yorkshire bluntness is in direct contrast to Smith's apparently diffident and reserved manner, which can be dangerously misleading. I know both men, and they share a toughness, even a stubbornness, that can withstand great pressure.

The final decision between them had to be made on the issue of which was the better judge of a player, and which was the stronger man in committee. The latter point was important, once the Board decided to revert to an old-style selection committee, because the new man's first task would be to break down the top-heavy influence of the captain – even a young man like Atherton, whose stamp had been firmly put on the touring party to the West Indies.

The postal vote was reportedly close – how close only Alan Smith knows, and there is more chance of the Vatican making a book on the next Pope than 'A.C.' releasing that sort of information – with Mike Smith possibly suffering from a reaction among the county chairmen against the initial wish of their executive committee to install him with undue haste after Dexter's resignation. Another factor in Illingworth's favour was the working party's decision to include him on their shortlist, knowing that Smith was already the choice of the executive. That can be construed in two ways: as a gesture to that body that fuller consultation with Board members was needed on such important policy decisions, or as a nod and a wink to voting members that the working party had found the best man for the job.

Undeniably, the counties were pleased that they were seen to be involved, and they felt that by voting they had contributed to a shift of direction in the running of the England team.

Either way, Illingworth was flown from Spain to attend the spring Board meeting in early March, when his appointment was officially confirmed and he met the press. For the first time at selection level, England had a man in charge who would run the show and deliberately maintain a high profile. As near as dammit, he wanted open government, mainly because the Illingworth neck was on the block.

Reaction to the appointment varied from an enthusiastic one from Ian Chappell to one of derision from Ian Botham. The former England all-rounder mocked Illingworth's age, and glibly stated that no man who had been out of Test cricket for over 20 years could possibly be in tune with the modern cricketer.

What Botham overlooked was that a shrewd and varied working party had chosen the best man for the job, irrespective of age or any of the so-called pro-Establishment views that Botham constantly denounces. He surely could not have believed, had he thought about it, that the instinctive judgement of cricket and its players which stood Illingworth, England, Yorkshire and Leicestershire in such good stead for over 20 years had suddenly deserted the man once he passed the age of 60? Furthermore, had Botham ever listened closely to Illingworth's television views, either as a player or on the odd occasion when he shared the same summariser's microphone, he would have realised that the content was rock-solid and never destructive. Botham has many qualities, but the ability to refrain from shooting from the lip is not one of them.

Chappell's view was apposite. 'Illy was the best captain I played against. He had and still has a good cricket brain, and he was always straight and aggressive. I think he is a good judge, and it is one of the best moves England have made in a long time.'

2
FIRST MONTH IN CHARGE

What qualities did Illingworth think he would bring to the job?

Illingworth
Firstly, I have always been a good watcher. Some cricketers don't like to watch when their side is batting, but I always have. Perhaps that is why my mind has always been trained to note what is going on in the middle, and why. It was always second nature to me to think a game through as it developed. Even in my young days with Yorkshire, I would always think about bowling and fielding changes, probably because I was brought up in a hard school. We could nearly field a team of Test cricketers, and while most of them would help you, it was normal Yorkshire practice for a youngster mostly to make his own way. It was rather like the approach by some Test captains – Colin Cowdrey, for instance – who believed if you were good enough to play for your country, you should not need telling how to play.

I agree with that as far as technique is concerned, because a player should not experiment with a change in method during a Test match. The time for that is back with his club and in his own nets. But I know, as captain, that at times you have got to tell some players what you want – be it quick runs with the bat, or a few tight overs with the ball. Games ebb and flow, and a good captain should always be flexible enough to have more than one game plan – especially in Test cricket where there are players who can suddenly take a match right away from you in a couple of sessions, unless you are able to counter them with something different.

Just think of that last mad session on the Friday evening of the Oval Test match against South Africa when Phil DeFreitas and Darren Gough hit their quicks all over The Oval. Perhaps it was because South Africa have only been back in Test cricket for a couple of years, but it surprised me a bit that Kepler Wessels just stood back and let it happen. He switched his bowlers, but not his field placings, and it didn't add up to have two or even three slips while the ball was disappearing to all corners in front of the wicket. In under an hour a potential lead for them of over 100 shrank almost to nothing, and that is where the game started to swing our way.

I also believe I am a good judge of a player. I don't have to see a cricketer score a lot of runs or take a stack of wickets for him to prove to me that he can play. Whatever anyone says about the modern game and how different it is from my day, basics are basics and always will be. What I find hard to understand is why so many of our batsmen have gone away from orthodox grip, stance and backlift. It's like golf – you can't get very far if the set-up is wrong. It governs everything, and you have got to have a method which repeats automatically.

Tony Greig started the stance with the bat held high, and I know Graham Gooch still does it, but I reckon he succeeds in spite of that, not because of it. I know he says it helps him to keep a still head and Greigy did it because of the extra pace of Jeff Thomson and Dennis Lillee, but why has there never been an Australian or West Indian who has ever tried it? Or Indian come to that. All the best players have stood with the bat grounded in order to make the pick-up a one-piece thing starting from the ground and not hip height. It is no coincidence that Graeme Hick seems a better player for England since he adopted a more orthodox stance with the bat now grounded first.

The same with bowlers. The first thing I look for is do they have a nice action, preferably sideways – and certainly so for the spinner. Even when I was playing at 51, I still made sure I got round and, as a result, I could spin it more than if I was chest-on, with the bowling arm and hand having nothing to pivot round. You can succeed the other way. Lance Gibbs did, but he was a far better bowler overseas where he could get bounce on the harder wickets with his natural loop. When he played for Warwickshire, he eventually learned to bowl around the wicket, but he never liked it, mainly I reckon because of his lack of a pivot which was shown up even more from around the wicket.

Again, look at Richie Benaud, who had a beautiful action in which he would look at the batsman across the outside of the left elbow and not inside it. Providing a right-arm slow bowler holds that position and leads with the left arm and shoulder throughout most of the action, he is bound to spin it more, if only because of the better hand and wrist action.

As for the faster bowlers, everything for them depends upon the hand action. I know some unorthodox bowlers produce the right results, despite a poor body action and feet placement, but, just like the batting pick-up I was talking about, they do it in spite of their unorthodoxy, not because of it. Phil Newport is a good example of someone who a coach would never think could swing a ball away. He is front-on, and looks bound to duck the ball in, but he has learned how to keep the wrist behind the ball and release it with the seam on a track towards the slips. Tom Cartwright was another one who learned to bowl the outswinger chest-on, and the inswinger with a nice sideways action, but that sort of bowler is an exception.

Phil DeFreitas and Devon Malcolm are the other sort – bowlers who depend upon not falling away as they deliver the ball. If they do, they are gone, but look what they did two summers ago, with DeFreitas only having one poor Test and Devon destroying South Africa at The Oval.

I can spot things in cricketers, some of them only small details, but often it is only a tiny adjustment that is needed. Another quality I think I bring to the job is that I always love to talk cricket to anyone, anywhere, at any time. My captaincy experience has taught me how to communicate, as well as how to deal with different players in different ways. My relationship with John Snow in 1970 was a typical example. He annoyed me with his attitude in the field, and I could easily have bounced him in front of the other players, who were brassed off with him anyway. Instead, I got him in my room and treated him like a sensible bloke. As a result, he delivered everything I asked and we won the Ashes.

When I was appointed as chairman, I realised that I had inherited very little from Ted Dexter – except a new captain in Michael Atherton. In a way, that was a good thing, because I could begin with a clean sheet and impose different selection policies. I also think it is important to give young players the security of two or three games when you first pick them. For instance, I did that with Dennis Amiss and Keith Fletcher, both of whom became fine Test batsmen after starting poorly.

Illingworth has picked two prime examples of keeping faith with perceived ability. Amiss scored 361 in his first 21 innings, passing 50 only once at Headingley against Pakistan in 1971, while Fletcher's first 536 Test runs took him 29 innings, with only two half-centuries. By coincidence, both young batsmen broke through on the tour to India and Pakistan on which Illingworth would not go.

Amiss scored 497 in 12 innings, including two hundreds and a 99, while Fletcher scored 514 in 14 innings, including a hundred, 97 and four other scores over 50. To summarise, between them Amiss and Fletcher followed an aggregate of 897 runs for England in 50 innings with 1030 in 26 innings.

Illingworth's appointment in early March gave the eager media plenty of scope for the 'quotes' features on which so many of their editors depend. The on-going series in the West Indies provided an easy topic for headline material which Illingworth was not shy of providing. He had decided that, if it was at all possible, he would rather work with than against the journalists, which is why, typically, he never ducked a question or offered a 'no comment', even if the answer might appear provocative or controversial.

Atherton must have been anxious about some of the remarks relayed back to him about some England players in the Caribbean, and also about the balance of the side. Optimistically, as it turned out, Illingworth was emphatic about the need for a 'properly balanced five-man attack, including two spinners when conditions warrant them'. In contrast, Atherton was a member of the Gooch school which thought a sixth batsman was essential.

Remember that the side that went 3–0 down to the West Indies and then recovered prestige and pride with the win in Barbados and the draw in Lara's match in Antigua was mostly Atherton's. He had publicly gone for youth and new faces, with the avowed intention of giving them a good run to prove themselves. Now here was a new chairman saying that he meant to have the last say, and as some players had already had ample opportunities to prove themselves, they would not be given many more chances unless they delivered. Hick was one who was under the microscope, and Chris Lewis another.

But firstly, the make-up of the remainder of the selection committee had to be determined.

Illingworth

It was important that we had the right committee if we were to work in the way I wanted. Firstly, I decided to do away with the observers, mainly because I felt they were not able to give me the sort of feedback I wanted. It was a good idea in theory, which I felt had not worked. For instance, a geographical split of their duties meant that they only saw certain cricketers at home under the same conditions, which I thought could be misleading. I wanted a couple of men I knew well, and whose thinking was similar to mine. Dennis Amiss was still a selector, although he was the new chief executive for Warwickshire. It was thought at one time he might do both jobs, but I couldn't see that. Not for the sort of job I wanted the selectors to have. I know other people in Dennis's position have been a selector – A.C. Smith, for instance – but I wanted the new men to be watching more cricket.

That way, we would have more first-hand information to swap in meetings, compared with reports from observers who would not be there and therefore unable to help us with things we might want to know which were not in the report. It would mean a lot more legwork for us, but I saw that as our best chance of doing the job properly. Various names were circulated to the counties to vote upon, and it is only partly true to say that I chose Fred Titmus and Brian Bolus. What I did do was star my preferences, and I was pleased that the counties went with me, but they need not have done so. There was some comment about not choosing David Graveney as a current player, but I honestly felt he could not see enough cricket to justify a place on the committee. Also there were bound to be problems in arranging selection meetings. We had enough trouble fitting in with the captain, and there would have been times when Graveney could not have travelled from wherever Durham were playing. Phil Sharpe and Bob Cottam were also on the voting list.

As for Fred and Brian, I knew them both well, and felt we could work together. They are very different in character. Fred is the quiet one, and Brian is never silent, but I knew they both cared passionately about English cricket, and therefore we could make a decent team. Like me, they were able to put in as much time as it took, so for the first time we had three full-time selectors. That meant we could watch everyone under consideration, and we first met at the Champion County (Middlesex) v. England 'A' at Lord's on 21 April.

We went through the fixture list until the end of May, and then drew up a list of over 50 players, which included everyone we thought had even a slight chance of playing for England. We saw them all by the end of May, so we did things methodically. Furthermore, just to show how flexible we were, the two touring teams we picked four months later to tour Australia and India included 10 players not on the list, as well as Stuart Lampitt who we put on standby for the 'A' tour. Joey Benjamin was the one 'outsider' who got into the senior side, with David Hemp, Paul Nixon, Richard Johnson, Min Patel, Michael Vaughan, Nick Knight and Paul Weekes the other nine who went to India with the 'A' squad.

To show what our original thinking was, here is the original list, split into counties.

DERBYSHIRE	DeFreitas, Cork and Malcolm
DURHAM	Morris
ESSEX	Gooch, Such, Ilott, Hussain and Stephenson
GLAMORGAN	Maynard, Croft, Morris, Watkin and Metson
GLOUCESTERSHIRE	Russell
HAMPSHIRE	Smith and Udal
KENT	McCague, Spencer and Igglesden
LANCASHIRE	Atherton, Crawley, Lloyd, Watkinson, Fairbrother, Hegg and Gallian
LEICESTERSHIRE	Millns and Mullally
MIDDLESEX	Gatting, Emburey, Tufnell, Ramprakash and Fraser
NORTHAMPTONSHIRE	Lamb, Taylor and Loye
NOTTINGHAMSHIRE	Lewis, Pollard and Johnson
SOMERSET	Caddick, Lathwell, Trump and Van Troost
SURREY	Stewart, Thorpe, both Bicknells, Brown
SUSSEX	Wells, Salisbury, Jarvis and Athey
WARWICKSHIRE	Reeve and Munton

| **WORCESTERSHIRE** | Hick, Rhodes, Illingworth and Newport |
| **YORKSHIRE** | Gough, White, Stemp and Blakey |

The list comprised 63 cricketers and, as Illingworth said, included every cricketer with the slightest chance of playing for England. The name of Athey might surprise some, as could the omission of Gladstone Small, whose revival earned him a mention in selection meetings later in the summer. Other facts of interest include 18 of the 63 playing for England against New Zealand or South Africa, with Robin Smith, Ian Salisbury, Angus Fraser, Peter Such and Paul Taylor not going to Australia, and Mike Gatting, Shaun Udal and Martin McCague the three who made that trip, despite not playing in a Test in the 1994 summer.

Illingworth's first month in charge, beginning with the Champion County fixture at Lord's against England 'A' on 21 April, was a full and lively one. His first press conference, held before England's return from the West Indies, was a typical example of the nationals' number two cricket correspondents plus several newsmen, trying to draw the new chairman into open opposition to Atherton. Micky Stewart had ended his days as coach armed with a tape recorder for such meetings with the media, but even that apparent insurance against a misquote does not solve the main problem – that of a remark taken out of context and, of course, the tabloid headlines that often shriek a message different from the following text. Where Illingworth will always score in such situations is in his ability never to swerve away from a straight answer. It is not in the man's nature to dress up a reply, nor is it to soft-pedal on what he sees as a key issue. Even though he could barely recognise the next day's press as a faithful report of what he had said, how he had said it and, more important, why, he went out of his way to accede to every request for an interview, no matter whether or not it concerned general policy or an individual player and whether he would fit into Illingworth's plans.

I was at New Road, Worcester for the New Zealand match on 4, 5, and 6 May, and watched and heard with amusement his chat with the national scribes, now back from the Caribbean. Several sides of tape were exhausted and pages of notebooks were filled with furious scribbling from delighted cricket correspondents, most of whose reporting lives had been filled with attempts to wring something out of the defensive waffle used by TCCB officials at such conferences. I had watched most England captains start by viewing relations with the media with an optimism that lasted as long as it took the first tabloid man to make something out of what the captain saw as nothing. Now it was Illingworth's turn to learn how the press related *his* utterances on the England cricket team's performances and prospects.

Men of contrasting character were inevitably sucked into a mood of non-cooperation, which manifested itself in surprising ways – varying from a scarcely veiled threat from Mike Brearley at Headingley in 1981 to a walkout by David Gower at Lord's in 1989. In the intervening period, I watched Ian Botham and Bob Willis become increasingly exasperated at what they saw as a banal form of questioning. Mike Gatting soldiered on better than most, mainly because of a transparent determination always to make the best of any situation.

Each press conference is like a game of tennis, although there is not much serve and volley on tap. Long rallies tend to develop about unimportant issues – how do you motivate the boys after such a crushing defeat, and is team spirit good? – at the expense of decent cricketing questions. I now do not attend these 'interviews' unless I have to, but often ask afterwards if the balance of selection – a spinner or an extra seamer – or the pitch had got a mention, and the answer is usually 'no'.

The press have a job to do, but their editors' obsession with quotes hamstrings men who, in different circumstances, would love to file copy that is more cricket-oriented. I have covered part or all of ten major England tours for the *Birmingham Post*, and became increasingly disenchanted with the way some of my colleagues approached their jobs. The only tour I can remember when relations between captain, manager and the media remained mostly cordial throughout was in 1985 in India – when England happened to win under the captaincy and management of Gower and Tony Brown. Such problems and concerns serve only to distract attention away from the main purpose of the tour – to win the series by identifying opposition weaknesses and enhancing the strength of your own side.

Illingworth was as bracing as an icy-cold shower. He told everyone that he would answer any question on any subject at any time from anyone – until he was let down. He said he was prepared to go off the record – always helpful for background – but woe betide anyone who attributed comments that were not officially on the record. While the game against New Zealand was in progress, he willingly discussed candidates whom he felt could address one of England's greatest weaknesses – a lack of runs in the lower middle order. He cited wicket-keeper Steve Rhodes as the sort of cricketer who could well bat at six or seven for England, and also mentioned his colleague, Phil Newport, whose considerable batting skills have still left him short of a maiden first-class hundred, mainly because he rarely bats higher than seven or eight in the powerful Worcestershire batting line-up. Illingworth was quite right to mention the all-rounder, but his comment turned out to be the ultimate batting kiss of death. Newport not only got a king pair in that match against New Zealand, but followed up with another pair in six balls in the next home match against Gloucestershire. His home batting record was slightly improved with three runs against Northamptonshire, but a duck against Essex meant that Chairman Raymond's hoped-for England all-rounder scored three runs in six home innings before he broke out with 35 on 24 June.

Rhodes was different. Since the introduction of four-day cricket, the always useful batting of the 'keeper took on another dimension. Promoted to number six by his county captain, he scored consecutive Championship hundreds towards the end of the 1993 season, added another for England 'A' in South Africa, and then hit his fourth in nine months in front of the new chairman. His unbeaten 100 against New Zealand was the best possible campaign address, and his accession to the England gloves at senior level could no longer be denied.

Illingworth

I concentrated on the quick bowlers for the first few weeks, while Fred and Brian watched the spinners. Fred had a good look at Peter Such and Shaun Udal, with the idea of playing the Hampshire lad in the one-day internationals. For several years now, I have thought he looked the most promising of the young off-spinners. He's got a nice action and spins it, and I often had a quiet word with him when the BBC televised Hampshire matches in the previous few seasons. Brian watched Kent's Min Patel and, of course, Richard Illingworth – again with the Texaco games in mind.

The only spinner I saw was Richard Stemp, who probably has the best action of them all, and I have always been impressed with his method. He does bowl from very wide of the crease, which means he has to turn it a lot from around the wicket, but although he is 27, he hadn't played 40 games before the start of the 1994 season, and he has got plenty of time to make it into the full England side.

Watching Yorkshire as I did in early May, I saw the good form Darren Gough was in, and he is my sort of player. There aren't many who are more positive, and he enjoys his cricket so much, there doesn't seem the slightest fear of failure. He's quick enough, and I marked him down as ideal for a try in the one-day games.

I also saw Derbyshire a couple of times to check up on Phil DeFreitas and Devon Malcolm. DeFreitas was impressive, mainly because he had got his outswinger back. It is worth so much to a captain if he's got at least one quick bowler who can consistently run the ball away from the right-hander, and DeFreitas had obviously worked hard in the winter playing for Boland under the guidance of Bob Woolmer. It wasn't just his bowling that was often the problem. It was his attitude. I am not saying that at times he did not try, but some cricketers' heads go down when things go against them, and that gives the same impression. I also had thought for a long time that he tended to pitch the ball half a yard too short. I remember a Test match at Edgbaston against the West Indies in 1991, when everyone said how unlucky he was because he kept on beating the bat. I pointed out on television that he was bowling too short, so when the ball did it off the pitch, it would be bound to beat everything. As kept on happening. Also, of course, a bowler sometimes has to bowl different lengths on different pitches. That certainly applies to movement off the seam, depending upon the pace of the pitch and how hard the surface is. Swing bowling is different, because you can't swing the ball from short of a length. Again, the length might vary a bit, but that is more to do with the pace of the bowler than the pitch, and Waqar Younis is a good example.

Because he is quicker than most, he only gets the big swing from full-length deliveries – yorkers most of the time because, at his speed, the ball simply will not swing earlier in its flight. Swing bowling depends upon so many factors, with the main one being the hand position at the moment of release. Someone like DeFreitas has worked it out but, because he has not got a genuine sideways action, he doesn't have to be much out of synch to lose it. He's also a lad who is sometimes short of confidence, so I told him that he would get a good run if he got more consistency into his cricket.

28

I spoke to him at Chesterfield in Derbyshire's first home four-day game against Durham, and told him what an important part of the England team he could become. I knew that Mike Atherton was a bit anti because of a few things in the past at Old Trafford. Phil said they'd fallen out and started to explain his side of it. I told him to forget it, because I have had too much experience of feuds being carried on to the detriment of both players and the side. It is pointless. Playing sport for a living is hard enough, particularly in cricket where players live and travel in each other's pockets for five months.

They spend far more time together than other sportsmen, and differences are bound to occur. If a captain does not sort them out, they fester and the side loses out. I told him that his move from Lancashire to Derbyshire had given him a fresh start, and I would ensure he started the season with a clean slate as far as England was concerned. He is such a good cricketer, but sometimes a player like that needs reassuring. I emphasised the benefit it would be to everyone if he could keep the outswinger going, and if he just got on with his cricket, I would back him to the hilt.

With his batting, consistency is also important because he is such a good natural striker, he really should get more runs. It was nonsense for him to be only averaging 12 for England at the start of the 1994 season with one fifty.

Whatever Illingworth said worked, because DeFreitas scored 207 runs in the six Tests against New Zealand and South Africa for an average close to 30, and his two fifties proved he could sustain an innings beyond 20 or 30.

Illingworth
As far as Devon was concerned, it was more a matter of seeing how fit he was, because of the knee problem he suffered in the West Indies. Derbyshire had always nursed him through a county season, which I wasn't sure was the right thing to do. I know they were trying to avoid over-bowling him, but any fast bowler needs regular cricket to sustain rhythm and the fact is that he had only played 120 games for them in 10 years, averaging around three wickets a game at a cost of 30. Allan Donald was four years younger, and made his county debut for Warwickshire three years after Devon, yet he had played as many games and taken more wickets.

I was in no doubt that Devon could be a match-winner, but it was proving an expensive gamble to pick him when you were never sure what he would do. Any fast bowler's form comes and goes, but even more so when he is being rested on a rota basis.

It was crucial as far as I was concerned to organise a reliable pace attack, but it was not going to be easy. For the last couple of years, England had tried all sorts, but most of them could not stay fit, and the anchor work was all on Gus Fraser, who bowled so well in the West Indies.

Chris Lewis was another who was getting towards his last chance. When you think that he came back from the West Indies with 25 appearances for England in 11 different series, and still only 66 wickets at 40 apiece, you realised enough was enough, unless he delivered better figures. His batting could be something special, but he had played most of his Test matches as one of four bowlers, so it was as a bowler he would have to take his chance.

The ironic thing was that Brian Bolus went to watch Kent play Nottinghamshire in early May at Canterbury, mainly to watch Duncan Spencer, Martin McCague and Alan Igglesden, and Lewis out-bowled them all. He took eight for 98 in a match Notts won by nine runs, and even though McCague and Igglesden each took seven wickets, Brian said that Lewis was the best bowler in the match. Spencer turned out to be a big disappointment, mainly because he could not stay fit and played only four games all summer. He is small for a quickie, but he has a strong action and hits the deck hard enough to shake up good players. He's only 23 and has hardly played yet, but we were prepared to look at anyone who might have that something extra which makes a Test cricketer.

I had a good look at the two Leicestershire lads, David Millns and Alan Mullally. The latter interested us, being a left-arm quickie who could offer variety, but in one way he disappointed me. He certainly beat the bat a lot, but seemed only able to move the ball one way – across the right-hander. At Test level, a left-arm pace bowler has to bring the ball back the other way, otherwise he has little chance.

Mark Ilott was also watched, but like the others he did not seem to carry the threat that genuine Test bowlers should. Aggression, penetration – call it what you like, some bowlers have it and some don't. Wicket-taking is something of a knack which the top bowlers find out about, and the ordinary ones don't. That is why I was so keen on Gough, and Craig White was beginning to get into that bracket. He had not bowled quick very long, and was mainly regarded as a batsman by Yorkshire, but as soon as I saw him switch to seam, I knew he had something. He has a good body action, and is sharp enough, even off what is only a short run. Unfortunately, Yorkshire's first two games were hit by rain and he had only bowled 13 overs in the Championship when we met to pick the squad for the two Texaco games.

We wanted to pick a squad to win the one-day games, and two batsmen we were keen to watch were John Morris and Matthew Maynard. Maynard did not look in great nick against Warwickshire and Northamptonshire, but I was impressed with Morris, who I went to see at the same time as I had a session with Graham Gooch about his long-term plans. He and I had plenty of press attention about the issue, but I didn't mind that as I regarded it as vital to our plans to know if he wanted to tour as well as play for England at home.

After all, he had just declined to go to the West Indies, and there were several times in the past when he made it clear he did not enjoy touring. I just wondered if, now that he was nearly 41 and coming to the end, he would be keener to make the most of what was left, but I was not going to pick him against New Zealand and South Africa unless he would go to Australia if picked. There was no real argument. He told me if that was what it would take to play for England again, then he would go. I was pleased, because I saw him as a vital part of our side, and someone we could build a top order around, either with him opening or batting lower down.

I was pleased to settle things within an hour or so of discussion, and told the press that I had told Gooch I could not pick someone who wanted to pick and choose when he played Test cricket. I was a bit surprised that none of them reminded me about when I opted out of the tour to India and Pakistan in 1972-73, but I didn't have to wait long. Simon Barnes in *The Times* picked it up a week or so later, but did not think to ring me up and ask me about it. Had he done so, I would have told him that I only dipped out after careful consideration. I was 41 then, and had had a long run without a break. I also had a winter job to consider, and I told the selectors straight that if I did not get the captaincy back from Tony Lewis, then I understood. I had never been to India and, at that time, hotels, travel and health in general were much more of a problem than nowadays.

Anyway, I understood the risks to my Test future, and acted accordingly.

When we met to pick the 14-man squad, I set down a few guidelines about future meetings. I wanted everyone to have their say, and I was particularly interested in the input of Mike Atherton and Keith Fletcher. I played a lot with Keith, and he had established himself as a good captain and coach with Essex.

Mike was obviously keen to stick with his players from the West Indies, but he accepted we needed a few new faces, especially for the two one-day games. We knew all about Dermot Reeve, and he has a good record in limited-overs cricket. Not only that, but we could bat him at six which helped the balance of the side. I pushed for Udal and also for Gough. The captain didn't need persuading about him, and went on record before the game as saying that he was capable of bowling as quick as anyone. Lewis caused some discussion, but we thought that, having played all five Tests in the West Indies, he should have another chance and I would make it my business to have a talk with him

We picked Devon in the hope that the pitches would suit him, and anyway he would be one of six bowlers – seven with Graeme Hick – in case he didn't fire properly. As it turned out the Edgbaston pitch was a slow nothing, not great for one-day cricket, so we left out Devon, Graham Thorpe and Phil DeFreitas. Once we went for five batsmen, Atherton, Stewart, Smith, Gooch and Hick picked themselves, so Thorpe was really there as cover. As it turned out, Lord's was washed out, so only 11 of the 14 got a game.

The Edgbaston pitch came in for a great deal of criticism about which it was difficult to argue. It was dreadfully slow and low in bounce, and batsmen could not trust the pace and bounce sufficiently to attempt much off the front foot. The turgid surface was a major disappointment for a showpiece one-day game – even more so because new head groundsman Steve Rouse had already produced the quickest pitches for years at Edgbaston in the first couple of matches of the season against Glamorgan and Leicestershire. He is a great believer in cross-rolling of the square, and much more of it than other groundsmen use. So what went wrong?

It seems that the Board's pitch consultant, then Harry Brind, visited Edgbaston a couple of weeks before the game and advised that a second pitch should be prepared, because Rouse's strip for his first international match was much too hard and well-grassed. As a result, he had no chance of preparing a decent pitch in such a short space of time, and everyone suffered – players and spectators alike.

Illingworth

Chris Lewis had a good match, and he was another player I had a long one-to-one chat with. I more or less talked about the same things with him as I had done with DeFreitas, particularly attitude and approach when things were not going well. I told him straight that some people were questioning his commitment, and only he could put the matter right. He had got to make up his mind what sort of bowler he wanted to be, and he had got to be seen to be putting everything in all the time. Not just when he was on top, but at times when a batsman was in and going well on a nothing pitch. There is no hiding place in Test cricket, and I told him he had had several anonymous games. The current England team could not afford that from anyone, let alone a key all-rounder. He had got the ability – now he had got to produce it consistently if he wanted an England future.

I told him that it is easy to knock a player, but the player with real heart rams that sort of criticism down people's throats with wickets and runs. As with DeFreitas, I told him that if he produced the goods, I would back him all the way, so now it was down to him. He took it in the right way and I felt we were getting somewhere. I have often found in the past that some top players need their minds concentrating – others don't and work it out for themselves.

All I knew was that three fine natural cricketers like DeFreitas, Lewis and Hick had played 81 times between them for England, but we were still unsure whether or not they would make it. I had come into the job determined to have a hands-on approach, and things like that were not going to drift any longer, with the people in charge just hoping for the best. Every member of a Test side has a vital part to play, and you cannot carry any passengers. Obviously, allowances have to be made for a youngster's first two or three games, but in the hardest school in cricket, a player must show quickly he can stand the heat or make way for someone else.

The main difference I saw in the modern game, compared with when I played for England from my first game against New Zealand at Old Trafford in 1958 to my last against the West Indies at Lord's in 1973, was that we used to hope and pray we would be picked, whereas too many current players think they should be chosen. I wanted to restore what I saw as some lost pride in playing for your country.

Just think of some top players in the past who struggled to establish themselves in the England side. Kenny Barrington went four years from his first two Tests against South Africa in 1955 to his third against India in 1959, and Fred Titmus went even longer. Like Kenny, he played two Tests against South Africa in 1955, but did not play again until 1962. Jim Parks was another – he ended with 46 caps, yet there were five years between his debut in 1954 against Pakistan and a second appearance in the West Indies in 1960. Even that second cap was only when he was called in for the final Test in Trinidad, even though he was not in the party. He was coaching out there, and the selectors called him in to strengthen the batting and he played instead of Roy Swetman.

I played in that fifth and final Test, which was my eighth cap out of a possible 12 from debut, and I always knew there were two battles at Test level. First, get picked, and then stay in the side. In that series I had a poor time with the bat – 92 in eight innings – but I did my bit with the ball, even though I only took four wickets. It was important that we bowled our overs economically, and I was pleased that I only conceded 383 runs from 196 overs. It was not a matter of bowling defensively, but figures like those give your captain control in the field, and he can work his attacking bowlers round you. David Allen was my partner, and he bowled 197 overs for 417 runs, which is why we were never batted out of the series by a top order which included Sobers, Walcott, Worrell, Kanhai, Hunt and Nurse.

It was a series like that which convinced me of the value of a properly balanced attack, which was why I was so outspoken about it as soon as I was appointed in March. I know the press made a meal of most of what I said, pointing out that a lot of it was in apparent contradiction to the thinking of Atherton. We met at Old Trafford during the Sunday one-day friendly match between Lancashire and Yorkshire, and I thought it was a good meeting. I was interested to see how it was reported in Monday's *Daily Mail*.

'England's supremo Ray Illingworth admitted there were "differences of opinion" after his first official meeting with captain Mike Atherton yesterday. The pair talked for an hour at Old Trafford just 24 hours after Atherton's return from the West Indies. Illingworth said: "There were one or two straight differences – but not disagreements. In fact, we are not a long way apart in our thinking. We discussed the players who went to the West Indies and the 'A' team who went to South Africa, and basically we seem to agree. Mike has quite a decent cricketing brain and I want to give him the chance to use it by getting him a properly balanced side with three seamers and two spinners." '

That last point was the most important, and Mike did not disagree with the principle. He was certainly reluctant to agree unconditionally, but said he would go along with it if possible. He also made the point that, in the West Indies, he did not have a batsman in the top six who he could count as a regular bowler. I wasn't so sure, because Hick bowled 77 overs in the series, and I still think he could turn himself into a good off-spinner. He has the basics – a good action and he spins it. What he needs is to get a lot of bowling under his belt – that is how an ordinary bowler can become a good one. I'm not sure how helpful Worcestershire have been, because he gets so little bowling with them. It can't be right that, at the start of the 1994 season, he had played in 260 first-class matches, yet still had taken only 170 wickets – and 92 of those came in four seasons between 1987 and 1991 from 86 games. That sort of bowling would put him well on the way towards 300 wickets, and the more he bowls, the better he will get.

I explained to Mike the quotes from me about bowlers and other things which were ferried back to him in the West Indies, and we honestly did not have a serious problem. I made the point that we had to play bowlers who could bat, because our shortfall in that department had cost Test matches which should have been saved.

Our first selection meeting was for the Texaco games, and there was no real disagreement from any of the five of us – Mike, Brian, Fred, Keith and me. Because we wanted Reeve, we only needed to pick six batsmen, and all the bowlers could bat, except Devon. Some people attach no importance to these games, but that is wrong. It gives the selectors the chance to see how players react to the atmosphere of a big game. I know that different techniques are required, but discipline is all-important, and it proves a lot if a player can maintain his discipline when a tight situation develops. Of course, you have to examine runs and wickets and the way they are obtained with great care, because there is no comparison between a one-day game and the approach to five-day cricket.

The Edgbaston game was one-sided, but I did not mind that. I was particularly interested in how Gough and Udal performed, because neither of them would have played in front of an 18,000 crowd before. They both did well, with Gough getting Martin Crowe out with genuine hostility. Unfortunately, the lad strained for extra pace and tore a muscle in the rib cage – the worst possible injury for a quick bowler. It usually happens in the left side due to the muscle being nipped as the ball is delivered and the side rotates and collapses under body weight. It is agony for the bowler – sometimes even breathing is a problem with the more severe tear, and I felt sorry for Gough that he was ruled out of the first Test at Trent Bridge.

Udal did well, and stuck to it when the Kiwis tried to get after him. Another plus was Lewis. First he smashed 19 off 10 balls and then ran in with the ball as though he meant it. He looked fiery and deserved his three wickets. All the batsmen got into double figures, with Atherton holding things together with 81, and I knew that 225 was enough on that pitch, providing we bowled well.

A win by 42 was a good start, and although the second match at Lord's was rained off, we could approach the first Test with greater confidence than the New Zealanders, who seemed to me to have problems in batting and bowling. When we left Lord's on the Sunday, we had six days before we picked the side for Trent Bridge and I watched the Yorkshire game against New Zealand at Headingley.

I was particularly interested in White and Stemp, and White had a good match. He batted well for his 59 and he looked the part with the ball. He took five for 43 in the first innings – all in the top seven – and made it possible for Moxon to enforce the follow-on. He got a couple more in the second innings, and I had seen enough to convince me he was worth a go. His batting could make all the difference at number six, and I thought he should make up into a decent fifth bowler. Like Gough, he is a positive cricketer and that is important in Test cricket, because that sort of player often affects and changes the course of a match, whereas others tend to drift with the tide.

Brian Bolus had also seen him, so it was not a case of pushing a particular fancy of mine, although I have never been afraid to back my judgement. We met in Southport where the captain was playing for five days against Somerset. Andy Caddick was injured, so that was one out of the side which played six weeks earlier in Antigua. Phil Tufnell was another one, because of personal problems which I made it clear to him he had to sort out before he played again. He is a lad who needs careful handling, and seems a sitting duck for the press. Some players cope better than others, but he is such a volatile character, I would not have been happy about him playing again until he could concentrate on his cricket.

Our first selection meeting was a bit of an eye-opener. I knew Atherton was a strong character, but I had not realised he had such black-and-white views about who could play and who could not. I know Brian felt the same, but it did not affect how the meeting went. It could have been a difficult one, because I could understand Mike wanting to stay with his players from the West Indies. It had been a funny tour, because they did very well to come back from 3-0 down, especially after the thrashing in Trinidad, but I did not think that should blind us to the faults which led to the series being over in three straight matches.

The batting order needed sorting out, with Gooch's return giving us several new options. More than that, should we leave out Hick and Smith to play Thorpe and John Crawley, who Mike was very keen to get in? Smith was the real problem, although he finished strongly in Antigua with 175. He still managed only 320 in the series – 145 in his other eight innings – and I was worried about his form. As against that, I knew we would be in for a tough series against South Africa and their all-pace attack, and I was worried that if we dropped Smith, it might destroy a self-confidence that was already a bit fragile. I always believe in doing my homework, and I knew that his last two series against Australia and the West Indies were worth 603 in 19 innings. Just about adequate, but disappointing from a senior player who we now thought should be a batsman around whom we could build a powerful line-up.

We decided that Hick would play so, with Gooch coming back, either Smith or Thorpe had to go if we were to pick five batsmen plus White. A lot was said about Thorpe, because he was another who had played a couple of good innings in the West Indies. But that was the trouble – 86 and 84, but only 69 in seven other innings, with one or two moderate-looking dismissals. The fact that he is a left-hander was in his favour, but someone was bound to be unlucky, and we decided it would be Thorpe.

That gave us a first six of Atherton, Stewart, Gooch, Smith, Hick and White, and we were more or less agreed on Steve Rhodes to keep instead of Jack Russell. It was not just a matter of extra batting ability to counter the popular view that Russell is a better 'keeper. Jack had fought it out as well as anyone in the West Indies – 195 at an average of 24.38 – but I come back to the same point I made about Gough and White. Rhodes is one of the most positive cricketers in the game, and he looks a natural fighter. Every now and again someone comes along who you would rather have with you in a fight than against you, and Rhodes is one of those.

Another thing I liked about him was how he had kept going for at least five years when a lot of people were talking him into a first cap. He had been on five 'A' tours which, like Thorpe, told him that he was close, but he even missed that when Stewart kept in India, and Russell went with the 'A' side to Australia. He was 29 then and it would have been easy for him to lose some enthusiasm, but he didn't. He is a bustler of a 'keeper, and can now be counted as an authentic batsman for Worcestershire, so we agreed that he deserved his debut.

That was the first seven, and DeFreitas was clearly a better bet with the ball than Lewis, who lost out once we picked White, as well as Mark Ilott in case we went for an all-pace attack. Fraser and Malcolm were near-automatic and we picked two spinners in the squad – Peter Such and Richard Stemp. Regarding Devon, the side can suffer if he bowls badly, and he is one of only four bowlers. That happened at Lord's against the West Indies in 1991, when Gooch was given – or asked for and got – him, Steve Watkin, Phil DeFreitas and Derek Pringle. A lot needed to go right for that sort of attack to work, and it didn't. At the end of the first day, England were nearly out of the game, with the West Indies 317 for three. In that innings, DeFreitas and Pringle carried the side and between them had figures of 66.1–12–193–7, compared with 34–5–136–1. The first pair went for just under three an over, and the second four. That might not sound a lot, but it is to a captain. It is not only the difference of

over 100 runs in a match, it is the fact that the tighter pair are
having to bowl when they should be resting, so the whole side
suffers. At least this time, the captain had got Mr Dependable,
Gus Fraser, a vastly improved DeFreitas and the back-up of
White, as well as a spinner. We never really thought we would
play both spinners, but I am a great believer in keeping all
options available regarding the balance of the side. I have seen
too many Tests where the captain, after seeing the pitch on the
morning of the match, wishes he had picked someone else.

Such was always going to get first crack, and we picked
Stemp, both as an extra option and to give him experience of a
Test match dressing-room. I was happy about the meeting and
the squad we picked. I know I had gone public on the final say
being mine, but I knew I would not push hard unless it was
really important to me. I believe that the captain should mostly
get his way, unless there is a big disagreement about a player,
because it is no good sending him out with a team he feels
could be improved. I had been in Mike's position as captain
with strong views about players, and I was only overruled once
when I dug my toes in. It happened with John Snow in 1971
against India. He had tangled with Sunil Gavaskar in the Lord's
Test when they collided during a sharp single and Snow went
across him for the ball.

Those sorts of incidents are usually 50–50, with the bowler
often holding back rather than going through for the ball at the
expense of a collision. Not with Snowy this time. He flattened
Gavaskar, probably because a few things had riled him – but
the players did not bear a grudge, and had quite a laugh about
it, Gavaskar included. Matter closed – or so we thought, but we
reckoned without the reaction of officialdom in the person of
TCCB secretary Billy Griffith. I objected to him coming into our
dressing-room, but he still ordered Snow to apologise.

He did, but was dropped as a disciplinary measure for the
next Test, despite all I said at the selection meeting. I suppose it
can be argued that, because he was left out for reasons other
than cricket, the captain's arguments did not carry the same
weight as usual, but I still think it was unwarranted over-
reaction. Now that I am chairman, things might be different,
although the chairman of the Board still holds a veto on any
selection.

As for the pitch, it was the first of several disappointments
to me. I don't see why England should always be at a

disadvantage at home. Every other country prepares pitches to suit their attack and I have never seen anything wrong in that, providing there is still a reasonable balance between bat and ball. By that I mean that, even if a pitch is giving one type of bowler some assistance, the good player can still build an innings. The pitch is the most important thing of all, which is why I tried hard to influence the groundsmen. I had a meeting with them and Alan Smith on 3 May. They were all there – Harry Brind, Mick Hunt, Keith Boyce, Ron Allsopp, Peter Marron and Steve Rouse.

I was quite hopeful, because I knew that two or three of them could get whatever they wanted, and I had already heard that Rouse had done well in his first few weeks at Edgbaston. Mind you, I had earlier met Donald Carr, who was in charge of the pitches committee, and he started by telling me that I couldn't do what I did at Leicester. By that he said the pitch must be evenly grassed – not just on the seamers' length with the spinners' length bare at both ends. I don't see what is wrong with that, because it encourages a captain to pick a balanced attack, and everyone in the game has got a chance. If the pitch is evenly grassed, then the spinner can only get into the match when the surface starts to go, and most Test pitches in England are prepared so that the surface lasts. Our climate makes it nearly impossible to produce the perfect pitch – one that starts off with consistent pace and bounce, and then starts to take increasing spin from towards the end of the second day onwards. That is fine in theory, but the preparation of a five-day pitch is such a delicate matter, with most of the real preparatory work done weeks before the match, that a few days of rain at the wrong time can spoil it. As can a lengthy dry spell, which means artificial watering has to be judged to perfection.

Our main problem is that I believe the groundsmen are frightened of a comeback from Lord's if they get one wrong. I reckon this could be solved by making them all employees of the Board and not the county clubs. At the moment, most of them are leaned on by captains to produce a suitable pitch for the home side, and they are petrified if they get it wrong. Look at the number of four-day games which are over in three or under. While we cover pitches, what is going on does little to help young cricketers learn how to bat and bowl properly. I made a report later in the season in which I suggested that, now that Brind has gone from The Oval, he should spend more time around the counties and leave the Test pitches to me. I cannot emphasise this too much, because I reckon the one thing in England we get wrong most of all is the preparation of our Test pitches.

We had one look at the Trent Bridge pitch and knew it would be slow, and also it would be of little help to the spinners. That was why we went in with three quicks, one spinner, Such, and White as a genuine fourth seamer, and Hick as an extra option.

Part 2
NEW ZEALAND, 1994

3

SMALL CLOUDS: TRENT BRIDGE

Illingworth's first Test team was mostly greeted with approval by the national media. The omission of Thorpe drew some criticism but, that apart, most discussion centred on the batting order, particularly the opening partnership. Atherton and Gooch had a wonderful record together, averaging over 60 per innings. Only seven pairings in history have achieved that sort of average while scoring over 1000 runs together, and Atherton and Gooch are third in the roll of honour, behind Jack Hobbs and Herbert Sutcliffe (87.81), and Allan Rae and Jeff Stollmeyer (71). Contrary to popular belief, Gordon Greenidge and Desmond Haynes are well down the list in 14th place, averaging 47 per partnership. Such pairings evolve because of a chemistry which, more often than not, is indefinable. Sometimes it is based upon a contrast in method, sometimes not. Left- and right-hand combinations are acknowledged to be the most difficult for bowlers, because of the constant need to switch line, and they provide seven of the top 13 pairings, although only Rae and Stollmeyer among the leading five. A feeling of comfort with each other is essential, as is trust. Not just about running between the wickets – John Edrich lost 3–1 to Geoffrey Boycott in 35 innings together – but in other things, such as rotation of the strike, and the ability to talk each other through difficult parts of an innings.

Atherton is so outwardly phlegmatic that he seems comfortable with anyone, and Alec Stewart deserved to keep his favourite place in the batting order, following his historic separate hundreds two months earlier in Barbados. That meant Gooch batting at three, with Hick and Smith to follow at four and five, although they had batted the other way round in the five Tests in the Caribbean. Craig White was picked for his debut, which meant an early abandonment of the theory that Rhodes could bat as six. That left four bowlers to be chosen from six, which, mathematically, gave the selectors 15 different combinations.

Illingworth

Once we had a look at the pitch, we knew we didn't want two spinners, or an all-pace attack. That meant Stemp missing out and, with DeFreitas and Fraser certainties, it was a straight choice between Malcolm and Ilott. Assuming that DeFreitas would hold his top form, we went for the extra pace of Malcolm, even though the pitch looked slow. As it happened, he bowled poorly, particularly in the second innings when his first three overs went for 25, mostly to cuts from short and wide deliveries. 'Daffy' was the big plus for us. He swung and seamed the ball away from the right-handers throughout the game, with six of his nine wickets coming from catches behind the wicket, and three LBWs proving how improved his line was. What pleased me most was that he was now bowling a fuller length, and I felt we were on the way to a decent attack, built around him and Fraser. White did a reasonable job, and his first wicket – Crowe caught behind down the leg-side – showed he might be one of those bowlers with a golden arm. He is just the type to unsettle batsmen, coming off quite a short run. Batsmen sometimes find it difficult to find a rhythm against that sort of bustler, and I was convinced he was worth a run. He only got 19 and holed out in the covers, but he is not afraid to go for his shots and, with a great gully catch as well as two others, he had a reasonable debut.

As did Rhodes. He took three catches in each innings, missed nothing and did not concede a bye. The thing with him is that he contributes so much more in a general way. He is something like Godfrey Evans was – a rubber ball of a man, who might not do everything by the book, but still pulls off some great catches, and is always geeing up the rest of the team. He is a good reader of the game and contributes a lot to his captain with advice and comments about which bowlers are doing what. To me, he looks a natural Test cricketer, and I know how much he enjoys the big time. He got a good 49 as well. 'Daffy' scored his second Test 50 at almost a run a ball and, with nine wickets, was unlucky to miss out on the Man of the Match.

That went to Gooch for his 210, and he certainly played a big part in the win, because the pace of his runs gave us extra time to win the match. He played as well as he has ever done, although the attack was not great and the pitch called for line and length, otherwise a top batsman could help himself. I was pleased to see Atherton get a hundred, and Smith 78, although he struggled a bit against their spinners.

Luck in cricket is often misunderstood. It is too facile to say that you make your own luck, although much so-called 'bad luck' is nothing of the sort. For instance, a catch might be brilliant, but the batsman has still put the ball in the air. Bowled off the pads is another dismissal than the unthinking batsman claims is bad luck. Nothing of the sort. If the ball would have missed leg stump, then it is poor footwork to put the pad on a line from which the ball can rebound on to the stumps.

A run-out is different, especially when a batsman is sent back after accepting or initiating a call. So often it happens to a man who is out of form or short of confidence – or both. Smith had scored 78 and was looking for a second successive Test hundred which would have quelled most of the doubts about him for the rest of the summer, only to be sent back by Rhodes, and then have to endure a lengthy wait before Merv Kitchen, as third umpire, was finally convinced that he was out. Smith could justifiably claim that that was bad luck, because his record is littered with big hundreds – and now one had been cruelly taken away from him. His next three innings in the series were to yield 42, and he was dropped both from the next series against South Africa, and the Ashes party to tour Australia in 1994–95. And all because of poor calling and the eye of the camera.

Incidentally, that decision by Kitchen came during his debut as third umpire. The day before, I played golf with the former Somerset batsman, and he confirmed what I already knew from other umpires – that they consider the role of the third umpire to constitute the shortest of short straws. They are in favour of the system, because it eliminates one of the most contentious areas of argument in cricket – the fast finish in a close decision. The argument that cricket has done without the cameras for over a hundred years is a footling one. As is the one that mistakes balance out. Try telling a team, when they suffer at a crucial stage of a big match, that the next time will be in their favour. Two wrongs have never made a right, and surely the argument for the use of cameras for line decisions is now proven. Never mind if the system still needs refining and improving with extra cameras. Never mind if the occasional decision is still impossible to give because of an intervening fielder or wicket-keeper masking the crucial part of the equation. The third umpire's answer is as always – if the batsman is not conclusively out, then he stays. The bull point is that, whereas LBWs and catches must remain within the umpire's interpretation of what he sees at close quarters, a run-out, stumping or a boundary line transgression by a chasing fielder can be settled for him, usually beyond argument.

I have been behind a BBC television microphone when a slow-motion freeze-frame shows a batsman out by two feet, only for a rerun at normal speed to show the batsman apparently in. Devon Malcolm, not one of the world's great backers-up at the non-striker's end, started late at Lord's in a one-day international, but finished like a train. The 'slo-mo' showed him out by at least a foot, but anyone looking at the subsequent normal-speed rerun would have bet good money he was past the back line, never mind the front, when the bails were broken. How can the naked eye compute bat, ball, bails and the fielder's hands – particularly in a fast finish? It cannot, but the camera can.

Stumpings can be more difficult, because the bat is usually put down over the line and not run in. The other advantage is that, now that the umpires in the middle know that they can refer those decisions, the unrelenting pressure on them is reduced. The traditionalists can grumble if they like, but cricketers and spectators have a much fairer game as a result.

The England win at Trent Bridge received muted praise on two counts. New Zealand's under-achievement meant that the home side did not beat much, although such comment must be tempered by the fact that any team can only play as well as they are allowed to. Also, an hour's drive away, at Edgbaston, Brian Lara was completing his second rewrite of the record books in seven weeks, almost to the minute, and his 501 naturally led on the following morning's back pages.

England's win by an innings and 90 runs was nevertheless conclusive and must have gone some way towards achieving Bolus's picturesquely phrased first aim – 'to stop the bleeding'. The low scores of Stewart and Hick, the poor bowling of Malcolm, and an unease about the bowling of Such, despite good match figures of 53–19–78–5 on a slow pitch, were small clouds. New Zealand must have reflected that, having been beaten with two full sessions to spare, they could still have escaped but for Crowe and Rutherford aggregating 83 in four innings, and debutant Heath Davis conceding 93 runs off only 21 overs. The Maori's middle name is Te-Ihi-O-Te-

Rangi, which means Salutations to God of the Sky, and the fact that he did not play in the remaining two Tests at Lord's and Old Trafford was a source of relief to broadcasters.

The crowd were robbed again on the first day when play was halted at 7 p.m. in bright sunshine, despite the so-called daily minimum quota of 90 overs not having been bowled. This artifical 7 p.m. curfew, together with an iniquitous recalculation of the daily minimum following an innings break, has frequently robbed the public of unbowled overs, not to mention the disadvantage often suffered by one side which has no chance of making up the overs sometimes deliberately lost by opponents trying to avoid defeat.

Illingworth

I enjoyed my first Test as chairman, and was sure that I would get along all right with the captain. What I wanted to get straight with him was the extent of my input in the dressing-room. As far as I am concerned, who comes in is the prerogative of the captain, and the last thing I wanted was for the players to look on me as an intruder. I just wanted to help where I could on general matters, and I was also keen to see how different players reacted to what was going on in the middle. You can learn a lot about a cricketer that way. If he's not a close watcher then, unless he is a genius, his cricket is likely to suffer because he might miss a trick he would not have if he had watched more closely.

Of course, it is different on a ground like Old Trafford, where the dressing-rooms are sideways on, but there is always the television to help out.

Mike told me before the Nottingham Test that the players would welcome me in with them, so I watched the whole game from the dressing-room. I was glad I was there the first day, because that was the start of three separate issues which the press got wrong. The first concerned Andrew Wingfield-Digby, who Ted Dexter had chosen to involve regarding any counselling or advice the players might need.

Alan Smith first rang me a couple of weeks before the first Test, and said it was my decision as to whether Andrew should be a regular in the dressing-room. Alan told me that Ted had involved him in case the players wanted a shoulder to cry on. My reply was that if a player needed that in a Test match, then he shouldn't be playing for England and, as it was my decision, then the answer was no.

Naturally, I thought that was that, so when Andrew walked in during the first day of the Test, I assumed that he had been told that the previous arrangement had been changed. It seems that he had not been told directly, because Alan had involved Keith Fletcher and the message had got lost somewhere. I am not sure why 'Fletch' was involved after being told it was my decision, but I was more concerned now about the embarrassment caused to Andrew by the headlines next day. 'Illy bans the Rev', and so on.

I rang him straight away to apologise for the way it had been handled, and told him, 'I always want to treat people in the same way I want to be treated by them, and I am sorry that has not been done this time.' He was good about it and accepted the situation quite readily. I told him he was welcome to drop in whenever he wanted, but it would be on that basis and not as an accepted regular arrangement.

I was not overjoyed about the press, nor was I about the way they went to town about the other two issues – mobile telephones and sunglasses. The headlines and stories made me look as though I was trying to rule the roost in every way, and that wasn't true. What I wanted to do was to cut out unnecessary distractions and focus the players' minds on getting the best out of themselves. I spoke to Mike about the mobile telephones and he agreed with me that they could be a distraction. Therefore the ban was with his consent, but not one journalist bothered to establish what was the most important fact of all. It wouldn't have made such a good story, so I was pinned as being the Great Dictator.

The sunglasses story was even more absurd, because I never banned them. In fact the reverse was true, because I tried them and found they enhanced a dull day, so I said to everyone, 'If you want them and they help, wear them.' I told the press that I felt I was being done, with too much reported as fact without them checking with me first. I told them I was always available to talk to them, and therefore there was no excuse for guessing. Time will tell if I can do my little bit to change them, but the more irresponsible writers will have to learn my way of doing things, otherwise they'll get nowt.

Part of the early problem was that most of the press could not get used to Illingworth never ducking a question. They had become so accustomed to assuming that it would be a waste of time trying to get an official line on a subject that they needed re-educating. The *Standard*'s John Thicknesse tells a good story about Illingworth's elephantine memory, which makes a neat point about the nature of the man. It happened on the eve of the second Cornhill Test match against South Africa in July at Headingley.

Thicknesse wanted to check something, and when Illingworth appeared in the press box he asked for a minute, to be taken aback when he was told, 'I want a chat with you first – outside.' Obediently he followed, and immediately received an outburst about the fact that he, Illingworth, considered that Thicknesse had stuffed him, so why should he co-operate? A confused 'Thickers' sought clarification.

'When did I do you?'

'Nineteen seventy-one, that's when, and I've never had an apology since.'

'In which case, I'm sorry. So can we start again?'

Marvellous. Michael Henderson of *The Times* was another one to fall foul of Illingworth's unerring ability to sniff out an inaccuracy. He was nailed in the same Headingley press box with an article in which he said that Illingworth had left the Old Trafford Test against New Zealand early in order to play golf.

As Illingworth reminded him, 'Due to a back problem for which I had an operation several months ago, I have not played golf for a long time.' The point he made with some force was that this was the sort of thing which he, Illingworth, believes should always be checked before a story goes to press.

4

A TOUGH LITTLE YORKIE: LORD'S

Illingworth

After the Trent Bridge Test ended on the Monday, we had five days before we met to pick the side for the next Test at Lord's, starting 10 days later. I went to see part of Yorkshire's home game against Somerset at Bradford to keep an eye on White and Stemp, and also to check on the progress of Darren Gough since he strained his side at Edgbaston three weeks earlier. He was still not right, so I concentrated on the other two. They both did well, with seven wickets between them in Somerset's first innings, and White batted aggressively for his 71 not out in the second innings.

I travelled to the meeting on Saturday, which meant linking up with the captain at the Cobham Hilton in Surrey, just off the M25, after the close of play in Lancashire's game against Sussex at Horsham. Sometimes it is a work of art to arrange a suitable place, but we must always travel to wherever the captain is playing. It wasn't a difficult meeting because the only problem we had was the groin injury Mark Ilott sustained against Gloucestershire in the match we sent him to play in when he was omitted from the XIII at Trent Bridge.

We were keen to pick 13 again, and also to give Mike as many options and variations as possible, so we went for Paul Taylor from Northamptonshire. He hadn't got a lot of wickets, but we wanted a left-arm quickie if possible, so we picked him. He is a funny sort of bowler, with no great body action, but he certainly moves the ball around at a lively pace. I always felt he would need conditions in his favour at Test level, but he was worth a go, if only because he never really got a chance the previous winter in India. It seems that one of the things against him was the management's fear of him providing the opposition's spinners with rough from his follow-through outside the right-handers' off stump. In which case, why take him on tour, and also, what about your own spinners? Surely you have to back your own selections.

What we had to decide was who dropped out if we played him, and I found the two days' practice interesting. I don't think we have the England set-up right yet – not in the coaching areas anyway. For instance, Geoff Arnold is on tap for the bowlers and Alan Knott for the wicket-keeper. Yet the batsmen have nobody – maybe because it is felt that those chosen should be able to work things out for themselves. I don't go along with that, so I decided to become involved, particularly with Robin Smith. At that stage, I was still not sure about Keith Fletcher's role, and I didn't want to tread on his toes.

But his hands seemed full in organising nets, so I had a session with Smith. The first thing I needed to do was to show him how much he was moving about and committing himself before the ball was bowled. Every batsman has an initial foot movement, usually to get into position for their strengths which are usually playing forward. The most successful are those who limit that movement to a minimum and make it as late as possible. A batsman cannot stand completely still against fast bowling, because a ball bowled at 80 miles per hour over 19 yards would not allow it, but batsmen like Barry Richards and Sunil Gavaskar are prime examples of what I mean.

Smith knows his problem, but even he was surprised at the amount of his movement when I got one of the bowlers to run in to bowl and simply hold on to the ball. Believing he would let the ball go, he had lunged all over the place, and I told him to work on the bad habit he had got into. Holding on to the ball might be an old-fashioned trick, but there is no better way for a coach to prove to a batsman where he is going wrong.

His biggest problem is a lack of self-confidence. He had followed his 78 in the first Test with 111 against Nottinghamshire, and he should have been bursting to show everyone what he could do. After all, he was now a senior member of the side, and that should have been reflected in his manner – instead of which he looked more like a bloke playing in his second Test. I am not trying to be over-critical, but so much of Test cricket is played in the head. It is rarely good enough just to be able to bat or bowl, because everyone chosen can do that at that level. It is almost like a game of chess, where the opposition is always trying to be a move ahead, and you can't match that if your own mind is in a muddle.

I told him what we wanted from him, and also emphasised what an important role he could play for us against South Africa. That was later misquoted by a section of the press, who tried to say that I had guaranteed Smith a place for the rest of the summer. Untrue. Of course I wanted him to play all the time, but only if he was playing somewhere near his best.

The other big story that blew up out of nowhere before the Test concerned Devon Malcolm.

The Lord's Test began on Thursday, 16 June, and, when I turned up at lunchtime the previous day to do my preview for the *Birmingham Post*, I walked straight into an impromptu press conference behind the Warner Stand. Devon Malcolm was surrounded by the national cricket correspondents, and was clearly upset that he had been given an early release from the squad of 13. I cannot remember a similar withdrawal, other than on the grounds of injury or illness, and the distressed Malcolm became a target for a bunch of journalists who are keen for a different story on the eve of a Test.

He said how shocked he was to be told he was not wanted 24 hours before the game, and it was impossible not to sympathise with his view that he had been unnecessarily humiliated. After all, Derbyshire's game the following day was at Cardiff against Glamorgan, and he could have quietly driven there early Thursday morning, with his omission causing far less comment than had sending him packing the previous day.

It was the culmination of a frustrating few months for Malcolm, who had been brought back after knee surgery in England to rejoin the party in the West Indies, only to sit out the last two Tests in Barbados and Antigua. He then failed to do himself justice at Trent Bridge, despite which he was included in the XIII for the second Test, only to be discarded after one day's net practice. He thus drove out of Lord's reflecting that his 27 England caps had come in 12 different series and, despite bowling well at The Oval against Australia in 1993 and the West Indies at Kingston in February 1994, those were his only two appearances in England's last 12 Tests.

Illingworth
It wasn't a case of being insensitive to Devon, but we knew

Wednesday morning he would not play because the pitch looked like the one at Trent Bridge, and he didn't bowl well there. Geoff Arnold had worked with him in the nets on Tuesday, and we were so keen to get him right that we sent Geoff with him to Cardiff to monitor him and work with him again. We wanted him to get plenty of match bowling, so once we had made up our minds he was not going to play, it made sense to get him to Cardiff as soon as possible. I suppose he could have travelled early Thursday morning, but a drive of nearly three hours on the M4 is not exactly an ideal preparation for a four-day match. Anyway, he bowled better at Cardiff. He took seven wickets and bowled more than 50 overs in the match, and Geoff said he was much better through the crease – in particular not falling away as he bowled, which makes him spray a lot down the leg-side.

On Thursday morning, we had a straight choice between Taylor and Stemp to replace Malcolm – that being the only change from the first Test. It was not an easy decision, but we finally settled for Taylor, although with hindsight we probably got it wrong. I felt a bit sorry for him, because he was obviously tight and tense after waiting so long for a chance. It is so difficult to draw a deep breath and convince yourself it is just another game, especially at Lord's. As a fringe selection, he was desperate to make an impression to keep himself in the swim, and he needed a bit of luck. Often you bowl well and get nothing, or badly and take wickets. Some days the ball keeps beating the bat, on others it will find the edge. Then again, you have days where the edges bisect the field or, worse still, go to hand and are dropped. Taylor needed two things which did not happen.

He needed to relax, bowl in his normal way and have a bit of luck, but that hardly happened in the game in which he had only four spells for 26 overs. Also, he should probably have bowled earlier than he did, to get him into the game, but as a past captain I know how difficult it is to get everything right for everybody. He couldn't have the new ball, with Fraser and DeFreitas playing, so he was always going to be third seamer anyway.

A breakdown of the three pace bowlers' figures shows that whatever faith Atherton had in Taylor soon evaporated. Fraser bowled 51 overs in the match, made up of nine spells, and DeFreitas bowled 51 overs, also comprising nine spells. Even Craig White, very much the fourth seamer, bowled 25 overs in the match – only one fewer than Taylor – and he was given six spells. In New Zealand's second innings, Taylor was the sixth and last bowler used.

Illingworth

The game was a big let-down after Trent Bridge, mainly because we batted so badly. All credit to Dion Nash for his bowling, but too many batsmen got out to indifferent strokes. Nash certainly outbowled our quicks, mainly because he got the line from the Pavilion end spot on. A lot of people reckon we talk nonsense about the difference in the two ends at Lord's, but I reckon it is greater than on any other Test ground in the world. It is not just the slope from the Pavilion end to the Nursery, because there are up and down slopes on other grounds – Headingley, for instance.

The real problem is the lateral slope from Grandstand to Mound, with a total drop of nine feet over 150 yards. That means that each pitch width carries an average slope of two inches from right to left as you stand in the batting crease at the Nursery end facing the Pavilion.

There are big problems for batsmen and bowlers alike until they get used to it – most of them bowling from the Pavilion end and batting at the Nursery end. For instance, a bowler's normal line of off, or off and middle, has to be shifted at least six inches towards the off-side. Even then, a straight ball will be carried back in by the slope, but it is difficult for a bowler to convince himself he has got to start on such a different line. It's almost like allowing for a cross-wind in golf – you have to aim off centre to counter it.

A bowler like Malcolm is a prime candidate for getting it wrong, because the first thing that goes wrong when he is not firing properly is that in falling away in the delivery stride, he pushes the ball leg-side. That's bad enough on a level pitch, but absolutely death at Lord's, where even a ball pitched middle and off will be whipped away by good batsmen.

Illingworth might not remember his words on television during the Lord's Test in 1991 against the West Indies, but they show that the problem was not a new one for Malcolm. A transcript reveals him talking of the same Pavilion end difficulty for the same Devon Malcolm, after his first six overs cost 33 including six boundaries, five of them leg-side. 'Devon is bowling into a stiff breeze, and I would have bowled him from the Nursery end with it. It would also have helped his action, because he bowls from the outer half of the return crease anyway. So does DeFreitas, but his hand action is still okay, but Devon's is not, which is why he is firing everything leg-side.'

Illingworth

Batsmen also have to make adjustments, particularly about what they can afford to leave outside off stump. On ordinary pitches, if a ball pitches a foot outside off stump it rarely does enough to hit the stumps, but at Lord's the slope will bring it back some of the way without anything happening off the seam. That's why you often see batsmen caught behind, playing at stuff they would normally leave.

Facing bowling from the Nursery end is more straightforward, although there again the good seamer can start something around middle and leg off a full length and still might hit.

I thought Nash bowled well for New Zealand, and you can argue it either way that he was helped by some poor strokes, or he forced them by good bowling. He had a good match, and became the first Kiwi to take 10 wickets in a Lord's Test and score a fifty, and he looks quite a prospect. Martin Crowe played an innings of pure class and, although we saved the follow-on with nine wickets down, I knew we had to fight to save the game.

There was a run-out incident which the press made a lot of. The only time we looked like competing when we batted was when Hick and White were going well. We were 193 for four, and they had put on 92 good runs. White had just hit Nash for three fours in one over and was beginning to motor when he went for a second run and was run-out by what was shown to be a couple of inches maximum. We had no problem with the decision, although the third umpire, Roy Palmer, gave it without calling for the freeze-frame which proved him right.

Atherton wanted to have another look at it, so asked for and was given permission by Clive Lloyd, the match referee, to see it again. Fair enough, although not according to some of the press who reported it as though Mike was disputing the decision and had demanded to look at the rerun. He did not, and what he did and how he did it was perfectly proper,

58

otherwise Lloyd would not have allowed it. It was a crucial wicket, because Hick got stuck after that, and only Rhodes got us past the follow-on. It was that 58 from Hick which led to me having a long chat with him in the next Test. He looked so good while White was in, but seemed to lose all confidence after the run-out. I was sure he would have batted differently had it been a county match, but the fear factor seemed to affect him.

The question now was whether we could avoid defeat. I thought England had lost too many games they could have drawn in the last few years, and I impressed on the team the importance of saving the match. Not just for the sake of the series, but also for their own pride. Sometimes it is all too easy to lose heart when nothing is going right, but I learned early on with Yorkshire that if you play your hardest all the time, you save matches you could lose, and rarely fail to nail down winning chances when they come along. A fighting attitude like that becomes a habit, and thank goodness we had one man in that match who proved himself a real toughie.

I mean Steve Rhodes, and he got us through in both innings. In the first innings he went in when we were in no real trouble, but a late collapse meant we could have followed on, and on the last day he batted for over two hours with the tail.

The England wicket-keeper batted for over five and a half hours in the match for his two unbeaten innings of 32 and 24. His sparky resilience gave the impression he was relishing the battle in the middle which, at times, was fought on two fronts – cricketing and verbal. The final session of the match had everything that a tense draw could offer: stern batting resistance against tight bowling to attacking fields, with plenty of work for the umpires as the tension grew. The light deteriorated so that Rutherford could not bring Nash back when he would have liked, but such was Rhodes's determination to keep New Zealand out that you felt he would have to be dragged from the crease. He was crowded and pressured, but soaked it all up without a tremor, and still remembered enough of his Yorkshire upbringing to ensure that no more overs were bowled than he thought necessary. Pitch repairs, glove adjustments and the odd fresh guard all helped to take the bowlers' feet off the accelerator, but all done with a fine sense of what was allowable and what was not. During the final half-hour, a few England players stopped watching, including Atherton, who retired to the showers, but Illingworth enjoyed the fight from the players' balcony.

Illingworth

I said afterwards that I could not have asked for more than a 'tough little Yorkie' to see us through and, after it was all over, I told the captain that if I could have chosen one England batsman to see out that last hour, it would have been Rhodes. He agreed with me, which I suppose is a bit of a comment on the other batsmen. In the second innings, Alec Stewart struck it well for his hundred, but too many of the others contributed to their dismissals in both innings.

After the match, Atherton expressed the wish that Lord's should inspire English players as well as the opposition, and his country's record proves the point. In the last 16 Tests there, only three victories have been recorded, two against Sri Lanka and one against India, while various touring teams have won seven times. It has become a jinx ground, as was to be emphatically evidenced on several counts two months later against South Africa. As for Nash, his match figures of 11 for 169 have only been bettered at Lord's twice in history – Bob Massie's 16 for 137 in 1972 and Sonny Ramadhin's 11 for 152 in 1950. Crowe's magnificent 142 was his 16th for New Zealand, his fourth against England, and he passed 5000 Test runs with a six off Fraser.

Illingworth will not need reminding that England's record at Lord's was no better during his career. He played nine Tests at Headquarters and finished on the winning side only twice. The first one was in the infamous 'Griffin no-balling' match in 1960 (when the South African bowler was called 11 times for throwing) when he scored 0 not out and bowled one over. He featured much more prominently in the other win – against India in 1967 when he took six for 29 in the second innings.

Illingworth

It was good to see us get out of the game with a draw, but that still did not excuse some of the batting and bowling. I was keen to give Smith and Hick every chance to prove to me they were worth playing, but I could understand the clamour in the media for Thorpe and Crawley. But for Gooch coming back, one of them would have played in the first two Tests, but I am a firm believer in picking your best side. Test cricket has changed a lot from the time when England used to rest players in order to try youngsters and, of course, we never took a full-strength team to India or Pakistan until about 15 years ago. People forget that

Fred Trueman and Alec Bedser never went there, and Statham only went once in 1951 when he managed eight for 293 in the five Tests.

I was also beginning to think about Such. He was steady enough, but I felt he was a bit stereotyped. He bowled a good line, but I never got the feeling that he would get people out. I know that Fred Titmus still thought that John Emburey was the best off-spinner we'd got, but he still had a problem after his eye operation for a detached retina. I suppose if he had been fit and we'd picked him, the press would have had a big go, but I can only repeat that you must pick your best side.

5

SERVICE WITH A SMILE: OLD TRAFFORD

Illingworth

There is not much cricket to watch between the end of one Test and the start of the next, particularly in a split summer. This time, we could watch a first-round NatWest match on the Tuesday – although with mostly minor county opposition, we could not learn much – and then the first three days of the next round of four-day games, before we met on the Saturday evening at the Copthorne Hotel in Manchester.

We weren't looking to make changes, so it was not a long meeting. Compared with Lord's we left Malcolm and Stemp out and brought in Ian Salisbury, who was now bowling better and had taken five wickets against Worcestershire the day before, including four out of the top six. We knew the Old Trafford pitch would offer more bounce than those at Trent Bridge and Lord's, and bounce is all-important for back-of-the-hand bowlers. It might have looked hard on Stemp, having been picked in the squad twice and left out on the morning of the match twice. The press had another go on predictable lines – 'perhaps he didn't carry the drinks properly', and so on.

We were influenced by several things. Firstly we thought it unlikely that we would want two finger spinners, and also Stemp had to attend a disciplinary meeting at Lord's on the Tuesday before the start of the match. He had been reported for some alleged verbals in the Somerset match at Bradford three weeks earlier, and if we picked him in the squad, it would give him a lot of travelling and also make it difficult for him to play in Yorkshire's next match against Kent in Canterbury. He had

63

to travel overnight to Lord's after the end of the Hampshire match at Headingley. The hearing was Tuesday, which meant he would miss that day's practice and would not get to Old Trafford until late Tuesday. Then if, as was likely, he was not picked, he would have a trip of around 250 miles to Canterbury. So, rather than lumber him with 400 miles of driving for nothing, and also because there was a real chance that Salisbury would play, we left him out.

As for Malcolm, he had only played one four-day game after we left him out at Lord's. Derbyshire had no game in the next round of Championship matches, and then they played New Zealand, although he was rested. I suppose, if Darren Gough was still unfit, we may have taken Malcolm to Old Trafford, but Gough had come back against Hampshire and had a good five days. He bowled over 50 overs and started off by nailing Robin Smith for a duck. In that innings he took six for 70 from 30 overs in what was his first match bowl for a month. I checked with him and the physio to see if there had been any reaction and was told 'a bit of stiffness', but nothing to worry about.

Mike, Fred and Brian did not need convincing, so we picked him instead of Taylor. As for Smith, he got a hundred in the second innings at Headingley, so we hoped that would bring him into the Test in form and in the right frame of mind. I knew the captain was keen on Crawley, but we decided to stick with the same batting line-up for the third successive game.

The first day was a bad one for Illingworth. Firstly, he lost the selection battle regarding Salisbury, which he was not shy about making public after the match.

Illingworth
I thought if ever we were going to play Salisbury, it should have been on that pitch. I said as much before we announced our team, but the feeling with the other three seemed to work out about 3½–1½ against, so I did not push it as Atherton, Fletcher and Titmus wanted such. I know I said in April that if I wanted something, I would get it, but I decided that this time it was only marginal in my view, so there was no point in forcing the issue. As it happened, Such did not bowl in the first innings, and only bowled 10 overs in the second innings, although Salisbury may have bowled more.

* * *

Having lost the first battle, Illingworth then watched Stewart, Smith and Hick get themselves out with rash-looking strokes for 57 between them, in three and a half hours' uneasy residence against a disciplined but ultra-defensive pace bowling tactic of a 7–2 off-side split to a wide line of attack. Also Gooch went first ball, to make him 13 for three since his 210 at Trent Bridge. Early days to talk about a decline in form, but the rest of his summer was to do little to keep the hack-pack at bay. Illingworth has always preached a message of discipline, which made it all the more galling to see two mispulls from Stewart and Hick, and a dragged-on attempted square cut by Smith, remove England's three best attacking batsmen and thus heap extra responsibility on the willing shoulders of Atherton. The chairman must have squirmed as England stuttered their way to 114 for four at tea, with a meagre 46 runs coming from 30 overs in the afternoon session. Atherton might have taken four and a half hours to reach 50, but where would his side have been without him?

At least the final session was more positive, with Atherton progressing from 59 to 96, and White's aggressive approach taking him from four to 42. The national press did not spare the England performance, although more credit might have been given to Nash and Co. for sticking so well to their game-plan, although a keener attention to the quick single might have caused a rethink.

The second day was different, thanks to Darren Gough, after Atherton became the first Lancashire player to score a hundred at Old Trafford as captain, and also the first Lancastrian to score two Test hundreds on his home ground.

Illingworth
I wanted Gough in the side from early in the season. He has an outgoing personality, looks like he is enjoying his cricket and is like a breath of fresh air, and not just on the field. He is partly responsible for what in now a good dressing-room spirit, and it didn't take him long to make his mark in a good-humoured way. Most lads are overawed in their first Test match, but Gough waded straight in. There is a small second dressing-room at Old Trafford, and he commandeered it with White. They put a notice on the door saying 'Yorkshire only', and told everyone that to get in, the password was 'Brian Close'. It sounds a bit schoolboyish, but how many young cricketers would have steamed into their first Test match and been able to act normally and have a bit of fun? I thought the dressing-room needed a bit more life, and he certainly lifted everyone.

Cricketers like that are few and far between, because either the senior players see it as cheek and sit on them, or it means they don't take their cricket seriously. But find one like Gough, and you know you've got someone who is afraid of nothing, and will usually express himself. As a bowler, he will always be a wicket-taker, so at times he is bound to go for a few. He will try anything, and maybe he is too inclined to experiment, but a bowler like that fits nicely with the steady performers. With the bat, he's got a simple method and, as he showed in his first Test and again against South Africa at The Oval, he can turn the game around in an hour if things go for him.

During the game I had a long talk with Hick about the need to be more positive. They've got a small room upstairs at Old Trafford they call the boot room, and I took him in there for half an hour. He told me he always thought he could make it for England at three, and that's where Brian Bolus, for one, wanted him. We couldn't put him there yet, but I had kept an eye on him in the first couple of games and he definitely seemed more outgoing. He had now been in Test cricket for three years and had been worked over by the West Indies and the Australian bowlers. He had had a good run, although he had never held his place throughout any of his first three home series against West Indies, Pakistan and Australia. He was unlucky in one way, because I can't think of any other young batsman who scored over 15,000 first-class runs and had hit 55 hundreds before he played in his first Test match. He was 25 before he made his debut against the West Indies at Headingley, yet Mark Ramprakash, who also made his debut in the game, was only 21. The point I am making is that, because of Hick's qualification wait, he was much more set in his ways than a more inexperienced batsman.

He would clearly have played for England earlier, had he been available, and early failures would have meant he could go back to Worcestershire and work on his method. But his debut came seven years after first playing county cricket, and it was then that much harder for him to adapt and recognise his faults. Also, the expectation level generated by the press and the public was greater than that for any other batsman I can remember, so it wasn't a total surprise to me that he took a long while to settle. But now his borrowed time was up. He had faced the West Indies and Australia twice, and was now playing in his 26th Test. He listened and told me that he wanted to play for England as he did for Worcestershire where he regarded every 50–50 ball as his. He had scratched around in the first innings – 20 off 67 balls in an hour and a half – and I thought the time was right to spell things out for him. I seemed to get through, and I was pleased about that because I don't reckon he is that easy to get to know. I just wanted to find out what made him tick, and I did.

Back to Gough, and what a day he had on the Friday. But for Atherton's 111, we could have been bowled out on the first day, but he gave the side the perfect platform for a respectable score, somewhere near 300, providing the lower order could do their stuff. He got out at 224 for six, and when Rhodes went at 237, it looked as though we could still be in trouble, when Gough joined DeFreitas. In the next two and a half hours, they were magnificent. They hit 18 fours between them in a stand of 130 and looking at them out there, you would never have known who was playing in his first Test and which one was playing his 36th. The crowd loved it, because it was not just the runs scored, it was the way in which they came, dictated entirely by an attitude which I loved to see – positive and full of enjoyment.

The joy of the onslaught was not entirely unconfined – at least not to me and my betting partner, Richard Hutton. We had gone for a spread bet on the England total, which we had wagered at £2 a run would be under 300. The former England and Yorkshire all-rounder vainly tried to persuade me to take a small profit when the new demolition firm of Gough and DeFreitas took the first few steps along their trail of destruction. 'Forget it, Richard. It can't go on,' was my utter misreading of the situation. At least I was in the good company of New Zealand captain Ken Rutherford, who could hardly believe the game was being rushed away from him so rapidly.

Wisden Cricket Monthly's David Frith wrote about Gough's 'West Point cadet march', as well as how the Yorkshire tyro 'carried on as if he played in these matches every Saturday afternoon'. Service with a smile indeed, a smile that became even broader when his first prized Test wicket took Gough just five deliveries.

Illingworth
I was pleased for the lad as well as for the side when he got Mark Greatbatch in his first over, and both he and 'Daffy'

carried on with the ball where they had left off with the bat. They shared the first four wickets, with two catches to Rhodes and one to Hick, and I thought we might rattle them out before they collected themselves. Often in cricket, when the tide of a game turns, it takes a big effort by one side to stem it. All sorts of strange things happen and, if you push extra hard, you can sometimes win the game in a couple of sessions. I think we might have done that, but for two things – Martin Crowe and the weather. We only lost a couple of overs on Saturday, but sunny Sunday was a rest day, and we only got 48 overs in on Monday.

Even then, we would have won but for Crowe. He played a funny sort of innings on the third day when New Zealand were struggling to save the follow-on. They wanted 183 and were 140 for seven, and he was then 70 off only 90 balls. He could have been caught hooking at Gough, who also hit him on the helmet. Perhaps that unsettled him, or maybe it was the bother about a substitute for him on the first two days, but he just had a go at everything, and finally was caught by Gooch, trying to hook again – this time off White.

He was another one I had a chat with. It seemed to me that, in the Lord's Test, he had only been putting the ball there, and I told him that wasn't what we wanted. The captain was looking to him as a shock bowler, not a stock one, and we wanted him to run in and bang it in hard as he did for Yorkshire in the early part of the season. At that stage, I did not know anything about his shin condition, but it had apparently already started to develop.

He certainly took notice, because he let it go so well that he finished with three good wickets for 18 and the lads reckon that he was half a yard quicker than Gough. He can be an unsettling bowler, and to get Parore out driving, Crowe hooking and Pringle bowled leg stump showed a lot of variation at a good pace. He paid for it, though, because although he only bowled 21 overs in the match, his shin condition flared up, and he was never right for the rest of the summer.

Regarding the substitute issue, the New Zealanders thought we were wrong to refuse one every time Crowe came off in the first two days. They said that he was feeling ill because of the antibiotics he took for a digestive complaint. All we knew was that he was doubtful before the match, and the fact that he felt too ill to field on Thursday and Friday, apparently because of something else, seemed too much of a coincidence.

Crowe cut a sorry figure crouched on the outfield in between deliveries, and was clearly unwell, as he had been before the game, so England's seemingly heartless attitude was understandable. Whatever the tourists' management might say about the cause of his disability, and despite their reference to 'inflammation of the alimentary canal', the original condition and its treatment were related, so there could be no substitute. Crowe's feverish innings could be traced to one of two things – a still-upset alimentary canal, or a cerebral upset at England's reluctance to take his condition seriously.

His 115 in the second innings was a masterly innings. It was his 17th hundred for New Zealand and his fifth against England, and the five and a half hours he batted were in stark disciplined contrast to his free-for-all in the first innings. He was finally caught by Hick at slip, but further rain denied England what would have been their first win on the ground for 13 years – the Ashes game in which Ian Botham hit his 86-ball hundred.

Illingworth

The Kiwis got away with a draw, but 1–0 in the series was about right. We could have lost at Lord's and we caught them cold at Trent Bridge, so it was time to assess where we were in the 17 days' break before we played South Africa at Lord's. They were going to be a harder side to beat, with their four fast bowlers, so we had to have a close look at our batting. Atherton, Gooch and Stewart had done well enough with 273, 223 and 196 respectively in the four innings they each had in the three Tests. They were virtually fireproof, so again it would come down to Smith and Hick. Their figures were moderate – 254 between them in eight innings and only one fifty each. They each had one piece of bad luck – Smith with his run-out in the first Test and perhaps Hick with a marginal LBW at Lord's, but otherwise they got out in disappointing ways.

Could we keep faith with them any longer? Maybe one, but definitely not both. Not with Thorpe and Crawley pressing so hard. It would be a long and lively meeting, but at least we had an extra week and that much more cricket to watch.

What were the other plus factors? For me, DeFreitas was the biggest, with 21 wickets and a couple of fifties in three completed innings. His outswing bowling was now quality stuff, and his batting at long last was beginning to count. His revival showed how much cricket is a matter of confidence, and I was pleased to see him react so positively to our talk at Chesterfield. Rhodes was also a great success.

He had done everything I hoped for. He saved a Test match, and had taken 12 catches, a couple of them outstanding. Like another plus, Gough, he was bubbly and a good bloke in the dressing-room. At least the charge against me that I was too Yorkshire-minded was proved wrong, with both of them taking to Test cricket so well.

White did well enough to justify his selection and, although it looked as though he would never be more than an extra seamer batting at six, at least it gave the captain a fifth bowler. So there we were, three batsmen, an all-rounder, a wicket-keeper and two bowlers to give us the nucleus of a good side.

As I always knew, we were short of bowlers, with the main worry being the form of Fraser and Malcolm among the quicks, and the need to find a penetrative spinner. Such was a good bowler up to a point. He bowled his overs for around two runs each, which at least gave the captain some control, but six wickets in 123 overs suggested we might have to look elsewhere.

At least I thought we had made a reasonable start, and had something to build on.

A half-term report would say of Messrs Illingworth, Titmus and Bolus that they had made a solid start. Criticised because of their age – they entered office at 182 for three – they provided a nice mix of character. The two former off-spinners were never in danger of overstatement, but what could have been misinterpreted as dour, defensive dullness was a good foil to the extrovert approach of Bolus. A hilarious after-dinner speaker, Bolus spread himself far and wide in the press boxes around the country in his first two months as a selector. It was a job he had been keen to do for several years, and he failed by the narrowest of margins in a vote taken at the spring Board meeting in March 1992. He dead-heated with Dennis Amiss on the first count, with Amiss winning a second vote. Widely experienced in personnel work, Bolus brought fresh ideas to the job and, as he was one of Illingworth's starred choices, the chairman must have been confident he could control the gush of a Bolus verbal tap that was often only a drop or two away from full flood.

Their first objective was to win the odd Test and save others that had been lost in recent years. Even though New Zealand were not the most fearsome of opponents, the new selectors achieved that first objective with the win at Trent Bridge and the draw at Lord's. Or, as Bolus phrased it, 'At least we've stopped the bleeding.' The next objective was to remove the dressing and see if the wound had completely healed.

Part 3
SOUTH AFRICA, 1994

6

CAPTAIN COURAGEOUS?: LORD'S

Illingworth informed Mike Atherton during the Old Trafford Test that he had been reappointed as England captain for the remainder of the summer. When the chairman told the press, he added, 'If he does well, he'll do the winter tour' – a remark that brought this rejoinder from David Frith: 'Such restraint was astonishing, for if ever England had stability of leadership it was now.'

Having made his point, Frith went on, unwittingly perhaps, to make the opposite case. 'It is a bewildering exercise to thumbnail down the list of England captains over the past 20, let alone 60, years. The Great Debate seems to return every couple of years, like a blight.'

Nothing new there, whether Frith's figure of 20 or 60 years is taken – or even 100 or 120 years. A trawl through the record books reveals the following astonishing statistic: *Peter May is the only man in history to have been appointed England captain for five consecutive years*. His first game in charge started on 9 June 1955 at Trent Bridge against South Africa, and his run ended through illness on 23 February 1960 at Sabina Park.

Some cricketers have led England over a longer period of five years, but their service as appointed captain was broken for various reasons – the main one, until the accession of May, being their unavailability to tour. The caveat to the unique performance of May is that Johnny Douglas and Walter Hammond were captains of their country either side of the two world wars. Therefore, the reign of Douglas was unbroken between 13 December 1913 in Durban and 14 June at Lord's in 1921, as was that of Hammond between 10 June 1938 at Trent Bridge against Australia and 6 February 1947 in Adelaide.

Hammond became the first England captain to lead his side 20 times consecutively, with Archie MacLaren (14), Bob Wyatt (13) and Douglas (12) his nearest challengers. The numerical pattern changed in the 1950s because of more countries playing Test cricket, but the length of tenure in cricket's hottest seat did not. Leonard Hutton, Ted Dexter, Mike Smith, Ray Illingworth, Mike Brearley, David Gower and Mike Gatting all led England more than 20 times, but none for longer than three consecutive years.

Captains have come and gone for different reasons, including winning the toss and putting Australia in (Denness), accusations of time-wasting and arguing with a spectator (Close, who has always disagreed), a Pakistani umpire and an English barmaid (Gatting), illness (May), as well as the sort of selectorial indecision highlighted by Colin Cowdrey. He captained England 27 times, losing on only four occasions, yet the selectors vacillated about him in nine separate series between 1959 and 1969.

Frith's next comment – 'As of now, the position seems to be perfectly filled, and, moreover, by a man with years ahead of him' – could have been justifiably applied to most of Atherton's predecessors, including Illingworth. Which might explain why the innately cautious Pudsey man was disinclined to write an open cheque for Atherton. 'If he does well he'll do the winter tour' was pithy and, as late July would show, remarkably prophetic. Atherton walked into Lord's with head held high for the historic Test against South Africa, but can hardly be said to have departed Headquarters in the same manner. He was to plunge English cricket into its biggest captaincy crisis since Gatting in Faisalabad, although the difference was that, whereas Gatting was only too keen to explain his actions and words, Atherton was not.

Before Gatting came Illingworth's argument with Lou Rowan in Sydney in 1971, followed, a few minutes later, by the England captain leading his players off the field in protest at the throwing of cans and bottles on to the outfield. Before that was the controversy involving Jardine on the Bodyline tour in 1932–33, but none of those three captains can have attracted the publicity surrounding the Atherton affair with its allegations of ball-tampering.

Illingworth
Our most important selection meeting so far was also the longest, going on until nearly midnight. The captain was playing in Blackpool against Derbyshire, so we met on Saturday evening, 16 July, at the Copthorne Hotel again in Manchester. What we

normally did was to have a chat for an hour or so before we got down to business, and from that it was clear that the batting was going to take some time to resolve. Smith was the one we discussed at length, because we had talked to him so many times to try to help him regain his confidence. He had now played 53 Test matches – more than anyone who played at Old Trafford except Gooch – and had got nine hundreds in 97 innings. He had scored 3677 runs at an average of just over 44, and he had only been dropped once before. The trouble was that that was 11 months previously at home against Australia, following scores in the first five Tests of 4, 18, 22, 5, 86, 50, 23, 35, 21 and 19.

He was then dropped for The Oval and scored as follows in the West Indies: 0, 2, 84, 24, 12, 0, 10, 13, 175. They are not bad figures – in fact for a young man making his way, they might have warranted a longer run. But we were now talking about, except for Gooch, our most senior batsman who was needed in a pivotal batting position. But in those 10 Tests, he had one good one against Australia at Trent Bridge, and two satisfactory games in the West Indies – at Georgetown where he scored 84 and 24 and his 175 in Antigua.

There were two problems – that only meant three good games out of 10, and yet he was out in single figures only five times in 19. He was doing a lot of the hard work by getting in, yet he was no longer going on as often as in previous years. Warne and May did him seven times in the previous summer, but he only had pace to deal with in the West Indies. Furthermore, we had lost both series by wide margins, so the time had come to make a change.

Some people might wonder about Hick's position, because in the same series he played four innings fewer for 572 runs, compared with Smith's 603 from 19 innings. Furthermore, Hick had not got a hundred, so should it not have been a case of both going, or neither?

With Mike so keen on John Crawley, I knew we must make a change, although it was not automatic whether Crawley or Graham Thorpe came in for Smith. We decided to stick with Hick, and we had quite a chew over which new batsman would come in and also the overall batting order, now that Gooch had had a couple of poor matches. I have often heard it said from chairmen of selectors that they never have a vote and, if the committee is split, they talk it through until there is general agreement.

I don't agree with that. The whole purpose of a committee is to have a cross-section of views and, if they are strongly held, I don't see why one man should back down. If he is out-voted, everyone knows where they are, and the majority carries the day. I know Mike had seen much more of Crawley than the three of us put together, and you have to say that anyone who scores big double hundreds must have something. I was not sold yet, because I watched him early in the season at Lord's for the 'A' side, and again at Old Trafford against Yorkshire, and he got out playing balls towards leg, which I would rather have seen him play straighter.

It is all very well being strong one side of the wicket, but top bowlers in Test cricket soon work that out and make you play somewhere else. In county cricket, you cash in more, because the quality of bowling is not so good or deep. Eventually, they work a batsman out, but Crawley was still only a youngster. I was worried that the quicker South African bowlers might find him out, but Mike was adamant that he wanted him.

Keith Fletcher went with him, which was not a great surprise, although I thought one of them might think that Thorpe had waited long enough. Like Hick, he played a couple of good innings in the West Indies, and I was keen to get a left-hander in if we could. I was positive we missed a big trick the previous summer against Warne by not picking a left-hander until we were 2–0 down, and Thorpe then averaged 46 in three games, missing The Oval Test because of injury.

The press had given us some stick for not picking him, who was averaging nearly 60 for Surrey, but I have never been influenced by them, and I was not going to start then. There was some sort of case for playing six front-line batsmen, because I knew White was beginning to struggle with his shins. Yorkshire beat Leicestershire at Harrogate, and he only bowled 15 overs out of 179 in the two innings, but in the end we reckoned he could get through a Test match as the fifth bowler, batting at six.

So it went on, Crawley v. Thorpe, until I called for a vote to see if anyone had changed their minds. No, 2–2, so it was down to me. I could prove my point to the press by overruling the captain, or I could go with him on a wider principle. That is what I did, because I did not think that was the issue to get heavy about – not if it meant denying the captain a batsman he clearly wanted. That was not compromising my views, either on the individual concerned or my declared intention to have the final say in selection. It was more a matter of common sense, and does not mean that I shall not overrule in the future.

The plain fact is that it is written into my contract that, not only do I get the final say, *I have a veto about any player except the captain, and that is held by the chairman of the Board.*

A final word about voting at these meetings. I have never been able to confirm it, but I was told on good authority that my captaincy to Australia in 1970–71 was only settled after a vote of 3–1 in my favour.

Illingworth of the elephantine memory again. He believes that Don Kenyon, Billy Sutcliffe and Alan Smith voted for him, but Chairman Alec Bedser wanted Cowdrey, and it would be a brave man who would risk money on him being wrong.

Illingworth
Crawley for Smith was the only change we made, although there was quite an argument during the game about the batting order. We certainly talked about it for a long time, particularly the number three spot. Fred and Brian were sure we had settled it with Hick at three, Crawley four and Gooch five, but the captain insisted that no firm decision was reached. I know how keen Bolus had been all summer to get Hick in at three, but all I can say is that it was a long meeting, which is where the confusion may have arisen. It was a big issue, because number three at Test level is a crucial position. What seems to have happened is that Mike, in the belief that it was left to him, asked Crawley where he would rather bat and acted accordingly.

This explains the different versions of the batting order floated in the national press, with each correspondent convinced he had obtained an accurate briefing before the start of the match. It was quite a permutation to get right, with Gooch *in situ* during the three New Zealand Tests, Hick keen to bat where he bats for Worcestershire and Crawley confident enough to want the spotlight. Crawley treads with sure foot the thin line between self-assurance and arrogance. Of his selection, he said, 'I'm not concerned about being written up. I went to play for England and if I'm selected, it's down to me to repay the faith. Obviously there are pressures, but it is down to me to learn how to cope with them. If the selectors think I'm ready, then I'm ready.' Atherton certainly did, emphasising, 'He is a strong character, and I am sure he will not be overawed by the occasion.'

The squad was announced on Sunday, 17 July, and I was covering the Surrey v. Warwickshire match at Guildford for my newspaper. The local media were there in the expectation of interviews with Thorpe, and reaction was predictable. Surrey's director of coaching, Mike Edwards, used the word 'disgraceful' to describe his player's omission. Thankfully, Thorpe refused to be drawn, perhaps because Illingworth had spoken to him about his situation.

Illingworth

I told him he was very much in our thoughts, and just to keep scoring runs. I couldn't promise him anything, but I did indicate that, if he stayed in form, he was likely to go to Australia.

We picked Salisbury, making two changes from Old Trafford with Crawley making his debut. The pitch was a bit damp early, but it proved a good toss to win because it crusted and started to crack from the second day onwards. The bounce was not consistent and, as usual on that sort of pitch, extra pace is the hardest to play against. Like Nash for New Zealand, Donald out-bowled our quicks and that is why we lost the match. I thought we had a reasonable first day, thanks to White nipping Rhodes out and Gough getting Wessels in the last half-hour, and I would have settled for their close-of-play 244 for six. If we could have kept them to around 300, the course of the match might have been different, but the way Matthews smashed us for 41 off 36 balls was a killer. As a result, their last three wickets put on 76, and a score of 357 makes it hard for the opposition to win. Our bowling was patchy, with DeFreitas having his first poor game of the summer. Also, he struggled with cramp on the first day, but we never bowled with the same discipline as the South Africans.

Matthews struck it well, but I was a bit disappointed how much room we gave him outside off stump. I know it was the first time we had seen him, but it shouldn't take too long to work out where a hitter likes to play. We now had to bat well to save the game, let alone think about trying to win it, but we were found out by quality pace bowling. We had four out of our top six caught behind the wicket, and the only time we looked like competing was when Hick and Gooch were together and we were 107 for three.

They were both going well but, once De Villiers got Gooch

LBW, it all changed. They put on 39 in 10 overs, but Hick dried up so much that we only managed 12 in the next 10 overs. I know a wicket makes a difference, but it was still disappointing that he seemed to draw back and just concentrate on survival. It emphasised the point I had made to Hick that he would not have batted the same in a county game. He was then caught behind and none of the last five partnerships were worth more than 20. Donald got three of our tail and was too much for them.

I know they bowled well, and were on an emotional high because of the occasion. But it was never a 180 pitch – more like 250 at the least. We never looked to try to get back a bit of the initiative, as is shown by the fact that from White down to Fraser at 11, the six of them faced 160 balls for 66 runs.

Yet again we were on the wrong end of it at Lord's, and there were nearly three days to go after we only lasted for 39 minutes on Saturday morning.

We needed early wickets, otherwise, with a lead of 177, they would leave themselves at least a day and a half in which to bowl us out. It was the hottest day of the match and I knew it would take a huge effort and some luck to get out of the game with a draw. The big difference between the two sides on the first two days was entirely down to discipline. By that, I mean few of them got themselves out, and their bowling was much tighter. Because it was such a big game for them, they must have been wound up to a degree where we should have been able to put pressure on them. Yet we were the side who struggled. Those first two days proved how strong mentally they were, but you couldn't say the same about us.

The South Africans are like the Aussies in that respect. They play tough and hard, and I suppose it's got a lot to do with their way of life and how they play their sport from an early age. The nearest we get to that in England is Yorkshire, or rather used to be, because I have to say that is not so obvious nowadays. Another reason why we never seem to match up to that sort of macho approach is that we play so much more cricket than in other countries. That does two things. For our players, it is bound to breed an attitude that there is always another day if things go wrong. For overseas cricketers, each match means that much more, and they play it as hard as in Test cricket.

You only have to add up the days of domestic cricket to see what I mean. In England we play 17 four-day games, plus 17

Sunday League games and a few knock-out matches. All that adds up to around 90 days – sounds like a prison sentence – which is far more than overseas. Our Test players miss on average seven four-day games and the same number of Sunday matches, but that is made up again with five or six Tests and the Texaco games. The South Africans don't even play half that amount of domestic cricket, and the Aussies play even less. *But*, their club and grade cricket is much stronger than ours, as is proved every year by the players who play for money in each other's country. The leagues in Lancashire and in the South all feature youngsters from Australia and South Africa who do much better than some of our young county players in Australian grade cricket. I am afraid it is a fact of life which won't change until the system does.

Lunch on that fateful Saturday, 23 July, must have been the last meal that the England captain, selectors and Board administrators enjoyed for several days. Almost exactly halfway through the pivotal day of the five-day Test – 2.50 p.m. – cricket was consigned to second place, a long way behind the storm that broke over the hapless head of Atherton.

In the BBC television commentary box, Tony Lewis was on microphone duty, and I was walking the 100 yards to the South African Broadcasting Corporation box at the other end of the Pavilion, away from the Warner Stand in which the BBC box is housed. When I got back to base, Lewis had finished his stint and asked me if I had seen what he, and the rest of the viewing world, had, thanks to a vigilant cameraman. He described the pictures which by now were going around the world, including, crucially, to South Africa, from where the instant backlash from viewers jammed the switchboards of the SABC in Johannesburg.

Their senior producer, Mike Demaine, had recorded the incident concerning Atherton, his pocket, right hand and what appeared to be dirt, and chose to show it several times back home. His BBC counterpart, Keith Mackenzie, decided to be more selective, with Lewis having reacted perfectly properly by carefully avoiding any on-air reaction that might be considered to prejudice an official investigation later. He confined himself to a reference to Aladdin's lamp, with the rubbing of that pantomime object comparable to Atherton's actions with the ball. Clearly a tongue-in-cheek comment by Lewis, but 20 years of broadcasting experience brought that instinctive response.

Being a Saturday afternoon, the Test match was not televised on the normal ball-by-ball basis, but shared the afternoon session with racing. During one of these breaks in live transmission, I asked for and was given a rerun of the clip that brought as much opprobrium on the head of Atherton as on any other captain in living memory – at least for purely cricketing actions. It looked horrible. A fumbling in the right-hand pocket, followed by the apparent transference of a substance on to the ball, which was then tossed to the bowler. Closer inspection of the pictures showed some of the substance falling away, as the first two fingers and thumb appeared to rub along the seam.

My next stint in the SABC box was after tea, by which time the lines to and from the Republic were red hot. Their commentator, Trevor Quirk, told me that he and summariser Andre Bruyns had already commented over the damaging pictures, and I would be expected to do the same. Like the rest of us, he was confused about the various interpretations of the pictures, which were already circulating. He even offered the theory that Atherton was spoofing the press because, surely, no Test captain would act so openly if his seemingly illegal actions were intended to alter the condition of the ball.

A good theory, except I could not believe that Atherton would perpetrate a practical joke in such poor taste when his mind should have been focused on how best to contain and frustrate the increasing tempo of South Africa's charge for victory.

Illingworth

The first I heard about it was when Mike Procter told me. I had been watching the game from the balcony, so had missed the television pictures. Then, the Board's media liaison officer, Richard Little, told me he had got a video of it in his office, so I went to see it right away. When I came back, shortly before the tea interval, I guessed that the press would be waiting for Atherton, so I got a message to him on the field, via Gooch at third man, to make sure he did not speak to anyone as he came off. I told him that he had to come straight to see me, which he did. I asked him to turn his pockets out, and I saw what looked like dry dust.

He told me he often did it to stop sweat getting on to the ball when he bowled, and did not see anything wrong as it was simply to soak up the sweat on his hands.

* * *

Former Lancashire colleague Paul Allott, now making his name in the world of commentary, later confirmed this to me, but it still seemed only half an answer. Much was made of Atherton's subsequent defence that, had the ball been tampered with, the umpires would have noticed, and they later confirmed that they had examined the ball several times and found nothing wrong. Again, that is only part of the answer, because any dust or dirt transferred to the ball along the seam would drop off, either in flight or on pitching.

The ball-tampering issue flared up on the same ground two years earlier in the Texaco one-day international between England and Pakistan, with threatened legal action by the Pakistan cricketers coming to nothing. Former player Sarfraz Nawaz was the only one to take Allan Lamb on, with his case being withdrawn once the third umpire in the match in question, Don Oslear, took the witness stand on the fourth and final day of the High Court hearing.

Allegations about altering the condition of the ball then largely centred on *the removal of parts of the ball to alter the equally weighted balance of the two sides.* Now, Atherton was being accused of adding weight, not removing it from the ball. Undoubtedly this can be done but, in order to make the extraneous substance, be it dust or dirt, stick, it has to be wedged under the quarter-seam; i.e. that same quarter-seam has to be lifted, and such an action is both illegal and easily detected, unless the section of the ball in question is quickly sealed again, and stays sealed with that side of the ball now heavier. Gouging achieves the same effect, but for opposite reasons, with that side of the ball being made lighter.

Any cricketer knows that, with a ball weighing no more than 5¾ ounces and no less than 5½ ounces, it needs only a few grammes to be added or removed from one side to create an imbalance in weight of the two sides which, roughly, weigh 2½ ounces each when the wrapper is removed. Those are all the aerodynamic variables, but what about the specific action of Atherton?

Or rather actions, because a couple of days later, match referee Peter Burge was asked privately about the two instances he had seen of Atherton delving in his pocket and then fingering the ball. 'Not two, but four,' Burge is said to have replied, explaining that since Saturday and his investigation of the matter he had watched the entire session on video – not just the recorded live play – and had noticed four similar incidents.

As to whether it would be folly to tamper with the ball in front of the camera, with its close-up technology, no cricketer on the field other than the bowler and batsman is ever sure when he is under scrutiny, so it is not true to say, in Atherton's defence, that he must be innocent because he knew his actions would be filmed. He could be off camera for several minutes, although, clearly, he is more often on camera than other fielders, because a commentator will ask the producer to feature him in between deliveries, if a point needs making about a bowling or fielding change. Even so, he could never be sure that he was being filmed, with 70 or 80 yards' distance between him and the cameraman.

As for the naked eye and binoculars, a mischievous observer might point out that Atherton's actions were made with his back to the Pavilion and committee rooms, but such speculation can only be just that and nothing more. What is fact is that he was filmed doing something more with the ball than a captain normally does when he is taking it to his bowler. The anti-Atherton lobby could thus argue that he was so desperate to give his bowlers every advantage that he hoped his actions would not be filmed and, anyway, they would not be picked up by the naked eye. Like the counter-arguments, these deductions are tenuous, but they must be put – if only to illustrate the difficulty of one man trying to read the mind of another. Even a rational man like Atherton can commit actions that are irrational – even to himself. That is only human nature, which never loses its capacity to surprise.

The South Africans were privately outraged but, to their eternal credit, did not utter one word either during or after the match. They kept out of an issue that was to engage the attention of Burge for a couple of days and Illingworth, his fellow-selectors and the Board's senior officers for a week and more. And then there was the press, some of whom will never forget that, to a man, they missed Gooch as captain being officially warned about the state of the ball on the field by umpires John Holder and Mervyn Kitchen at The Oval against the West Indies in August 1991.

Again, the incident occurred on a Saturday, which meant that the day's play and incidents were not under the same close scrutiny by the national daily correspondents and their number twos. Instead, the Sunday boys had moved in, with much tighter deadlines for their various edition times, so reaction to the story was understandably delayed.

Illingworth
At the end of play, I went for my usual hour or so over to the Cornhill hospitality room at the Nursery end. As I left the

dressing-room, a message came from Peter Burge that he wanted to see Atherton and Fletcher. I guessed he would want to see the captain, but I was satisfied then that what he had done was silly, but not culpable.

I chatted about it with Mike Procter in Cornhill, and did not have a clue when I left the ground at about 8 p.m. that the thing was still dragging on in the Pavilion. It was only by chance that I ran into Burge back in the hotel opposite Lord's at around 10 p.m. He told me that he had issued a statement saying that he accepted Atherton's explanation, and I must admit, I did not dream that the press would make so much of it next morning.

Having got their match reports out of the way, the media could now concentrate on the drama unfolding in the Pavilion. Burge interviewed Atherton and Fletcher, and also brought in both umpires, 'Dickie' Bird and Steve Randell, to confirm that the ball had not been altered in any way. Time dragged on, most of it devoted to finalising Burge's statement which was to exasperate the media, largely because of what it did not say rather than what it did. Even Richie Benaud thundered his disbelief next morning about what he saw as an abrogation of duty by the authorities in not being more forthcoming to the public.

Consider the strength of Benaud's feelings as he penned these words.

Has everyone in this cricket world gone bonkers? We have had controversy after controversy and for most of the time cricket authorities seem to live behind a veil of secrecy. The telling phrase in Burge's statement was 'I have accepted the explanation given and no action will be taken.'

What was the explanation given by Atherton? We don't know because Atherton was instructed by England's cricket authorities to say nothing. Regarding the ball-tampering allegations against the Pakistanis of two years ago, I said then that the cricketing authorities should know better than to think they would be able, deliberately, to deprive the cricketing public of such knowledge.

I say it again in this Atherton matter. If there has been an explanation given and accepted by the match referee, then the cricket authorities have a duty to their public to make that explanation known for the benefit of this and other cricket countries. People paying their monies at the turnstiles and watching on television and buying newspapers keep the game going, along with all those who play club cricket and engage in other aspects of the game.

If the explanation is given and accepted, then the match referee should have been completely satisfied. If he is completely satisfied, then everyone should know about it. By sewing tight the lips of the referee and refusing to allow cricket followers to know the facts, the cricket authorities are doing a grave disservice to the game.

Those words should be written large on the walls of the Lord's cricket committee rooms.

The missing link was perceived to be Burge's statement that he had accepted Atherton's version of the incident, although he did not reveal what that explanation was. As Benaud said, such an omission could only further inflame a hostile press, who now had the sniff of a cover-up. That was untrue, but it is a sad fact that cricket's authorities appear to have an instinctive ability to repeat mistakes concerning what should be said and what kept secret. Open government is one extreme that the ICC and the TCCB will never be in danger of adopting, but the other extreme of point-blank refusal to abandon a self-defeating policy of secrecy is illogical, unreasonable and doomed to failure.

As was illustrated again, once Illingworth awoke and read his Sunday press.

Illingworth

I got to the ground at 9.30 a.m. and saw Atherton immediately. I told him we simply had to do something, otherwise the heavy mob of the Monday morning press would crucify him and everyone else. I said that the Sunday boys were only net bowlers compared with what was to come, and I went through everything with him before he went to practise. I told him we had to show the rest of the world we were clean, otherwise other countries – especially Pakistan – would have a field day. Once I found out he had not told the whole truth to Burge, I was even more determined to try to stop things festering by some sort of strong, public action.

We were in a mess, and if the matter went back to the ICC, anything might happen, including a heavy fine or even suspension or a banning for a period. There were two issues. The dirt in the pocket, and the fact that Atherton hid that from

Burge. I told Richard Little as much and, as soon as play started, I saw him again – this time with Alan Smith.

Atherton had seen Smith and Doug Insole the previous evening after the official hearing and statement, and had apparently been told that he must not make any further statement. In fact, Atherton deviated from this strategy slightly, by informing writer Rob Steen that 'I will not be making a statement, nor do I anticipate making one in the future.' Again, the Board reverted to type, thus further strengthening the point made by Benaud and others. What Smith and Insole did not know was that Atherton had not been frank with the match referee, but it would be naïve to assume that, even with that knowledge, their instruction to Atherton would have been different.

I have known both men for 40 years, as players and then administrators, and know both as honest and honourable men. As are people like Donald Carr, Dennis Silk, Ossie Wheatley, Colin Cowdrey and many others – all of whom nevertheless instinctively close ranks on big issues. It is too simplistic to say that they must work with the press, but so much adverse comment of recent years could have been avoided with a more forthcoming attitude from the authorities. If, as in the Atherton matter, the press believe they have to force things out into the open, then column inches by the dozen are filled for many more days than would otherwise be the case.

Illingworth
I have to say that I had to instigate what happened later on Sunday. I told 'A.C.' that we had to sort it out by announcing something to show the world we meant business. I told him that it would not die a death, and the only way we could stop it going back to the ICC was to take firm action. I said that what Atherton had done was against the spirit of the game, if nothing worse, and we had to punish that as well as the concealment. I don't think the Board would have gone that far on their own, but I was pleased that they went along with what I wanted to do. 'A.C.' brought Doug Insole in on it immediately, and also the Board chairman, Frank Chamberlain, came in on things after lunch. The cricket suddenly seemed a side issue, and I wondered what I'd done to get in the middle of something like this in my fourth Test as chairman of selectors. Whatever it meant, I was not going to duck it, so while we were being bowled out to lose the game easily, the three of us,

together with Richard Little, hammered out what we would do.

I thought the best way out was the most painful – that Atherton should be asked to attend a press conference where he would own up to hiding part of the truth from Burge, and I would announce that I had fined him the maximum I could of £1000 on each of two counts. My statement had to be worded very carefully, and it all took so long that I could not watch any cricket after lunch on that fourth day.

I also went to Burge and told him what I was going to do. As I expected, he was not impressed, and told me that, had he known the truth on Saturday evening, he would probably have suspended Atherton for two matches. I think that, had he done that, the player would have put the matter in the hands of his solicitors, which would have undermined the whole structure of the code of conduct and the match referee. Anyway, thank goodness we pre-empted that, because cricket and lawyers should never mix – at least not professionally. Nobody wins, except for the lawyers' bank managers.

I have known Burge since we played Test cricket against each other in 1961 and 1962–63. We are the same age and speak the same language, so I could talk straight to him. I told him what I was going to do and he agreed that he would not take any further action. He told me that he would issue a statement saying that he would regard it as sufficient punishment that the England captain would be heavily fined and have to admit in public that he had not been frank with the match referee. And it would be in public, because the press conference was widened to include television and radio and, as it turned out, it went live into Sunday *Grandstand*.

We had announced that Mike would face the press before we knew that the match would be over that day, so we had to get the normal after-the-match ceremonies out of the way first. Being the hottest day of the summer, and with the Pavilion library having no air-conditioning, I knew it would be uncomfortable, but never dreamed it would turn out like it did. There must have been 50 or more people crammed in there. That was bad enough after we kept them waiting for over half an hour, but then there were the arc lights of the television cameras to make it worse than a hothouse.

I was spared the thermal roasting, thanks to the presence in the library of the BBC cameras. Keith Mackenzie ensured that we could hook in to the hearing from the comfort of the commentary box, and my thousand words or so for the *Birmingham Post* were kick-started by an early sight of the statements before they were publicly read by Illingworth and Atherton.

Illingworth

Those statements took for ever to agree. Richard Little was in charge of them and altered them at least three or four times. Mike would not accept one, but we eventually came up with a wording that satisfied everyone. I didn't want any apology to me because my overall view is this.

Mike was more stupid than anything else, and the condition of the ball was not altered. I think we made the right decision to go public. If we had swept it under the carpet, we would really have got some stick, and not just from the press. Just think of what some countries would have made of it, which is why I included in my statement that England had to be seen to be whiter than white on such an important issue.

I was soaked with sweat within a couple of minutes, and I read my statement first. The press made something of the fact that I did not believe Atherton had done anything illegal, yet I had still fined him the maximum £1000 for his actions. I did not mind that, because the definition of what is illegal is not clear. Law 42 (5) refers twice to the forbidding of 'artificial substances'. You can polish the ball, but not with an artifical substance. Is sweat artificial? If it is, then every bowler in the game breaks Law 42. It also says that no artificial substance may be used to change the condition of the ball. I know the ball was not changed, but is the dust and dirt Mike admitted to having in his pocket artificial or not? As I have said, he acted stupidly and deserved something, which is why I fined him.

I was questioned at some length about what I had done and why, but I made it clear Mike accepted the two fines, and this would therefore be the end of it. At least the thing had been dealt with publicly, even if it was the day after. I can remember many incidents which have dragged on, simply because of inaction by the authorities. I pointed out that I had only established all the facts before lunch that same day, and the fact that I was now announcing disciplinary action after the game hardly proved I had dragged my feet. I was pleased in one way, because the whole mess showed I was right in asking for bottom-line authority in my contract.

Illingworth was right. He achieved several things by his strong and rapid action. He pre-empted a second strike by Burge and therefore, probably, saved Atherton his job. It is unlikely that the Board would have kept him in office after censure and punishment by a match referee. In doing this, Illingworth also made a nonsense of the theory, widely advanced in the national press, that he and Atherton did not get on and that the chairman would not be averse to a change of captaincy. Had that been the situation, Illingworth had a perfect opportunity to let Atherton dangle until he hung himself. All Illingworth had to do was to do nothing, but it was no surprise to me that he acted promptly, fairly, with his action underscored with the touch of instinctive loyalty he usually offers unless an individual convinces him otherwise. Atherton must have come close to doing that and, had their relationship really been that strained, nobody could have pointed a finger at the chairman if he had watched his captain float down the river.

Not only that, but the events of the following week, in which Atherton asked for time to consider his position, further proved the point that Illingworth, by acting according to his own rules of life, achieved what few other men in his position could have done.

Illingworth's statement closed with: 'I have fined Michael the maximum I can on each count, and as far as I am concerned, the matter has been dealt with and is now closed.' If only that had been true . . .

Atherton's statement said this:

Having spent some time looking at television footage and discussing it with Ray Illingworth, I felt that the sooner I explained the situation the better. Yesterday evening, I was asked to attend a meeting with Mr Burge, and after that he issued a statement that he accepted the explanation I gave and that no further action would be taken. In my explanation, I did not present all the facts.

I am here to explain what I did and to answer any questions. As you are aware we use sweat to get the bruises out of the ball and then rub to maintain the shine. It was very hot and humid out there yesterday, your hands get wet and this in turn dampens the ball when you handle it. You all saw me reach into my pocket, dry my fingers with some dirt in order not to dampen the ball. Whilst I told Mr Burge that I put my hand into my pocket to dry my fingers, I did not tell him that I used the dirt to dry them; therefore my response to his questioning was incomplete.

I would like to add that at no time in my career have I ever used substances to alter the condition of the ball. I would apologise to Mr Burge and the South African team. I hope everybody accepts my apology.

Replying to a question, Atherton said: 'I made a huge mistake in not doing what other bowlers and fielders did in the middle when their hands got sweaty. They rubbed their hands along the ground to dry them. All I did differently was to have the dirt in my pocket.'

He was then asked, 'If you had that problem, could you not have taken a towel out with you?'

'Yes, I could, but I didn't. I can only repeat that at no time did I alter the condition of the ball or set out to do that. We wanted to get the ball to reverse swing, and it won't do that when it is sweaty.'

However, overseas bowlers, who frequently use spit and sweat in order to make one side heavier than the other, seem to manage to make it reverse swing in such circumstances, but perhaps English bowlers use different methods. I wrote the following in the *Birmingham Post*.

'It is a well-known fact that a ball swings more when one side is heavier than the other, either through spit and sweat to increase the moisture content – which Atherton specified he wanted to avoid – or to increase the weight by adding dust and dirt to the seam and quarter-seam.'

I ended the article with these three paragraphs.

Nobody is pointing that particular finger at the England captain, but he is lucky that he has been guaranteed that the incident will not affect his position as England captain.

He is lucky, full stop. He was caught doing something he should not in front of 28,000 people at Lord's, and in full close-up view of the cameras. He hid the truth from the referee, and now he hopes the matter is closed.

If it is, he can thank Illingworth and his lucky stars.

Well, it was far from closed, and the rumblings would continue right up to the end of the first day's play of the Headingley Test, 11 days later.

The unique press conference accomplished much, even though it

92

The only four England captains in the 20th century to regain the Ashes in Australia, from top left: Sir Pelham Warner, Johnny Douglas, Douglas Jardine and Raymond Illingworth. (*Allsport/Hulton Deutsch* except bottom right by *Patrick Eagar*)

Illingworth's first selection committee in 1994. Fred Titmus, Brian Bolus and Illingworth before the Lord's Test against New Zealand. (*Patrick Eagar*)

New selector David Graveney, who replaced Brian Bolus in 1995, talks to Michael Atherton and Illingworth during The Oval Test match against the West Indies. (*Allsport/Adrian Murrell*)

Darren Gough, celebrating his first wicket for England against New Zealand in the Texaco Trophy match at Edgbaston in May 1994. He had Martin Crowe caught by Alec Stewart. (*Patrick Eagar*)

Craig White run out against New Zealand in the Lord's Test, June 1994. The third umpire was called upon before Steve Bucknor gave him out. (*Patrick Eagar*)

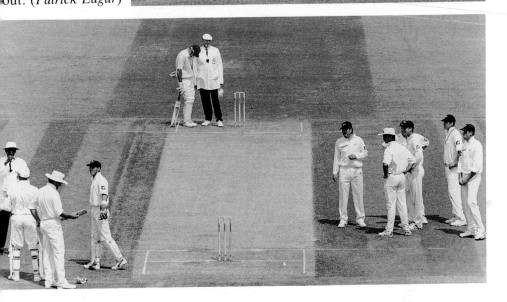

Michael Atherton transferring dust and earth from his pocket to the ball in the Lord's Test against South Africa in July 1994. (*Patrick Eagar*)

The start of the grilling of Michael Atherton about the 'dust in the pocket' incident, at a press conference immediately after the end of the game on the fourth day. (*Allsport/Adrian Murrell*)

Glory denied. Michael Atherton caught and bowled for 99 by Brian McMillan in the Headingley Test, August 1994. This innings occurred 11 days after the Lord's press conference when Illingworth fined him £2000, and only six days after he decided he wished to remain captain of England. (*Patrick Eagar*)

Everything looks correct for batsman and bowler. Cronje's middle stump disappears during Devon Malcolm's devastating nine for 57 against South Africa at The Oval in August 1994. (*Patrick Eagar*)

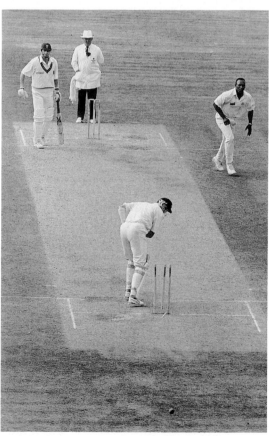

Malcolm's ninth and final wicket, Allan Donald bowled at The Oval, August 1994. (*Patrick Eagar*)

Michael Atherton given out LBW to Fanie de Villiers at The Oval August 1994. He was fined half of his match fee by match referee, Peter Burge, for looking at his bat to indicate he thought he had hit it. (*Patrick Eagar*)

Dennis Silk, chairman of the Test and County Cricket Board when Illingworth was appointed manager as well as chairman of selectors in March 1995. (*Patrick Eagar*)

England bowling coach Peter Lever, formerly of England and Lancashire, talking to Darren Gough at Newlands, Cape Town, in January 1996. (*Patrick Eagar*)

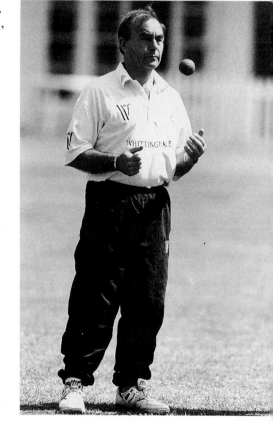

England batting coach, former England and Surrey batsman John Edrich, seen here supervising nets before the Lord's Test against the West Indies in June 1995. (*Patrick Eagar*)

was hardly an edifying sight to see an England captain wriggle like a pinned butterfly as he tried to justify the sequence of events in the previous 28 hours. No captain in history has gone through the same administrative mangle before. The match referee system had been in existence only for three years, and England had never had such a no-nonsense man as Illingworth in charge . . . at least not since he was captain of his country, 25 years earlier.

History will make its own judgement on the two men. Suffice it to say now that the traumas of that Lord's Test established a bond between the two that was not obvious before. Not that astrologists would expect an Aries (Atherton) to sit comfortably with a Gemini, which, surprisingly, Illingworth is. Anyone with a less obvious split personality is hard to imagine, but it seems that even the stars occasionally throw up an exception to the rule.

Illingworth

I drove away from Lord's completely knackered. Mentally as well as physically, because of all that went on behind the scenes from lunch onwards. The cricket was forgotten, yet there we were, being bowled out in under two sessions for 99. Not much more could have gone wrong, either on or off the field. Our batting was blown away in 46 overs – not by Donald, but mainly McMillan and Matthews. The batting order did not work, and we were clearly going to have to do something about it before Headingley. Titmus and Bolus chuntered all through the match about it being different from what they insisted we agreed when we picked the team.

We lost early wickets, but we still got as far as 74 for three in 32 overs, with Gooch and Stewart fighting it out. From that position, half an hour into the final session, we should have taken the game well into the fifth day, yet it was all over in an hour. Matthews did it. He got Stewart caught behind the very next ball after he changed his bat, and then got White playing at a slightly wide one next ball. Donald came back to get Gooch LBW, and generally created mayhem for half an hour, in which he hit Gough on the arm – it looked a bad one, and he had to retire – and also got Salisbury out. What with Fraser also getting a cracked little finger, we were well and truly stuffed.

All credit to South Africa, especially their bowlers, but we should never have lost 20 wickets for 277 runs, with nobody scoring 40.

* * *

It was a curious match for batsmen. South Africa scored 635 runs from 221.2 overs, yet only Wessels (105) and Gary Kirsten (72) passed 50 in the first innings, with nobody at all doing so in the second innings.

The historical highlights for South Africa included their second-ever win at Lord's. The previous one was in 1935 when an England top order of Wyatt, Sutcliffe, Leyland, Hammond, Ames and Holmes were rolled over for 198 and 151. Were the good old days really that good?

Also, the South African win by 356 was their biggest runs margin in all Tests, while England's score of 99 was their lowest at Lord's since 1888. Then there was the curio of Wessels scoring a hundred on debut against England for two countries, having previously done so for Australia. For England, Gooch became the first batsman to score more than 2000 Test runs on the same ground, and Gough's eight wickets gave him figures for his first two Tests of 95.2–18–274–14. A rare find – an English bowler who looked to be a natural wicket-taker.

Illingworth thus had to face two crises – the issue of the captaincy and the morale of a side thrashed inside four days. Atherton, by nature phlegmatic and with a public image usually on an even keel, showed himself to be human, in that the volume and ferocity of media comment had got to him. It would have been extraordinary if it had not, with instant judgements passed by some reporters and ex-players whose lives have not entirely been spent outside glasshouses. He led the news on television and radio. Tabloids ran phone-in polls to see whether he should go or stay, and he rang Illingworth to say he needed space and time to consider his position.

Illingworth

Mike rang me on the Monday to say that he was having doubts about whether he should resign. He wanted to know what my feelings were, and I told him not to rush his decision. If he thought it all through properly over the next few days and he decided he wanted to step down, that would be that, but I told him to weigh everything up first. He asked me if he had my support, and I told him 'yes'. I had also thought about his position carefully. If I thought he had done anything wrong with the ball, he would have gone, but I put it all down to stupidity. And, of course, he was 26. In the context of captaincy that is young. I tried to imagine myself captaining England at that age in 1958, and I could not.

* * *

That remark makes a nonsense of the oft-repeated criticism about the age gap between the 62-year-old Illingworth and the modern player – less than half his age. That private comparison between Atherton and Illingworth at the same age has certainly altered the course of history. How much, is down to Atherton.

Illingworth

I also guaranteed Mike the support of the other selectors, although I know Bolus had reservations to begin with. He attached more importance than I did to our first selection meeting, where he thought Mike was a bit too dogmatic, but eventually agreed with the rest of us that if he wanted to carry on, then he should.

Our selection meeting for the Headingley Test was arranged for that Saturday and, with Mike having no match and having spent a hectic few days trying to keep out of the way in the Lake District, it was set up for the Ladbroke's Hotel in Leeds. He spoke to me a couple of times in the middle of the week, and it seemed to me that he was clearing his mind, even though he was being chased by everyone. I know he spoke to people whose views he trusted – David Lloyd was one – and so I wasn't surprised when he rang me on the Thursday to say that he wanted to stay on.

Atherton's announcement prompted yet another press conference – this time at Old Trafford on Friday morning – where, so he hoped, he would lay the matter to rest. Easier said than done, because of the two extreme views held by the so-called *cognoscenti*. The issue divided the cricket world. BBC Radio cricket correspondent Jonathan Agnew thought Atherton should go, and had been outspoken in stating his views.

He and I were co-commentators for the BBC's television coverage of Durham's home AXA Equity & Law game at Durham University two days later, and he was clearly agitated about the furore he had created.

My view was simple. He had been appointed by the BBC to report and comment. He had played Test cricket and was closer to the county cricket circuit than any of his predecessors. Perhaps that was why he was more sensitive to criticism than previous correspondents who had not played first-class cricket. I told him that if he held strong views about an issue, then it would not be honest to remain silent and paddle a diplomatic canoe through safe waters. What I did believe was that he clouded the issue by referring to his friendship with Atherton. That had nothing to do with the principle of a cricket correspondent commenting on an England captain. It was wrong of him to personalise the matter as one between Agnew and Atherton.

The press conference was, if anything, even more uncomfortable for a now contrite Atherton. The anti brigade pursued what they saw as inconsistencies in his account of Black Saturday, and this time there was no Illingworth beside him. Nor, surprisingly, was there any representative of the Test and County Cricket Board – his main support was provided by Lancashire's chief executive, John Bower. As at Lord's, five days earlier, the first part was broadcast live – this time on Radio 5 – and the mood of the assembled national press was little different from Sunday. It ranged from scepticism to something approaching outright hostility, but Atherton could hardly have expected much sympathy.

He had given the press a terrific story, and they were not going to let it die that easily. Nor was it only the tabloids who were against him. *The Times* leader page said, 'If the captain of England's cricket team fails to uphold the values of his society – or the values to which his society aspires – he is unworthy of that uncommon honour which the captaincy represents. He should be replaced.'

In the same newspaper, Simon Barnes asked, 'Why is a nice boy playing boys' games considered more blameworthy and more newsworthy than a bent politician? Atherton has now realised that sportspeople are expected to have higher moral standards than the people who run the country.' Still with *The Times*, John Woodcock offered this telling comment. 'Michael Atherton leads England into the second Test against South Africa at Headingley today. On the basis of all the available evidence, he is fortunate to do so.' Right, left and middle, so to speak.

The *Today* newspaper did not understate its view. 'He has dithered and obfuscated and what bits of truth we know have been dragged out through television evidence. If it had been a Pakistani captured on film doing what Atherton was doing, or an Indian who then withheld part of the truth from the match referee, or a West Indian who then admitted such a lack of frankness, we would never hear the end of it. And quite right too.'

Asif Iqbal, former Pakistan captain, said, 'The Pakistanis were branded cheats on far less visual evidence than has been produced in Atherton's case.'

All of which must have shown Atherton that those who did not want to listen would not . . . no matter what was in his second prepared statement. He explained how and when he had picked up the dirt from an adjoining pitch 'in full view of anyone who was watching me at the time. What I did could have been seen by umpires, players and spectators. My mind was solely on keeping the ball dry and ensuring that sweaty hands had not dampened the ball.'

On his lack of frankness to Burge, Atherton said this: 'I have expressed my full apologies to the match referee, Peter Burge, for my foolishness in not telling him of the dirt in my pocket. Thinking back to that meeting, I gave my response without considering the consequences and believing that I had done nothing improper, but not wishing to raise any suspicions about my actions. I cannot turn the clock back, but I fully accept that on this occasion I was thoughtless and should have given him the full picture.'

So there it is – the most instinctive human reaction of all when someone is afraid of being falsely accused of a crime. Massage the reply, even at the cost of complete veracity, if the white lie will help prevent a miscarriage of justice.

Human nature again – there is no escape from it.

7

THE VULTURES WAIT: HEADINGLEY

Illingworth
The Saturday selection meeting was not a long one, although we had problems with the fitness of White, Gough and Fraser, and we had to talk about the spinners in contention – as well as settle the arguments about the batting order. White's shins were worse, Gough's bruised arm had bled internally, and Fraser's broken little finger kept him out of Middlesex's game against Essex at Uxbridge.

White played in the five days against Durham, but Gough only played on the Sunday to see if the severe bruising in his bowling arm would allow him to bowl properly.

The BBC televised the Sunday game and, from the commentary box, I watched the two Yorkshire pace bowlers with interest, because they had both been named in the England squad for the Headingley Test earlier that morning. White was obviously struggling, but Gough was able to get through his spell with no trouble. The game was played on a newly cut pitch that was soft and took a lot of spin, and Gough impressed me with his mixed bag of tricks, including a slower genuine off-spinner, and the big inswinger that was becoming his trademark.

Illingworth
The big problem was which spinner to choose. I wanted a real turner but, as soon as I saw the pitch for the first time a couple of days before the selection meeting, I knew we would not get one. Keith Boyce would have had to have taken a lot more grass

off for that, and I don't think he could risk it in case the surface broke up. Nevertheless, we still needed one front-line spinner, but which one? I didn't think Salisbury bowled well enough at Lord's, and neither of the two left-arm spinners we had looked at for most of the season were quite there yet. Stemp's time will come – I'm pretty sure of that if he works hard – and Min Patel never quite convinced Fred Titmus that he was ready.

We had tried Peter Such, but I was in favour of the ball leaving the right-hander, which brought us round to Tufnell. I know that earlier in the summer I told him that he could only expect to get back after he had sorted his private life out, and he was playing regularly again for Middlesex. Mike Gatting knows how to handle him, and I noticed that he came back into the side at the end of June against Derbyshire.

He didn't get a wicket – it was in the second innings that Johnson got his all ten – but had a decent bowl of 30 overs for 57 runs in the first innings. He picked up six wickets against Sussex at Arundel and bowled 57 overs in the game, so I knew he was getting plenty of bowling. He got another 40 overs in against Lancashire and then, even better, bowled 80 overs against Essex. We talked around him, and the captain was all for picking him and forgetting the past, so he was in.

Regarding the quicks, we picked all three who were injured, with the proviso that White and Gough played next day as a fitness test, and we were assured that Fraser would be all right. We needed cover, so Joey Benjamin was picked after a lot of talk about other bowlers. Warwickshire's Munton was having a fine season, and his name kept cropping up. I could not honestly see how we could get him and Fraser in the same side, so he was unlucky. I spoke to a lot of people about him, and the overall view was that, good bowler though he is, he lacks half a yard of pace for Test cricket. We might be proved wrong, because there have been many successful bowlers of his type, but selection is all about judgement, and that was ours. Benjamin was having a good season, and Stewart told us what a good attacking bowler he was. He might have been 33, but he didn't make his debut with Warwickshire until he was 27, so there weren't that many miles on the clock.

We did a major surgery job on the batting order – and this time I made sure that it was all agreed before we broke up. Hick had to go to number three – we all agreed that. That meant Crawley dropping down ... how far depended on whether

Thorpe played. He had been so close to being picked at Lord's that it was nearly automatic he came in for this Test. The real problem came with Stewart and Gooch. Who was to open? Stewart wanted to, but in the end we went for Gooch and dropped Alec down the order. As it turned out, with White unfit and our decision to play six batsmen, Thorpe came in at number four – the right place for a left-hander – so Stewart batted at five and Crawley at six.

The top of the order is the most important to get right, especially after Lord's. With a South African all-pace attack, it is crucial to get a good start because that gives the middle and lower order a much better chance if they are coming in against an older ball. Lose a couple quickly, and everyone struggles. I know we had yo-yoed Gooch from three to five in four Tests, but he was still our best batsman, and we were in real trouble, 1–0 down in a three-match series.

I was glad we got Thorpe in. Earlier in the season, when I spoke to him, he told me how disappointed he was. I told him, 'I should think you are, otherwise something is wrong.' Fortunately he listened to me and kept his mouth shut when the press got to him about not playing. By doing that, he did himself and all of us a big favour, so it was nice to reward him for his patience.

We had a long look at the pitch on the Thursday morning, because it was damp and looked as though it might do a bit, particularly early on. You never know with Headingley, and a lot of rubbish has been talked about past pitches. The big thing is that it swings a lot there, and a lot of people think that, if the ball moves around a lot, it must be the pitch.

Swing is a largely unexplained phenomenon. Bowlers and scientists all have their theories, which include the angle of the seam, humidity, the speed of the ball allied to length, and so on. No one can explain why one ball will swing and another one will not in the same conditions, and no one can explain why relatively open grounds like Headingley and Edgbaston offer more swing than a built-up arena like Lord's, or other open grounds like Old Trafford, Trent Bridge and The Oval. That is not to say that the ball does not swing at the latter three Test grounds, but it does so more often at Headingley and Edgbaston.

Cloud cover is supposed to be another factor, and Illingworth will tell you that a westerly wind is more conducive than one from the east, presumably because of the usual difference in temperature.

Illingworth
We decided that we would bat if we won the toss and take our chance, because we felt that the bounce would be more predictable in the first innings. I would agree that Headingley pitches tend to go up and down as the game evolves – mostly down. It would be a cop-out to say that the toss would be a good one to lose. I've never believed that. If you are a good judge of pitches and conditions, then you should back yourself. I always have. Occasionally, you get one wrong, but more Tests are lost than won because of sides being afraid to make a proper put at the start. A captain will consult his team about the best course of action, but he must not be swayed by defensive ideas; for instance, if his openers don't fancy batting first because of a bit of moisture, or the opposition bowlers. Most Tests are controlled by the side batting first and building a big score, so I was pleased when Atherton won the toss and chose to bat.

What the toss meant to the press box was that the Red Rose Atherton would appear first in front of a White Rose crowd, as one of two opening batsmen and not, more inconspicuously, as one of 11 fielders. Furthermore, any Test opener can get a first-ball dismissal. The vultures waited.

Illingworth
The decision about the final XI did not take long. White was unfit, and we wanted the spinner, so Tufnell played and Benjamin did not. A last look at the pitch confirmed my first impressions – there was enough damp there to make batting first a bit of a problem, certainly until lunch, against the South African pace attack. But much more important to me was that it looked as though it would do a lot up and down as the game progressed, and you don't choose to bat last on a pitch like that.

As it happened, other than a ball from Fraser which torpedoed Richardson on the third day, very little happened on the last couple of days, and that surprised me. The odd one did it, but never enough to cause much bother, which is why over 1300 runs were scored and only 28 wickets fell.

The start of the game was tense – more so than usual, because of all the media attention on Atherton. I can't remember any other Test captain who went through what he did in the 10 days between the end of one Test match and the start of another. He was pursued all over the country by the media, and even the second press conference he gave on the previous Friday at Old Trafford did little to ease his situation. I repeat – I tried to think back to how I would have dealt with it all at the age of 26, and I can't begin to imagine.

I was pleased he won the toss, because batting first would concentrate his mind, whereas had we been in the field, his concentration could have been broken much easier, either by the crowd or his own thoughts. I also recognise that he could hardly have been in the best-prepared frame of mind to play a big innings against quality pace bowling, but it was the lesser of two evils for the lad when he took guard.

His reception from the crowd was good. He got a big hand as he walked to the middle with Gooch, and it was probably a relief to everyone, after all that had happened, when the first ball was bowled.

If the cricket gods had a pow-wow about the most improbable scenario they could devise, they finally came up with a winner. They could have dealt a first-ball dismissal, or a run-out, or a controversial decision, or a chanceless hundred, but they decided on something different.

They let him stay most of the first day, and survive the loss of Gooch and Hick in seam-friendly conditions that limited the captain to 19 painfully gathered runs in the two-hour pre-lunch session. He was dropped at 41 by McMillan, and then watched Thorpe come in to blaze away in startling fashion.

Illingworth
Having waited for so long, Thorpe could have been forgiven if he had come in to play safe and push the ball around, especially with his captain having been there for over two hours. Instead he decided to go for his shots and he played a smashing innings. The way he hooked and cover-drove made me wish I had forced the issue with him earlier, and what was also impressive was that they came off for 40 minutes for rain just when he had got going, but he picked up in the same way as soon as play restarted.

Confidence is a a fragile thing, but suddenly some of it rubbed off on Atherton. He had got to 50 off 123 balls while Thorpe had got there off only 60, yet when Thorpe was third out at 226, his 72 was only fractionally over half of the 142 they put on for the third wicket.

The changed batting order worked out well, with Stewart coming in to join Mike, because they have always played well together. Also, providing Alec survived the final hour, he would be there for the second new ball, with his wide experience as an opener proving invaluable.

The gods were ready to spring their ambush. With the Headingley crowd vocal and supportive, they let Atherton get to 99 with a good cover-drive off Donald. The bowler then 'spliced' him, but the ball dropped safely – and then there was an orchestrated shout for a leg-side catch to Richardson which was turned down.

Then they struck down a man who, the previous year, was run-out for 99 at Lord's after slipping to his knees. Other than hit-wicket, there is no crueller way to die in the hole – except, possibly, to be caught and bowled. And so it came to pass.

McMillan took the catch and an exhausted Atherton walked off after 320 minutes of sheer bloody-minded, gutsy batting to a tumultuous ovation from the White Rose to the Red Rose.

Illingworth
You have got to admire a performance – it was more than just an innings – like that. Although I did not need convincing what a tough, strong character he is, others might not have realised it. I knew a little bit of what he'd been through, because I also had the odd brush with the authorities when I was the England captain. Mine was more resentment about the Establishment's attitude towards complaints I made on our successful trip to Australia, but I could guess at his satisfaction at ramming a few words down a few throats. Not for the first time, I realised that there is something of Geoff Boycott in his mental make-up – and that is meant as a compliment to both.

More is the pity that Atherton could not let things lie. He agreed to give a press conference at the end of the day, but sullenly allowed himself to make the next day's headlines for the wrong reason again. He felt obliged to have a dig at 'the gutter press', and of course they crucified him.

Not only them, but no less a writer than the doyen of the press box, John Woodcock of *The Times*, felt obliged to tackle Atherton face to face, and another doyen, Richie Benaud, took great exception to being lumped with 'the gutter press', simply because he shared the view that Atherton's explanations were not wholly convincing.

Woodcock was quoted in a tabloid as saying that he had joined in the demand for Atherton's resignation. Imagine the scene next day when the Squire of Longparish happened to run into Atherton in the dressing-room area.

'Michael, I just want you to know the report in today's papers that I called for your resignation is not true.'

A mollified cricketer began to make a polite response, when Woodcock, in his inimitably understated way, made a lethal incision with: 'No, what I actually wrote was that I thought you were a very fortunate young man still to be captain of your country.' The mollified look vanished without trace.

Illingworth

I was sorry Mike had used that 'gutter press' remark. It was a silly comment to make and I just hope he learns as he goes on.

We did really well on the second day thanks to Stewart and Rhodes batting at their best and Crawley getting in for two and a half hours. He still worries me about how much he favours the leg-side, but he knows he needs to work on it, so the next 12 months should show us how good he is.

As for Alec, he took them on and, with Donald unfit because of his big toe, we got to 477 – the sort of score which should put a side in charge, even if it took 160 overs to get there. We nicked a wicket that evening, but even when we had them five down for 105 on the Saturday, I knew it was going to be hard work to finish them off.

A lot of South Africa's supporters moan because they don't have a top batsman, but it is also one of their strengths that numbers six, seven and eight are just as likely to get runs as the top five. This time it was Peter Kirsten's hundred that held us up, although our bowling was disappointing. A pitch like Headingley calls for bowlers who keep on getting the ball in the right place. It's not just automatic length and line – it is also working out what the best line and length is on different surfaces.

Headingley has never been a quick pitch, so a fairly full length is essential. As for line, that varies from batsman to batsman. Some love off-side width, others, like Crawley, work the leg-side, so it is always a matter of a captain and his bowler deciding on their main plan of attack against each batsman and setting different fields accordingly.

That did not happen, particularly with their bowler Matthews, who had shown everyone at Lord's how he can play on the off-side. A lot of tail-enders are like that, but they are nowhere near as effective when the ball is tucked into their body and they are denied the room they want.

It was almost as though we had not learned one thing about him from the first Test where he scored 66 in the match from only 74 balls, with most of his 11 fours coming between extra cover and third man.

He did us again. After all, when he came in at 281 for seven, the follow-on had been saved but we were still well on for a lead of around 150 at least. Gough got carried away a bit, but DeFreitas and Fraser should have been able to keep him quiet – instead he hit 62 from 100 balls, and we even let Donald bat with a runner and smash us for 27 out of 37 for the last wicket.

A lead of only 30 meant we had to force the pace but, even though Hick got a good hundred and Thorpe played well again, given their slow over rate, we could hardly declare before lunch. We left ourselves 60 overs to bowl them out but, unless we got a good start, the pitch was playing too well to give us much hope.

Nevertheless, I think we could have pushed harder at the start and got more men round the bat. That is something a young captain can only learn as he goes along, but I reckon we missed a small trick there.

Crawley could have been forgiven for thinking that his captain missed another one when, with one over to go before lunch and the closure, he was sent in to bat when either DeFreitas or Rhodes could surely have gone in. It was hit or miss, and Crawley missed for an unnecessary sacrificial duck.

Illingworth
I understand the point, but it is only another indication that Mike believes Test cricket to be a hard game, and sees no reason to protect his players from anything. I suppose it was the same thing when he declared on Hick six months later in the Sydney Test. I would have sent someone else in, but I can follow his reasoning.

Looking back at the game, it was disappointing we could not force a win after our 477, but the pitch was the biggest factor.

Looking at how Tufnell turned it in their second innings, I suppose a second spinner might have made a difference, but they bat so deep, I doubt it. There were several plus factors for us.

The way Atherton bounced back, the second innings played by Hick, although he needs to bat more like that first time around, and the form of Thorpe and Stewart. I am always keen on a left-hander, so Thorpe's 145 runs in the match were especially pleasing. The bowling was not so satisfactory, and we needed to do some hard thinking before The Oval Test.

The game threw up several statistical quirks. England's 477 was the fifth highest in Test history not to contain a hundred. Kirsten became the second-oldest batsman at 39 years and 84 days to score a maiden Test hundred. Hick's 110 was his second century for England in his 28th Test, and it was the 76th of his first-class career.

Atherton became the fifth player after M.J.K. Smith, G. Boycott, R.B. Richardson and J.G. Wright to score 99 twice in Tests. Since then, Salim Malik and Mark Waugh have also done it.

England declared twice for the first time since Lord's against India in 1990. And so to The Oval.

8

MALCOLM'S MATCH: THE OVAL

Illingworth

We met at the Hilton in Leeds to pick the side for The Oval, and the bowling caused most of the discussion. The Oval pitch is one on its own in England for pace and bounce, and we were all agreed that Devon Malcolm should come back into the squad. That meant a straight swap for Fraser, whose 14 wickets in the first five Tests since West Indies had cost 543 runs – not far off 40 per wicket, which I found worrying.

We decided to keep Benjamin in, with White now ruled out for the season, so apart from the one change, it was an unchanged XII for a win-or-bust game. I knew when we finished the meeting that we would have a difficult decision to make on the day, because I knew that Mike would never go along with five batsmen and five bowlers. I have banged on and on about it, but it is as though he has been brainwashed by Fletcher and Gooch, who insist that you can only win a Test match by scoring enough runs to put a side under pressure.

All I know is that in my 31 Tests as captain of England, I agreed to the extra batsman only four times, and twice I was talked into it against my better judgement. It's all very well people writing and saying that, because I played Test cricket over 20 years ago, I cannot understand how it has changed.

Some things never change – like the proper balance of a side with an all-rounder batting at six, whether he is the wicket-keeper or a bowling all-rounder. It has so many advantages. To start with, it concentrates the minds of the top five a bit more. Subconsciously, I reckon they relax a bit, knowing that there is one extra batsman to come to the rescue. Also, I ask how many times the sixth batsman succeeds when the others have failed? And even when he does, at what expense?

A four-man attack leaves a captain at the mercy of form and fitness. Only one bowler has to be not firing and, unless you are lucky, you are struggling. Each bowler knows he is going to have to bowl roughly a quarter of the day's overs, so tends to pace himself accordingly. That also does not help the over rate, but the biggest advantage of all with a fifth genuine bowler is that it makes life so much easier for the fielding captain.

His options are many and varied. He can use all his bowlers in shorter spells, and switch them around more easily. It is not just a matter of having one extra bowler – it is the tactical elbow room it allows. You cannot always quantify it, but I do know that you usually have more control in the field with five than four.

Especially when your four contain an out-and-out strike bowler like Devon Malcolm. He is always a gamble, and if it goes wrong, there's nowhere to go with only three other bowlers.

Illingworth's point is perfectly illustrated by the Lord's Test against the West Indies in 1991. Gooch went in with the same four-man attack as had won the first Test at Headingley – DeFreitas, Malcolm, Pringle and Watkin. Not one gamble, but two – with the inexperienced Watkin holding his place after taking five for 93 in 21 overs on debut on a helpful pitch.

On the morning of the match, I would have lost good money betting that Illingworth would press hard, if not for a five-man attack, then for Tufnell as one of four to give Atherton some sort of lifeline if Malcolm and Gough fired too many blanks. When the side was announced, and it excluded Tufnell, I found it difficult to believe that the chairman had shifted his ground so much that, from a starting point in the summer of wanting five bowlers including at least one spinner, he had agreed to a four-man attack with no spinner at all. I should have known better.

Illingworth
As soon as I saw the pitch on the Thursday morning, I had sympathy with Mike wanting an all-pace attack. I know it went against all my principles, and I know that it left him with little variation – only Hick to spin it – but I just could not see what

110

part a spinner would play. The surface would offer him nothing, and I thought we would be better off giving Mike what he wanted – four quicks. He made it clear to us that he was reluctant to go in with no spinner, but really felt that he needed four front-line pace bowlers.

Brian and Fred were not in favour, but did not argue, which is why the captain got his way in the end. It looked defensive, it looked all wrong, yet we honestly did it as our best way to win the game and halve the series. Also, I know we keep on about Hick's bowling, but I still believe he can make up into a decent bowler. Whether or not he has got it in him to work properly at it, I am unsure, but I was quite prepared to see him used, if necessary, at The Oval.

I know that four bowlers is a dangerous, thin policy, but it can work if things go for you. For instance, days can be split, either by innings breaks, or the weather. I know the argument the other way is a better one, and I keep coming back to playing five batsmen and five bowlers. For instance, the England number six scored 19, 51, 9, 42, 10, 0, 38, and 0 in the first five Tests against New Zealand and South Africa. A total of 169 in eight innings is very moderate.

Take off any runs that a genuine fifth bowler might have got, and the benefit of a fifth bowler in those five Tests is there for everyone to see.

The point was proved again in South Africa's first innings, when they recovered from 136 for five, with Jonty Rhodes retired hurt, to 332 – a total that should have kept them out of trouble. Malcolm and Gough took one wicket for 166 runs from only 44 overs, and Atherton had nowhere to go once he was stuck against McMillan and Richardson, and the last four wickets added 196.

Illingworth

In the end, Benjamin saved the day with his four for 42, otherwise we would have been facing 400, and that would have been that. A first-day score of 326 for eight, with McMillan still there, reflected some poor bowling and, at that stage, the gamble of a four-man pace attack looked to have failed. They were unlucky that Rhodes could not come back, but we were on the wrong end of it for most of the second day as well.

They bowled well, but it was disappointing to be 222 for seven after Hick, Thorpe and Stewart all got in on as good a batting pitch, regarding consistency of bounce, as they will ever see. Gough told me he would play his shots before he went in, and I was not going to tell him to desert his natural game. The last half-hour turned things right around.

Not just because they smashed 59 in eight overs, but because they shocked Wessels and his bowlers so much that they lost their way. The Oval is the biggest playing area we have but, although the ball kept disappearing in front of the wicket, they kept slips in when they should have tried to defend. Donald went for 30 off two overs, and he should have had someone back for the slog.

It reminded me of Botham at Headingley in 1981. Once Gough and DeFreitas started, Wessels should have altered his field. He needed a fly slip for the top edge and a deep mid-on, but he didn't react and I reckon he let us off. The funniest thing was when, with a few minutes to go, Gough looked up at our balcony to see if he should carry on hitting or defend for the close of play and start again next day.

I know how hard that is to do, particularly as the fielding side have then had a chance to regroup, so I waved my hands telling him to keep going. What I didn't know was that Keith Fletcher was signalling the opposite at the other end of the balcony. The lad could have been confused, but fortunately he kept hitting to end 35 minutes' play in which more damage was done than the 59 runs scored. It knocked South Africa sideways to see their best fast bowlers being hooked and driven like that, and it lifted our dressing-room a lot.

For the first time in two days, we felt we were on top, and, as far as I am concerned, all that happened from then on started with that eighth-wicket partnership. We got to 304 and were back in the game, providing we bowled better than first time around.

I had made a point of going into the dressing-room at the start of play to have a word with Malcolm. He hadn't bowled well, and I believed he held the key for the rest of the match. You can't treat every cricketer the same. Some need a soft approach, others need a bit of a jolt sometimes, and I reckon the time had come to remind him that he was playing in a Test match, that he was representing his country, and just a general reminder to him that he had been picked as a nasty, big fast bowler, and it was time he focused on that.

When I saw him, he was sitting in a corner, eyes closed, with the cans on, listening to music. I wasn't too impressed, because I confess I thought he was probably listening to pop music and I was even more determined to roust him.

I tapped him on the shoulder and when he lifted one can to listen to me, I heard the pop music coming out and said: 'You should be listening to "Land of Hope and Glory".' I then had a general chat with him for a couple of minutes about his bowling and attitude and left him to it.

I had had an earlier word about bowling to the tail. I told him not to bowl on or outside their off stump, but to bang it in at them around leg stump. He was magnificent. He bowled fast and straight and, once he had whipped the top three out for one run, we knew we had them.

It's not easy to face up to a genuine fast bowler on his day, and only Cullinan, Wessels and McMillan shaped up. I was surprised at Kepler, because he started to get them out of trouble with Cullinan. They took the score to 73 – an overall lead of 101 – and with their depth in batting, they looked capable of setting us something approaching 300. But it just shows how Devon had unsettled them.

He came back and went around the wicket to Kepler, and got him caught behind off a wild slash. It looked an awful stroke, but that is what fast bowling can achieve. Actually, that second spell of Devon's was a costly one – 36 from six overs – and again they were getting away from us, with McMillan supporting Cullinan well.

At that stage they were 137 for four – 165 ahead – but back came Devon for a devastating spell in which he just wiped out the last five. You can always tell the quality of a performance by analysing how a bowler gets his wickets. Devon bowled two, had one LBW, and five were caught either by Rhodes or Thorpe at slip. Like I said, fast and straight.

We had plenty of time to score 204 – 108 overs – but Gooch decided he was going to take them on. When he got out in the fifth over, the score was 56 and Atherton and Hick carried on in the same way. I know we should have won comfortably, but it was especially satisfying to get there inside 36 overs.

England's first win in England against South Africa since Trent Bridge in 1960 was clinched by the sixth-best innings analysis in all Tests. Devon Malcolm's nine for 57 was the best ever at The Oval, beating eight for 29 in 1912 by Sydney Barnes. Jim Laker's 10 for 53 is top of the shop, but what illustrious company Malcolm joined at the head of the list of bowlers who have taken nine wickets in an innings.

Only George Lohmann with nine for 28, Laker again with nine for 37, Richard Hadlee's nine for 52 and Abdul Qadir with nine for 56 are ahead of the Derbyshire fast bowler, whose bowling was truly inspired.

Kepler Wessels became the first batsman to score 1000 runs for two different countries, and Graham Gooch's 205th innings for England broke the previous record held by David Gower. At 33, Joey Benjamin became the oldest new-ball bowler to make his England debut for 13 years, since another Surrey bowler, Robin Jackman, first played for his country in the West Indies at the age of 35.

Match referee Peter Burge worked overtime. He imposed fines of 50 per cent and 25 per cent of their respective match fees on Mike Atherton and Fanie de Villiers, both for dissent. The South African team were fined 70 per cent of their fees for a slow over rate, and England also forfeited 30 per cent for a similar offence. Because a touring team's fines are based on their home fees, and because the South African players had had their fees lowered at the same time as they were put on an annual retaining contract, the visitors paid £980, and England £750.

The Atherton incident provoked most comment. Burge ruled that his head-shaking and other gestures when he was given out LBW to de Villiers constituted unreasonable dissent. The England dressing-room, including Illingworth, thought it harsh, with the captain making much of the fact that what he had seen on the television replays was unexceptionable.

Burge's statement did, however, make it clear that he had reached his decision based on what he had seen with his own eyes, much of which was not on film, with the main camera switching to bowler and umpire once the appeal was made. The press had a field day, with the general conclusion being that Burge had exacted revenge for having been misled in the Lord's Test.

Certainly, the Australian referee had warned Atherton that 'if you as much as sneeze, you'll catch pneumonia', but the thin line between disappointment and dissent often becomes blurred. The argument is debated by two schools – the one that insists that a player must accept unquestioningly every decision by the umpire, and the one that believes that players are only human, therefore a cricketer cannot be expected to swallow a clear injustice without showing some reaction.

114

It then becomes a matter of degree and interpretation by different umpires and referees, and that is where the trouble starts. On that Friday evening, Atherton was pursued by the media but, thanks to the wit of the editor of the *Wisden Cricket Monthly* magazine, David Frith, he was able to slip the net entering and leaving Greens Restaurant in St James's – the venue for an editorial board dinner.

Few expected the England captain to attend but, to his credit, he did, and I listened with some sympathy to his aggrieved comments. His theme in a subsequent column for the monthly was that 'surely common sense rather than the ICC Code of Conduct should be the overriding factor'.

In an ideal world, he would be right, but it was the absence of that common-sense factor in the 1980s, particularly on the part of players, which persuaded Sir Colin Cowdrey in his role as chairman of ICC that the only chance of reversing a trend towards a roller-ball approach by some teams was the introduction of the match referee and the code of conduct. The system is still being refined, but few cricket lovers would deny that the system has more plus factors than minus.

Illingworth is the last man to be carried away on the euphoric wave of victory, but his considered verdict on the dramatic Oval Test shows how highly he rated the England performance.

Illingworth

I have thought about it carefully, and I rate what happened in the last couple of days of that game as good an exhibition of positive cricket by England as I have seen in 30 years. I was also happy at how the team spirit had developed throughout the summer. There was life in the dressing-room, and I was sure that we had the nucleus of a team that would do well in the next 12 months against the toughest opposition of all, Australia and the West Indies.

We carried that spirit on into the two remaining one-day games, even though the personnel was slightly different. We brought in Fairbrother, Cork, Udal and Lewis and left out Malcolm and Tufnell and won both games well. The captain thought Stewart might keep wicket, but we said no, because of the outstanding summer Rhodes had, and as Mike rated him his outstanding player of the season, he didn't mind.

Illingworth reflected on his first summer in charge. The results were good, the series against New Zealand won, although by a narrower margin than he would have liked, and the series halved against a tough, resilient South African team, plus a clean sweep of the four Texaco games. He, Bolus and Titmus had picked 13 players against New Zealand, and five more against South Africa. Among the batsmen, Robin Smith had gone, and Graham Thorpe and John Crawley arrived.

Among the bowlers tried, Malcolm maintained his astonishing record of single appearances in a series, which he had now extended to six in six series. Paul Taylor was tried and discarded, as was Ian Salisbury. Fraser, most significantly of all, was dropped and Benjamin given his chance.

So how big were the ticks and crosses, with the Ashes selection close at hand?

Illingworth

I reckon we got about a 20 per cent improvement during the season in general terms, particularly with cricketing confidence. Some of our changes helped that, such as Rhodes, who had a fine debut season. We knew that there were still areas we needed to work on, but we had several big pluses. I've mentioned Rhodes, and there was Thorpe and Hick, once we moved him up to three. Among the other batsmen, Gooch had a moderate second half and did not play up to his own standards. We still believed he had one tour left in him, especially against the Aussies and Warne.

Back to Thorpe. He came through well, but he has got to learn to make hundreds. I would not want to stop him playing his shots, but he has got to be a touch more selective, particularly when he has got in. Anybody can get rolled over early but, once a Test batsman gets to 20 and has batted for an hour or so, the top ones then make it count. With Thorpe I am sure it is only a matter of time, because he is one of only a few home batsmen who can play off the back foot. That, plus the left-hand factor, makes him a key member of the top order.

As for Crawley, he has got the big match temperament, which is a start, but he needs to work on his technique. I know David Lloyd at Lancashire is helping him to avoid playing too much leg-side, but it is a big problem for him. Also his fielding. It is only ordinary for a youngster, and he should work much harder on his general fitness.

Alec Stewart had a good summer, and he is good for the side. He's got plenty about him and can lift other players.

We did well with the bowlers, especially DeFreitas and Gough. My early-season chat with DeFreitas was not wasted, and he did exceptionally well to pitch the ball up and take 30 wickets in the six Tests. I have always thought he tended to pitch half a yard too short, and often said so when I was doing television and other people would say how unlucky he was if he beat the bat a lot.

Nobody in this game is ever always lucky or unlucky. It is also only part truth to say that you make your own luck. What that means is that your method will dictate, day in, day out, what your returns will be. Botham was supposed to be a lucky bowler because he seemed to get wickets with long hops and other bad deliveries. What people forget is that he was always prepared to experiment and try something different to unsettle a batsman and get him out.

So when DeFreitas kept beating the bat and getting nobody out, it was because he was pitching too short, so when the ball moved, it would beat the lot. The same applies to Mike Hendrick, also of Derbyshire, who played in 30 Tests, took 87 wickets at 25 apiece, yet never took five wickets in an innings.

Gough did better than I had hoped, although I knew what a live wire he was from watching him with Yorkshire. He is fearless on the field. Nobody scares him and there is no match situation he does not believe he can't turn around, even if it looks hopeless. People shouldn't compare him with Botham – they are not the same sort of cricketer – but I will agree there is something of the same attitude in both of them. Apart from his bowling and batting, he is also a great bloke to have in the dressing-room.

Craig White has got something, and I know some people think I am blinded to some extent because I have seen him a fair bit for Yorkshire. Well, only time will tell if my judgement is right or wrong, but I am not stupid enough to push a player for the crucial number six position if I don't genuinely believe he will do a good job. That is the quickest way to failure I know.

He has suffered a lot with injury, and mostly in the couple of years since he switched from spin to seam. He is a bit like McMillan and Mark Waugh. They come in off quite a short run, but have strong body actions and hit the pitch hard. That often means they surprise batsmen with pace and bounce. For instance, Rhodes told me that at times he and the slips stood a pace or so further back to White than Gough. I think he's got plenty of rough edges and needs to tighten up quite a bit, but I am sure he has got an England future. The same with his batting. He got one 50 from number six, and he averaged nearly 50 for Yorkshire in 1994. I am in no hurry to write him off until he has had more opportunity.

Among the other bowlers, Tufnell did well enough at Headingley, and his attitude was good. Another plus for him is how hard he has worked on his fielding. I have a gut feeling that Stemp is potentially better but only time will tell.

That leaves Malcolm and Fraser. The trouble with Devon is that he does not have a natural-length ball. That is why he goes for so many, because you cannot set attacking fields for someone like that. His control so often deteriorates when he goes wide of the crease, and he cannot then bowl a consistent line. At times, he must drive his captain spare, because just when you are prepared to forget him, he clicks for a few overs and has the sort of game he had at The Oval. I am not sure what the answer is, but that is why in the 18 months leading up to The Oval, his six Tests came in six different series.

Fraser had what I thought was a disappointing summer. His 14 Test wickets cost 40 each and came from 211 overs, which is a poor strike rate. I know he gives you control, and I know that by bowling tight he creates pressure and so helps other bowlers to take wickets, but there is a limit to the value of that, compared with his own wicket-taking ability.

I watched every ball of the summer, and came to the conclusion he had lost some vital nip. He does not swing the ball, therefore relies entirely on seam movement, and the extra bounce which was one of his strengths comes from zip. He never took four wickets in an innings once in the summer, and only managed three in an innings once for England.

Part 4
THE TOUR TO AUSTRALIA, 1994–95

9

SELECTING THE TOURING SIDE

Illingworth
We met at the Copthorne Hotel in Manchester on Thursday, 1 September. The press had a big grumble, because that meant we would not announce the two parties until the following morning, and they made the point that their Saturday morning coverage would clash with the previews of the NatWest final at Lord's.

Quite an argument took place on the timing of the meeting. The press could not see why, as Atherton started a four-day game at Old Trafford on the Tuesday, the meeting could not be at least one day earlier. In my capacity as chairman of the Cricket Writers' Club, I approached Alan Smith on the morning of the Texaco one-day international at Old Trafford the previous Saturday.

By this time, we had been told that it was impossible to bring the meeting forward, so I requested as early a press conference as possible on the Friday morning. This would not prevent the Saturday morning clash with the biggest one-day occasion of the season, but it would enable the national number ones to write their tour party reviews in good time for them to arrive in London for their own annual dinner – one of the big cricket occasions of the year.

Illingworth
The problem about not being able to meet until the Thursday was that Brian and Fred were committed some while previously to be at Scarborough for the cricket and a function. We sat down at 6.30 p.m., and I suppose we created a bit of

history by being the first panel of selectors who were not augmented by other officials.

There were just the three of us, plus the team manager and the captain, with Tim Lamb there to take notes. That was it, whereas in my time the room was full and I didn't know half of them. The total attendance then was certainly well into double figures, and I reckon that made for longer meetings than otherwise would have been the case.

The senior party for Australia did not take all that long. It didn't exactly pick itself, but once we had written down the certainties, we were more than halfway there in a few minutes. We were all agreed on Atherton, Gooch, Stewart, Hick, Thorpe, Rhodes, Gough, DeFreitas and Malcolm.

The captain said we should identify a group of young players and stick with them. I asked him to name a few, but there was not a great deal forthcoming.

We then took each department separately, and listed anyone who had even a faint chance of going. The batting first. Out of Gatting, White, Crawley, Ramprakash, Hussein, Maynard, Fairbrother, Bicknell and Wells, we wanted three, and went for the first three.

Regarding Gatting, he had had a good season – only Gooch scored more runs – and I had not forgotten that he was unlucky to be dropped after his last innings for England of 59 at Lord's when he got the wrong end of a marginal LBW decision against Shane Warne. We knew Warne would be a problem, and as Gatting has always played slow bowling well, none of us had any reservations about picking him.

Obviously at that stage we could not second-guess what the side would be for the first Test in Brisbane, but with fielding so important on the Australian big grounds, I could not see a situation, other than injury, where Gooch and Gatting would play in the same side. The captain was perfectly happy to have both in the party for their ability as well as their experience.

We talked around the other candidates, but they all fell a bit short in one area or another.

The spinners took a bit of time, not because there were that many candidates, but two or three of them were much of a muchness. We thought Tufnell did enough at Headingley to be first choice and the captain was very keen to have him so that left one other. We could not really see two spinners playing in a Test, even at Sydney, so Udal was picked for several reasons.

He had a good Championship year with Hampshire, with 62 wickets taken at a good strike rate of a wicket every 10 overs. We talked about Patel, Stemp and Such, as well as Richard Illingworth, but I have thought for a long time that Udal has the makings of a really good cricketer. The others agreed, so that left the pace bowling.

We must have considered at least a dozen, but in the end it came down to the final choice between McCague and Fraser. Benjamin did well enough in the first Test, so he was picked first. There were various question marks, either on form or fitness, regarding bowlers like Ilott, Igglesden, Caddick and Mullally. Youngsters were considered, like Cork, Martin and Chapple of Lancashire, and Munton's great season for Warwickshire got him a mention.

The general feeling was that he still lacked half a yard for Test cricket, and anyway we could not pick him if Fraser went. He was to cause the longest discussion of the lot.

We also thought about Millns of Leicestershire, because the thinking was slowly pointing towards trying to pick a shock attack. A lot of my views were coloured by the belief that White would do a good job at number six. It is nonsense to say that I am biased towards Yorkshire players. It is my neck that is on the block and I am certainly not prepared to risk it by picking any other than what I believe to be the best player for each position.

Just like when I was captain, I would be crackers to risk my reputation for someone who I genuinely did not believe was the best man for the job. As captain, if I pushed extra hard for a player, it was down to me if he succeeded or failed. Similarly as chairman. I know the high profile I was given when I took the job, but responsibility of that sort has never bothered me.

All I have ever tried to do with selection is to make sure the reasoning is right at the time. You can be proved wrong by form and fitness, or even bad luck with a brilliant catch or a poor decision, but that is not the point. It is what the reasoning was at the time that is the important thing. As for White, everyone was happy about him, always providing he was fit. In case he was not, or if there were any other problems with the quick bowlers, Millns was put on stand-by until the party left England.

I have never been a gambler at cricket. That does not mean I do not subscribe to attacking cricket, because I have always tried to be positive. There are times when you have to regroup if things are not going right in the field. That is one of the arts

123

of good captaincy – to sense when to make a big push, and also when to sit back and frustrate the opposition if they are on top.

For that reason, I could understand Mike wanting Fraser. A captain feels more comfortable if he has one bowler he can turn to if the flak starts flying, and Fraser's reputation has been built on being the sort of old-fashioned, line-and-length stock bowler who is worth his weight in gold.

I just reckoned he had lost his nip, and therefore was not getting wickets as he used to. It's all right doing a stock job, but if you are one of four bowlers, you have still got to be able to bowl people out, rather than bowl them in. His returns in five Tests were ordinary – 14 wickets from 211 overs for 541 runs – and I thought he would struggle in Australia.

The captain was adamant he wanted him but, for once, I went all the way against him. I thought with DeFreitas and Benjamin in the party, he had two bowlers who could do a job for him, and I was in favour of an out-and-out strike bowler like McCague. We had watched him and checked up on fitness. He only played nine Championship games for Kent but got 54 good wickets at 17 apiece, and the rest of us thought he might just respond to the challenge of going back to Australia.

Keith went with the captain for Fraser, which was a bit of a surprise to me as he'd agreed with me about him when I spoke to him earlier. In the end, McCague won the day to complete our party of 16. I never thought he would be a Malcolm-type blaster, but he was sharp enough and could swing it away from the right-hander.

I cannot emphasise too much that the captain was only knocked back on one player – Fraser. That is why I was surprised and disappointed about quoted remarks from Atherton to the contrary that the party was not his side, because there were two or three others he was against taking. Journalists close to him kept mentioning Gatting, but he certainly did not object or have any reservations at the time.

He never said as much, but I reckon he might have had a few reservations about taking two senior ex-Test captains, but that is only a guess.

Then we picked the 'A' party, and that took much longer and was much more difficult, mainly because I reckon we could have selected two parties of, more or less, equal strengths. We decided that, other things being equal, we would go for the younger cricketer.

We started with the captain, and that did not take long. Alan Wells was the front-runner, and the only other man we spoke about was Mark Nicholas. We went for continuity, with Wells having done well on the previous tour of South Africa, and anyway, he could still be considered as a fringe candidate for the senior side.

We next picked the wicket-keepers. I had spoken to Jack Russell during The Oval Test and asked him what he wanted to do. He said that he would go to India if we really wanted him, but he would not mind staying on stand-by for Australia.

That meant we could take two younger men, and we talked about Nixon, Piper, Metson, Blakey, Hegg and Marsh. The first two had had outstanding seasons, and we also took into account the opinions of Alan Knott, so they were chosen. Nixon was the first 'keeper to score 1000 runs for Leicestershire – and that surprised me because I was sure Roger Tolchard had done it. Not so – 999 was his best aggregate.

We knew that the batting would cause most discussion, so we picked the bowlers next. We knew that spin would play a big part in India, so we went for a full hand of spinners and, as Stemp, Such and Patel had all got a mention for Australia, we settled on them, as well as Salisbury. He has had a few rough spells in the last few years, mainly because of a shoulder problem, but he is a good cricketer and, at the age of 24, he has plenty of time to come through. Having picked three spinners who all make the ball leave the right-hander, and only Such who spun it the other way, we decided on one more off-spinner. Weekes and Neil Smith were the two candidates, and we went for the Middlesex lad after Fred Titmus said he thought he was the better bowler.

I know a lot of Warwickshire supporters and officials were upset that several of their successful players in what was a marvellous season did not get a tour. They also got upset when I was quoted as saying that they were only average players. I must have seen that misquote thrown up a dozen times or more by Bob Woolmer and Dermot Reeve, but I never said it. What I did say was that often a good side is made up of good players who might not be Test material. I stick by that, because although batsmen like Ostler and Twose had good seasons, so did the players who were eventually picked.

As for Weekes and Smith, the Middlesex lad averaged more with the bat in the Championship – 30 against 25 – and he got his wickets marginally cheaper. Also he was 25 compared with 27, and Fred Titmus said what an improving cricketer he was.

As for the quick bowlers, we saw little point in taking out-and-out strike bowlers, but instead considered men who pitched it up and swung it.

Cork and Chapple were the best in this category, and we added Ilott and Johnson, mainly because of his age, to complete what we all thought would be a keen and varied attack. Munton was again unlucky, because I am sure he would have done a good job, but we preferred Johnson purely on age.

Worcestershire's Lampitt got close following a good all-round season, and he was put on stand-by. That left the batting, and that took up more time than anything else in a meeting which lasted all of six hours and took us past midnight. That is why I cannot accept the criticism later levelled at us that we had not informed Fraser and others who missed out that they had not been chosen.

It might seem heartless for a front-runner to find out from the media that he has not made the side, but I am not sure what else we could have done, bearing in mind that we did not break up until after midnight, and the press conference to announce both parties was timed for 8.30 a.m. next morning at the request of the press.

We considered every young batsman in county cricket before we narrowed them down to about a dozen names. With decent batting available from bowlers such as Cork and Weekes, we could only fit in six, and Ramprakash was an automatic pick. He is another young cricketer who has had his problems, which is why we decided to see if some extra responsibility would settle him down. It surprised a lot of people when we named him as vice-captain, but it proved to be one of the best things we did.

We wanted a couple of left-handers, and Nick Knight and David Hemp had both showed enough to earn selection. That left two other places, and filling them proved the hardest thing of all. Players such as Ally Brown, Paul Johnson, the Warwickshire pair Ostler and Twose, as well as Darren Bicknell and Mal Loye, could all have been picked, but in the end we chose Jason Gallian and Michael Vaughan – only 23 and 20, but already good enough to score five hundreds between them in 1994.

Finally we had finished. The 'A' party included only one player over 26 – the captain, Wells, who was 32 – and only three who had full Test caps – Ramprakash, Salisbury and Ilott. It would be a hard tour played under difficult conditions, and would provide an ideal test of character as well as technique. Regarding pre-tour preparation, it was decided that the 'A' party would have a break and then go to Malaga in December, while the senior players would have a complete rest before they flew to Australia only a month after the end of the season.

I am sure that such a pairing of tours to West Indies and Australia in the same calendar year is wrong, and I am glad it will only happen once again in the next 10 years. It is not just that they are two such difficult countries to tour, but the timing means that, with the home season to fit in in between, the England players are involved in Test and county cricket non-stop for the entire year.

Also the itinerary in Australia was poor, which is why I got involved in the one for South Africa in 1995–96. In that one, we cut the travelling to a minimum during the five-match Test series, and we left the seven one-day games until the end of the tour, which provided a good run-up to the World Cup.

Illingworth faced a large press conference within eight hours of the meeting breaking up and, as expected, the majority of questions centred on the inclusion of Gatting and McCague and the omission of Fraser. He was understandably shocked at being left out, and provided easy quotable ammunition for those ready to fire charges about the unfeeling England authorities.

It might be argued that, providing Atherton knew where to contact Fraser, he could and should have done so – even in the middle of the night. Another school of thought says that no man has a divine right of selection, and there is nothing wrong in the players learning of their fate through the media.

Illingworth
After the final selection meeting, my only remaining official duties included a visit to Edgbaston on 8, 9 and 10 September to watch the England Under-19 match against India, and the writing of my report to the TCCB on my first series as chairman.

I was asked more than once about Micky Stewart and whether or not I ever talked to him. The answer is yes, just as I go out of my way to talk to and listen to anyone whose judgement I respect, and who might be able to tell me something about a player I don't know. When I talk to Micky, it is, more often than not, about general things such as temperament and reaction to the good and bad in cricket, rather than purely technique.

I wanted my report to be wide-ranging and comprehensive. I had nothing to hide and simply wanted a factual account of all that had happened. This included any relevant corrections of things wrongly attributed to me in print, and I was particularly anxious to clear the air about the age of myself, Titmus and Bolus, and any possible drawback this might have.

I know the modern game is different. It always has been, and I remember what I thought were big differences in the 1960s compared with the first 15 seasons after the Second World War. But certain basics will never alter, and it is those on which I try to concentrate. On the specific question of a selector's age, it is too simplistic to say that over 60 is not too old, just as it is to assume that any ex-player under 50 is bound to be a better bet.

As far as I am concerned, it all comes down to judgement and, within obvious certain limits, I do not believe that age is a factor. As for identifying with the selected players, I found no trouble with that during the 10 years or so in which I was in the television commentary box. I repeat that not only umpires but players often came to me to have a chat about aspects of the day's play. That must mean they thought I had something to offer, and I didn't think that being in my 60s puts me at a disadvantage.

Again, it depends upon the individual, and I can think of plenty of 50-year-olds who never could talk cricket sense and never will. As for Brian Bolus and Fred Titmus, they are lively characters who have succeeded in whatever they have done, on and off the field. They have good minds and know the game through and through. What more do you want?

Therefore, I asked the captain if he had any reservations about the three of us. When he said no, I also told him I proposed to put that into my report for the Board, so he knew the situation on that score, as far as both the Board and I were concerned. I have always tried to prevent wires getting crossed, which is why I always speak my mind. Not too many people can accuse me of waffling, even if at times I have ruffled a few feathers.

That is how I operated as a player and captain, and how I will always perform as chairman.

10
THE WRITING ON THE WALL: BRISBANE

Illingworth

I went to Spain for a month before the first Test in Brisbane, but was back well before it started. Atherton rang me just before the match and told me that the pitch was dry and did not have much grass. He was undecided about the number six spot, and could not make his mind up between White, Gatting and Crawley.

Being so far away made it difficult for me to offer an opinion but, as he had asked me, I told him I was in favour of White. Neither of the other two were in top form and, apart from the bowling insurance White would give, I reckoned he would save between 10 and 15 runs in the field in an innings. Also, if neither Gatting nor Crawley was in good nick, White was just as likely to score a few runs.

I was quite surprised when I watched the game on Sky and saw that Gatting was the final choice. So much for sticking with younger players. That is not a criticism, just a comment that even someone like Atherton, who was so strongly in favour of a youth policy, sometimes settles for proven experience when a tough situation arises.

My honest feelings about the Brisbane Test match were that we were slack in the field. It doesn't stop there, because such slackness creeps into the other departments. And, as it happens, it was not all down to Gooch and Gatting. It is not just a matter of agility and diving around, it is all about attitude, and I thought the two older men were exemplary throughout. My feeling that others were not, and lacked all-round commitment, went into my memory bank.

The writing was already on the wall that we were giving a big start to the Aussies in general out-cricket, and I knew we could only get away with that if we were the better side in batting and bowling. That clearly was not the case, so I knew it would be a long hard tour.

I received a telephone call from John Thicknesse of the *Evening Standard* from Tasmania at what I calculated to be around 4 a.m. local time. He was reporting on the match against the Australian 'A' side and was unusually keen to know what the current betting was on the Ashes series, particularly regarding the odds for Australia to win the series by more than a one-game margin.

My punting antennae started to twitch and I asked him why he was so apparently certain that a rare betting opportunity was at hand – rare enough to plunge all you could afford to lose, and then some more.

'Simple. We are giving away at least 20 or 30 runs a day, either in running between the wickets when we bat, or in general fielding when we bowl. That means 100 runs a Test and 500 runs in the series. We might occasionally bat or bowl well, but such a consistent downside of runs gained and lost in general approach is guaranteed to settle the series.'

I was sold, and a few hundred pounds were wagered by Thicknesse and Bannister on Australia to retain the Ashes by a margin of more than one Test. I am still talking to 'Thickers' – just – after the frights in Sydney and Adelaide, before all was safely gathered in at Perth.

Illingworth
I don't think we started playing in Brisbane before the start of the third day. We wasted the new ball by poorly directed bowling, and a score of 167 on a good pitch was pathetic. After all, it was no great disaster when they got 426 first up, and an ordinarily good batting performance would have kept us out of serious trouble. I know McDermott bowled well, but to be bowled out in 67 overs was poor.

At least in their second innings we made them bat longer than they wanted. We kept them to under three an over compared with 3.5 in the first innings, and we applied ourselves with the bat so well that we made them bowl 137 overs before we lost the match. The match was won and lost in the first two innings, and it annoys me that that is down to temperament and lack of application, rather than skills.

Not many games are won against an opposition first-innings score of 426, and the first priority should have been to bat as long as possible and score a minimum of around 300. But when two batsmen get out hooking and another one trying to hoick May, plus a caught and bowled – well, such soft shots get what they deserve.

When you think that they only got 248 for eight second innings, it shows you how easy it would have been to save the game if we had batted anything like the first innings. At the start of the fifth day, we were 219 for two, with Hick and Thorpe having gone so well on the previous day that I thought we were in with a shout of at least saving it. But Warne did them both early on, Gatting got a good one from McDermott and, once Gooch was out top-edging to Healy off May, that was that.

I spoke to Atherton afterwards, and was anxious to know about McCague, who played because of Malcolm's chickenpox. His figures of 19.2-4-96-2 were awful, but sometimes a bowler can be unlucky. Not this time, the general opinion being that he was totally overwhelmed by the occasion. If true, that is a major disappointment, because an important part of playing Test cricket is the ability to stand up to everything – the opposition, the tension and everything that goes with playing for your country.

In terms of age and experience, there is not much between Gough and McCague, but just look how Gough actually enjoys every minute of every match. I know he is an exception to the general rule, but you could not get two more opposite appearances in a match than him and McCague. I pushed for him ahead of Fraser, so it was particularly disappointing for me to hear that he more or less froze when it mattered in Brisbane. Everybody is tense in Test cricket, particularly if you have not played much, but one of the qualities needed is to perform somewhere near to your best in spite of the nerves.

11
DARK HOURS: MELBOURNE

Illingworth

I flew into Melbourne a couple of days before the game, which started on Christmas Eve and then had a rest day on Christmas Day. There were no problems between the captain and me regarding the Tetley lunch in London at which I answered questions and was generally stuffed. I sat next to him at the pre-match dinner and talked to him mainly about how to get the side's confidence back. I kept stressing the positive side of things, and I was quite hopeful before the match.

The pitch was corrugated in appearance and was bound to be up and down. The problem was that it was damp as well, which meant that Warne would have turned it square. I reckoned that it was a worthwhile gamble to put them in if we won the toss for two reasons: with the dampness there, we could well bowl them out cheaply and, with the next day being a rest day, the pitch would have dried out for the second day of the match, and Warne would not get so much help.

We did well enough to get them 220 for seven before Steve Waugh got them to 279, but when we were 119 for one I thought we could get a lead. I don't often moan about decisions, because they are part of the game, but this time we really got the rough end of three – Atherton, Hick and Thorpe – and the handicap was too much, especially as Stewart broke a finger.

There is nothing that can be done about decisions, but there is about your tactics, and I reckon we were wrong when we fielded again not to attack more. We should have had more men around the bat for the new ball and really pushed them hard,

133

because a lead of 67 is not significant if you can get two or three quick wickets. The captain must take the major responsibility for that, although surely the management could put him right at an interval break if they recognised he had got it wrong.

As a result, we allowed Australia to build a strong position. Even when a new batsman came in, Tufnell bowled over the wicket to him, and that is a tactic which should be used only sparingly, and when other things are not working. I thought Tufnell had a disappointing game, because he did not spin it a lot on a surface on which Hick showed it would turn, even though he hardly got a bowl.

The second innings was embarrassing. I know the captain got another rough decision, but how can a decent side allow themselves to be bowled out for 92 in 43 overs? We were given a bowling lesson by McDermott, whose line now is superb. As for Warne, he is as good a leg-spinner as I have ever seen. If he can avoid the shoulder problem caused by the extra rotation needed for the googly, he will break all records. Richie Benaud had a higher arm and got more bounce, although his side-spin was less.

The biggest problem for batsmen is judging the amount of turn he will get, because he does not spin them all the same amount. He can give it the biggest rip possible without losing accuracy, but he will mix in some other leg-breaks which turn less but bounce more. Not only that but his flipper is a good one and getting more accurate all the time. Also his pace is not slow, and he has the ability to get in-drift from the big-spinning leg-break.

Remember the Gatting dismissal at Old Trafford? What really did him was that he started to play to a line of about middle and leg. The ball then swerved late in flight to pitch outside leg stump, and Gatting was committed to following and playing at something which pitched six inches outside the line and took the off bail.

He is now the complete bowler, because he is the one bowler I know who can pose just as many problems from around the wicket. Most bowlers switch as a defensive tactic, and it is a simple matter to kick them off. Warne is different. Because he can spin it so much he can pitch it so wide of leg stump you can't tread on it and often you cannot judge the turn well enough to put a pad in the way. The only answer is to play French cricket, as Emburey did at Edgbaston in 1993. It looks

134

ugly, but it works, as Emburey proved by batting for six hours in the match.

I got one laugh out of the game. I was watching it from the Australian Board box together with Keith Fletcher and his wife Sue. On the opposite side of the ground, the Barmy Army had been going non-stop for hours, and Sue had had enough. She borrowed Keith's binoculars to have a close-up of the sort of people who could go to cricket and make such an incessant row.

She adjusted the 'bins' and suddenly froze in horror. There, right in the middle of the huge choir, was her daughter Sarah, singing her head off. Any thoughts the Fletchers had of getting an explanation that evening vanished when Sarah turned up unable to utter a word. Her voice had long gone.

I have detailed various events involving Mike Smith, Keith and myself in the three weeks I was there. I did not agree with several things, including the blanket refusal by 'M.J.K.' to allow any players to talk to the press. I can understand some of the reasoning behind it, because I well know how a touring bunch of journalists operate, but you have got to swallow most of it and use them for your own ends. This should have happened after the Sydney Test when Gough had such a brilliant game and, naturally, the English writers wanted a few quotes from him.

'The message is clear. England need a young, mobile and refreshing team to remove the memories of tired defeatism. It needs people with character and "spunk", players of fiery egos and burning desires. Patience must be shown, for there will surely be some dark hours.'

Almost Churchillian, or redolent of an utterance from the Iron Lady, but the stark message was from Michael Atherton, following a Test match which brought scorn and abuse from, among others, Denis Compton ('this England team is a disgrace to the nation'), Keith Stackpole ('this team seems to have no spirit and it is sad to see'), Ian Wooldridge ('the captain says how much he despises the British press for not getting in behind the England team in its hour of need. Tiresomely, at the moment, there is no England team we can get behind'), and from chairman Raymond ('it's amazing to me in two or three months how things have drifted. It's very disappointing').

Bob Massie was one of many who were critical of the decision to give the toss away, although he admitted that 'the slow pitch rarely contributed to a dismissal, and the defeat by 295 runs was more attributable to a deterioration of mental approach than the pitch'.

Just as penetrative with the written word as the new ball, Massie's specific analysis of England's shortcomings was devastating. 'In addition to poor decisions and the injury to Stewart, a distinct lack of application in the three crucial areas of the game – batting, bowling and fielding – made for a humiliating capitulation. Australia's fielding is light-years superior to England's. Examination of every department of England's game in this Test highlights a lack of the basics, and therein lies the area for rapid improvement.

'There is nothing you can do about poor decisions, but you can about line and length, sub-standard fielding and indiscreet batting – *hard work*. Gough is raw about the edges, but shows great pride in playing for England. Some others do not.'

That is not just a knife going in, it is a surgical scalpel with not an unnecessary word used. After all, Melbourne produced the 14th win in the last 21 games between the two countries, with Warne's hat-trick the seventh in Ashes Tests, but the first for 91 years. Regarding Warne, he took his 150th Test wicket in his 31st game and his 50th against England in his eighth Test.

McDermott also climbed a few rungs on the historical ladder, with his 254th wicket taking him beyond Benaud, McKenzie, Holding and Statham, and putting him 13th on the overall list in Test cricket. On the batting front, Boon closed in on 7000 Test runs, while Atherton passed 3000. Ian Healy, then only 30, moved into fourth place on the wicket-keeping roll of honour behind Rodney Marsh, Jeffrey Dujon and Alan Knott.

12

SOME BRIGHT SPOTS: SYDNEY, ADELAIDE, PERTH

Illingworth

When we picked the Ashes party, it was felt that Sydney would offer spin the best chance, as it has in recent years. Not a bit of it. It was a flat, well-grassed pitch which, on all appearances, might turn a bit on the fifth day. Otherwise, it looked as though only the quicks would get anything from it.

The party now was more than slightly different from the original one. Gone were McCague and White, and Stewart was unavailable. Before the end of the series, Gough and Hick would also go, and Udal would sustain a side strain. Ilott had come and gone, but first stand-by Fraser was now in the shake-up and played because of the last-minute drop-out of DeFreitas. When we were in the middle, he was playing, and only when Atherton got back to the dressing-room did he find out that Fraser would have to play because DeFreitas complained about a hamstring.

We won the toss again and had to bat, even though we might get into trouble early on. That is a risk you have to take sometimes, and it looked as though it had paid off when the captain and Crawley took us from 20 for three to 193 before we lost four wickets for three runs, including the stupid run-out of Steve Rhodes.

The second day showed what could be done with a bit of fight and luck. Gough and Malcolm threw the bat and it came off so well that we got to 309. I am all for a cricketer playing his natural game, and Gough proved the point with the bat for the third time in seven Tests. He can disrupt an attack as well as anyone in top cricket, and it is amazing how fielding captains seem to freeze when hitters like him come off. That is the time when you have got to defend in certain areas, but the trick is in identifying those areas and stopping your bowlers becoming rattled.

He then bowled brilliantly, although we just failed to make the Aussies follow on. If we had succeeded, we would have won the match, but even so, we still had 120 overs in which to bowl them out, although the declaration with Hick on 98 caused such a fuss. I can understand it, because there was no real reason why we could not have batted for at least another over. It's all very well saying that the team comes before an individual, and so it does providing time is really tight.

It wasn't on this occasion and, although I was not in the dressing-room, I believe the declaration came as a complete surprise to everyone, including Fletcher. It was therefore no surprise to me that when we took the field after the 10-minute break, we looked flat, as though we were on the wrong end of the match.

We should have bounced out of the dressing-room, with an 'up and at 'em' approach, but the attitude of the players told me that the dressing-room must have had an uncomfortable atmosphere just when it should have been bubbling.

We had a bit of luck with the rain which juiced the pitch up at the right time, and Fraser bowled superbly. I am not trying to defend my original opposition to his selection, but you cannot pick a bowler in the hope that typically damp English seaming conditions will suddenly appear towards the end of a five-day Test. All to his credit, he was suddenly presented with ideal conditions, and he made the most of them. It was a shame we could not nail down the win, but at least we showed more fight and proved what I always believed – that there was not that much between the two teams, if we played to our potential.

If Gough and Malcolm had shown the same control as Fraser, we would still have won, but you can't have everything. We were actually the better side in the match, although the fact they stayed on when it rained helped us no end.

I have referred earlier to Mike Smith's unwarranted gag on the players, and there was no better example than Gough. Individual performances like his don't come along that often, and should be milked for everything, especially on a tour where so much went wrong. It was a decision which I firmly believe did nobody any good at all. It got up the noses of the press, and it denied the reading public the chance to read something good for once. If 'M.J.K.' was so wary of them, all he had to do was to sit in and veto any out-of-order question. An ideal chance to promote the game was lost.

I returned to England on 17 January, and my overall view was this: there was a general slackness which I found worrying. We had ended the 1994 series against South Africa on such a high that something serious had gone wrong in a few months to produce defeats of the sort we suffered in Brisbane and Melbourne.

I felt frustrated, because they were mostly the same players, and bubbly types like Rhodes, Gough, Stewart, Gatting and Tufnell don't change overnight. As the captain subsequently admitted, he found it difficult to motivate his players, and the management must shoulder some of the responsibility for that.

I know from past experience that Mike Smith feels that playing for England should be sufficient motivation, but that is begging the issue. Some players think and act differently from others, and it is the job of the captain and management to get the best out of everyone. I always believed as captain in making sure every player was always involved and knew what we were trying to do. That did not seem to happen in Australia.

I was not there long enough to interfere – and that was the trouble; any suggestions from me about the dressing-room spirit were interpreted as interference, so I kept my distance. I was criticised by the press for not spending more time in Australia, but I was asked by the Board only to go for long enough to see at first hand how the tour was going. The day-to-day involvement, which I reckon I handled well enough at home, was the responsibility of the appointed team and general manager, and I would only act differently under different circumstances.

We all got tangled up with the press, so I backed off.

I watched the last two Tests at home, and was thrilled at the Adelaide win, and deflated by Perth. Gatting's hundred was a terrific exhibition of guts. On the playing front, Hick and Thorpe batted well, and Crawley made progress, although he must be made to pay greater attention to his general fitness. He is a young specialist batsman, and he should take a long look at the young Australian batsmen and their approach to training and practice.

Atherton fought hard and had more than his fair share of poor decisions. Gooch and Gatting disappointed me although, as I have already said, I never thought they would both play in the same side unless there were injuries. DeFreitas proved to me that he is a better bowler in England, and Gough made the biggest strides of anyone. He can become a genuine all-rounder.

Chris Lewis did well in Adelaide, but until he rams home wickets and runs consistently, he won't establish a regular place. I wish we could transplant a bit of bloody-mindedness into him – the sort that Trevor Bailey in my time and Allan Border had more recently. They were good players, but so is Lewis. The difference is that they made the most of their ability, while he has not done that yet. It all boils down to attitude and you can't coach that.

There were several disappointments, especially Benjamin. He was unlucky to start with, when they misdiagnosed shingles, but part of being a good tourist is to put up with whatever comes along and still contribute on and off the field. Tufnell did a reasonable job and the captain thinks a lot of him, but he still has work to do on his general attitude. He worked hard at his fielding, but I just sense that he has gone back a bit as a Test bowler, mainly because he does not spin it a great deal.

Udal and White showed they have got the right approach to top cricket, but injuries did not help on what was always going to be a hard tour for them.

The biggest disappointment was Rhodes. Not for his wicket-keeping, because he kept reasonably well, if not up to his very best. He was unfairly criticised for missing something which was not a catch anyway, and I thought he did well in taking Tufnell from over-the-wicket bowling into the rough. His batting fell away to nothing, and that surprised as well as disappointed me after his fine first season against New Zealand and South Africa.

Team manager Keith Fletcher has an interesting theory about Rhodes. 'He was only getting, on average, an innings every week or so, compared with three or four knocks a week in county cricket. He is the sort of cricketer whose rhythm depends upon regular cricket, and that may be why he suffered in Australia.'

Yet Rhodes has had a series of successful 'A' tours, so it could be a matter of the sort of bad trot that comes to every cricketer.

* * *

Illingworth

That leaves Fraser. Much was made of his original omission, and I know how strongly the captain fought for him. He had one great spell in Sydney, but as good a judge as Richie Benaud twice referred to his bowling in other parts of the series as 'ordinary'. I hope he recovers his nip and plays for England many more times, but it could be that the debilitating hip injury he battled so bravely to overcome will prove too big a handicap in Test cricket.

My overall view of the tour is that we under-achieved, never mind all the injuries and the bad decisions in the Melbourne Test match. I also feel that the under-achieving went largely unchecked by the management, and that is why we got a little bit at odds when I was out there. There were two problems as far as I was concerned – the roles of Mike Smith and Keith Fletcher. It was not up to me to complain because I had nothing to do with their appointments, just as they did not with mine. Keith was already into the second year of a five-year contract when I was elected chairman and, of course, 'M.J.K.' was the candidate I pipped for the job in March 1994.

13
ILLINGWORTH AND THE PRESS

Illingworth's initial honeymoon with the press survived his first home season in charge. Unilateral comments from the new chairman and the captain, mostly made before the end of the tour of the West Indies in April, were seized on by the popular papers as evidence of a schismatic split about Atherton's expressed determination to stick with his Caribbean choices, but a potentially difficult situation was quickly defused by both men before the start of the home series.

They had their differences, but what chairman and captain do not? The Lord's Test against South Africa proved a catalyst, nailing once and for all the canard that Illingworth was looking to replace Atherton. The dirt-in-the-pocket row provided him with a golden opportunity. All he had to do was to stand back, stay silent and let Atherton take the heat until the match referee, Peter Burge, suspended him – as he surely would – and England would have had a new captain.

It needs emphasising that Illingworth used the word 'stupid' as opposed to condemnatory language to describe Atherton's actions and initial subterfuge, but if the marriage really was that unsteady, a divorce was there for the taking. Instead, links were forged out of mutual respect, and the rest of the summer passed relatively uneventfully.

The Oval Test and the two Texaco games against South Africa provided three thumping victories but, typically, Illingworth did not let the euphoria deflect him from delving deeply into one issue before he made his detailed report to the TCCB.

Illingworth

I had read so much about the age of myself, Fred Titmus and Brian Bolus, and how much better it would be with younger selectors who would supposedly be more understanding towards the modern player, that I tackled Mike about it before I wrote my report.

I asked him specifically if he was happy with the make-up of the panel, and he told me he was, so I included that in the report. I am glad I did, bearing in mind his remarks to the contrary in Australia, and the fact that the manager, M.J.K. Smith, went out of his way to identify himself with the comments.

A function in November 1994 provoked the biggest press reaction of the year. I was invited to a luncheon in London at which Tetley were to announce a new £50,000 sponsorship deal. I knew that there were plenty of journalists present, and I knew that I would be on the record.

I also know full well that if the press want to stuff you, they will, no matter how careful you are. The fact that all the papers next day made no mention of Tetley, but went head first on the basis that I was criticising Atherton, proves to me that that was what they were after.

None of them made the point that I did not stand up and make a speech in which I volunteered comments – it was strictly a question-and-answer format. I therefore responded to specific questions, and to several of them in a light-hearted way. There were no cricket journalists there as such and, as far as I am concerned, the headlines and my reported answers were twisted and given a different slant from what was intended to a degree I have never experienced before.

I have always been straight with the press, right back to the time when I was captain of England, and mostly I have been treated fairly. Not this time.

For instance, how about the *Sun* headline on 23 November, a couple of days before the Brisbane Test match, 'ILLY DISHES THE DIRT ON CAP'N MIKE'? Or the *Today* headline, 'ENGLAND AT WAR'?

That is just cheap journalism. Brian Woolnough of the *Sun* wrote, 'In an explosive speech yesterday, Illingworth hammered Atherton for never phoning him since England arrived in Australia a month ago.' He uses other emotive words like 'raging chairman', and qualifications preceding quotes like 'Illy slammed Athers', and 'Illingworth stormed'. All this via an 11-paragraph wedge of quotes, apparently given by me in an unbroken speech, instead of making it clear that on each topic I was asked a specific question by a different journalist.

When I was asked if Mike had telephoned me, what was I supposed to say? 'Yes' when he had not? Then when I was asked what I would have said had he rung me, the only thing I mentioned was that I would have asked him why he let Steve Rhodes open the innings when there were other batsmen in need of time in the middle.

I was then asked if I thought there should be one supremo, and I gave the same answer as I always have in the last ten years or so, ever since I was first spoken to about the England team job Micky Stewart eventually took. Yet that answer was reported by Woolnough as 'showing my bitterness'. What have I got to be bitter about?

I had been happy enough since then doing my television and newspaper work, and had no thought about getting back into top cricket. Remember, when I was approached about my availability for the chairmanship, I was totally surprised, and never before or after that first approach did I do any lobbying. All the running was made by other people, which is flattering, but still did not weaken my resolve to take the job on my terms regarding bottom-line accountability and responsibility. I was only being consistent there, because it was the failure to agree on those crucial matters which made me walk away from negotiations in the mid-1980s.

I was also quite happy to confirm at the lunch that Mike wanted Gus Fraser and I did not, but also made the counter-point that, for the first Test against South Africa, Mike wanted Crawley ahead of Thorpe, whereas I thought the opposite, but let him have his way.

As for Nigel Whitfield in *Today*, he got me 'blasting' Mike and 'fuming'. That is untrue, and all those journalists know it. You can't even excuse it as journalistic licence. It is mischievous writing aimed at creating headlines out of nothing.

Anyway, it didn't work, because as soon as I caught wind of what they were up to, I rang Mike to tell him he would have the press on to him and I explained what I had said and, just as important, how I had said it. Fortunately, he is too level-headed to take exception about that sort of rubbish, and he told me he had already been approached by the press in Australia to deal with my comments.

There were other things written on the same lines in the following month before I flew to Melbourne. The most sensible and accurate were in a piece I did with Richard Williams for the *Independent on Sunday*. My quotes were as given, and not sensationalised into conclusions drawn by the writer. Even then, one of my closing quotes about not flying 13,000 miles to watch England play like prats was lifted by a tabloid and used the day I flew out.

The point was that the paper said I had told the England players this, yet here I was, reading it in Heathrow before I had even got on the plane. Jet-lag in reverse perhaps.

The argument that Illingworth should have recognised he was stepping into a journalistic minefield is a powerful one. So was he, as he believes, ingenuous? Or does the section of the media that believes he is no stranger to the art of dissembling have a point when they insist he knew exactly what he was saying and how it would be reported?

How, they ask, could he ignore the fact that he was talking to hard-nosed journalists, most of whom are under instruction from sports editors who are rarely interested in news over which they cannot fly a sensational banner?

Knowing him as I do, the starting point is that rarely does he duck a question. He has no great command of parliamentary language, nor is he inclined to coat a verbal acid drop with sugary words. If he has something to say, he says it in a way that leaves little room for misinterpretation.

Which is different from the conclusion drawn by the *Mail on Sunday*'s Patrick Collins. 'Atherton and his men should not expect an apology, for being a professional Yorkshireman means never having to say you're sorry.' Not the most objective sentence ever crafted. Nor is this summation of Illingworth's reference to his pre-emptive action in the Lord's Test against South Africa helping to 'save Atherton's neck'. Collins dismisses that with 'A curious rendering of history, this, since I recall Illingworth's defence of his captain as having been rather more inept than anything seen at White Hart Lane this season.' A short telephone call to match referee Peter Burge would immediately have dis-abused Collins. Or is it possible to disabuse a writer who believes 'Illingworth's performance was the boorish, self-regarding whine of a man whose every public utterance proves his unsuitability for office'?

Collins – dare one say it, with typical Yorkshire tenacity? – returned to the attack about Illingworth's remarks after the heavy defeat in Melbourne. 'But the greatest problem of all for Atherton is the man who spent his Christmas hols in Australia, watched a bit of cricket, then hurried back to his holiday home in Spain to watch the rest of the series on Sky TV.'

Illingworth
For the record, I watched the Brisbane Test on television from my Farsley home, as I did the fourth and fifth Tests in Adelaide and Perth, and did not return to Spain until February. I am not sure what difference it makes where I watch a game on television, but as Mr Collins chooses to make a point of it, I must correct him.

Collins wrote on 8 January 1995: 'Raymond Illingworth was responsible for the selection of this touring party (by common consent, one of the weakest that England has ever sent abroad with a spectacular capacity for self-destruction), and some of the selections were made in defiance of the captain's wishes.'

Illingworth
Not some, just one. Fraser was the only player Mike was knocked back on. He agreed with every other player chosen, including Mike Gatting.

Collins clearly knows better. 'Craig White was selected, despite Atherton's conviction that he fell short of Test class. So Mike Gatting, an old Illingworth favourite, was given a place and now has a batting average for the series which is lower than that of Devon Malcolm.'
Which is a nice comparison, except that after the next Test, in Adelaide a month later, Gatting had scored a hundred and Malcolm's average of 16.66 was greater than the combined averages of Chris Lewis, Steve Rhodes and Phil Tufnell. The big drawback about facts and figures is that they have an annoying habit of spoiling a good story.

Illingworth
When I refer to bowlers of the past, it is usually to make a point. For instance, Collins wrote that because I said that the Melbourne conditions cried out for bowlers like Derek

147

Shackleton and Tom Cartwright, and because they had played their last Test matches 30 years ago, I must be suffering from jet-lag. The point of my remark was that not since then have England had that sort of true artist as a medium-pace seamer.

Collins went on to mock Illingworth for his change of stance compared with a good opening day for England and the subsequent terminal decline in Melbourne. He wrote: 'He addressed the team on the eve of the Test. England enjoyed a productive opening day, and Illingworth was swift to seize the credit. "I told them that they must play as if every ball was coming to them." One correspondent described this mundane chatter as "Churchillian oratory".

'England lost by 295 runs and the chairman began to side-step like a latter-day Phil Bennett. When England decided not to practise next day, Illingworth was asked for a reason. "It's not my job, it's Keith Fletcher's. It is their jobs, not mine, that are on the line if they don't do the business".' He also queried Illingworth's reply to a question about Fletcher's future, in which he rightly said that it was nothing to do with him. As Fletcher was not halfway through a five-year contract, Illingworth pointed out that it was a matter for the Board who had appointed both of them.

Collins ended his onslaught with a reference to Ian Botham's charge that 'Illingworth is out of touch and sympathy with modern cricketers'.

Illingworth
If that is true, why did Mike gladly invite me to spend so much time in the dressing-room in the home Tests against New Zealand and South Africa? I decided not to do the same in Australia because, with Mike Smith there as well as Keith, I thought three extra people would be too many.

I believe that Illingworth answered each question at the fateful lunch with no regard to how loaded it was – a mistake. I believe he chose the wrong time and place to be 'light-hearted' – a mistake. But that does not make him a mischief-maker, out to undermine an England squad he helped to pick. If he could go back to 23 November and speak again, he might respond differently with hindsight.

A fair conclusion to draw is that his trust that the assembled media would report him accurately, and not lard the quotes so sensationally, was a misplaced trust. Foolish and naïve? Yes. Culpable? I think not.

148

Illingworth

I ran into the media again as soon as I landed in Melbourne. It was around midnight when I got to the hotel only to be met by about 20 journalists, so I knew it would be difficult to keep a low profile. Also, I did not see why I should. If I was asked a straight question, I would give a straight answer, and I assumed the same would apply to the captain and the manager. It did not work out that way, mainly because of interviews Mike did following a feature he did for the *Mail on Sunday* with their cricket correspondent, Peter Hayter.

The thing which surprised and disappointed me most was that Mike was quoted again about wanting younger selectors. He said: 'What we require are selectors who are more in touch with the dynamics of the modern game, ideally Test players who are able to communicate with current players more effectively because they have played the same game.'

He also floated the idea that he should have the final say in matters of selection. He and 'M.J.K.' called a press conference in Melbourne where they were playing a one-day game. I had stayed in Sydney after the third Test match. When I heard that Mike said that, rather than the final say in case of disagreement, he wanted control over selection and that Mike Smith endorsed the remarks, I rang them and said I wanted to clear things up when they got back to Sydney.

I reminded the captain of my talk with him four months previously about the same subjects – age of selectors and whose was the ultimate responsibility – and also of the fact that I told him then that his answers would feature in my report to the Board, and he agreed that he was now saying something different.

He did say that he had asked Hayter to delete certain passages of the article, but Hayter had not done so. He also agreed that he had said what was reported at the Melbourne press conference, and 'M.J.K.' also agreed he had confirmed that there would be no censure for Mike and that he backed his remarks.

That did not surprise me as, clearly, the article would have had to be cleared by the manager. I know it was cleared, but how closely it was read is another matter. I asked them both point blank if they were criticising selection and, if they were, what was going on? They denied they were criticising, so I did the best thing possible under the circumstances to defuse the situation. I told them that I would not say anything more in public about the matter, and would leave all future quotes to them.

The story got around that Illingworth had been gagged, but he insists that was not true. As now seems inevitable on a major tour, the collision course between management, players and the travelling media is an ever-shortening path, and the disappointing early results, culminating in England losing the first Test, had produced an unusually early siege mentality within the management. How else to explain Smith's reply to a request for a radio interview? 'We have come here to play cricket, not talk about it.'

Illingworth

I understand from past experience what they have to put up with, but it does not help if you overreact. For instance, how can you justify Mike Smith's blanket refusal to any requests made for individual players to be interviewed when they had done well? The prime example was when Darren Gough had such a brilliant game in Sydney and yet he was not allowed to talk to the press. I know the players have got to be shielded against some aspects of publicity, but how on earth can a young man get stuffed when all they want is some quotes after one of the best days of his career?

I have long known that you are in a no-win situation with the press. That is why I went out of my way in my first couple of months in the job in April and May 1994 to seek out the cricket correspondents when they got back from the West Indies. I was open with them, and said I would be unless I was done with inaccuracies or slanted reporting. I was always available for comment, and I wanted them to understand I was prepared to talk about things which I know previous chairmen of selectors would not.

Perhaps I was silly ever to imagine I could change the system, but I do not regret it. I have always been straight with people – I know that was one of my big strengths as captain – and it is their loss if they want to revert to the old system. They should remember I was chosen by the counties to try to rectify a declining situation in the England set-up. It might take a lot longer than my two-year contract, but I am sure that if certain basics are restored, such as guts and sheer pride in playing for England, then the improvement will be more consistent instead of, as at present, just happening here and there in the middle of some pretty poor performances.

It should be easier to develop a good dressing-room spirit on tour than at home, where the blokes only get together for a week at a time. Yet that was not the case in my first 12 months in the job. We got a good spirit going against New Zealand and South Africa. I know, because I was invited to spend all my time with the players. Yet, for whatever reason, not only did we not build on that in Australia, it actually went the other way.

Illingworth was reluctant to criticise the management publicly, but clearly M.J.K. Smith and Keith Fletcher had a big influence on tour, and therefore must bear the major responsibility. As Atherton surprisingly confirmed immediately after the final Test in Perth. He commented: 'I don't think we were perhaps as united and focused on the job as in the West Indies.' Perhaps unwittingly, he made exactly the same point after a four-month tour as Illingworth made when he arrived in Melbourne.

The decline in dressing-room spirit identified immediately by Illingworth can only reflect on the captain and both managers. Smith and Fletcher are reserved and diffident men by nature, they fight shy of tub-thumping, even when blunt speaking is necessary. Clearly, changes were needed, and Illingworth had long advocated the virtues of combining the roles of chairman and team manager.

Illingworth
The chairman should manage the side abroad, because it would establish continuity, which is important, as well as allow him to see everything abroad as well as at home. I know that figures are more important at Test level than in other levels of the game, but temperament and how a player approaches his game are also important.

I have toured most countries, and know the extra problems players face abroad, often playing in front of hostile crowds when you think you haven't got a friend in the world. It takes a lot of character to stand up to that, and also on-field discipline is crucial, with the match referee system now firmly established.

Take the Chris Lewis incident in Adelaide. If, as I read, John Reid had specifically warned Mike about such gestures in his pre-match talk, it is disappointing that either the captain did not pass the warning on to the players or, if he did, that Lewis did not heed it. I don't care how excited a player gets when he gets a wicket, there is no room in the game for behaviour like that.

What also disappointed me was that our management seemed to regard that as natural aggression and not to be condemned. At least, I did not see one word of criticism from anybody about Lewis, nor did Mike make any apparent effort on the field to cool him down. They should remember what Bob Willis did to Robin Jackman at Headingley against Pakistan in 1982, when Jackman waved a batsman off. He got a public dressing-down – finger-wagging, the lot. And that, remember, was to an experienced 36-year-old bowler.

If the chairman of selectors managed abroad, I believe it would short-circuit most of those problems.

He would not have long to wait.

14
THE UPHEAVAL

The night of the long knives was Monday, 6 March. Many versions have been given of the events that led up to Fletcher's dismissal. Not unexpectedly, Illingworth was named in several newspapers as playing a large part in the upheaval. The truth is different.

Illingworth
After I got back from Australia in the middle of January, I had one meeting at Lord's with Alan Smith before I went back to Spain in early February. He had been in Australia for longer than I had, and other Board officials had also been there, including Doug Insole, Dennis Silk and Duncan Fearnley, all of whom were on the executive committee.

I outlined to Alan my reservations about the set-up in Australia, and again stressed that my reason was the decline in the dressing-room spirit. I have been in the game too long not to sense the wrong sort of atmosphere, and I told Alan that I thought a lot of it sprang from the fact that nobody seemed sure of what Keith Fletcher's role was.

The question of replacing him was never discussed – just a suggestion from me that it might be a good idea if somebody spoke to him on an official basis. I can smile about it now, because I was neither surprised that Alan seemed to agree with me, nor by the fact that he did not volunteer who should do it. I asked him if I should, and he quickly agreed that that would be a good idea.

That was it. Nothing more, and I left for Spain wondering how the Board would tackle what I thought was a big problem.

While I was away, I gave it a lot of thought, and became more convinced than ever that Keith was not able to get to the players as he should, especially the senior players. He is a smashing bloke and I have never had a cross word with him, either playing with or against him, or when I captained him 17 times in my 31 games as England skipper.

I always made a point of getting to know every player in my sides so that I could get the best out of them. As a batsman, Keith was a fine player, and perhaps his diffident appearance when he went in to bat was misleading, because he was brave enough. But, as a team manager and coach, I reckon he needed to be more outgoing and go out of his way to identify more with individual problems. I was sure we could make more of our players if he did that . . . it was just a matter of getting him to switch to a higher profile.

I flew back to London on Saturday, 4 March and was contacted to ensure I could attend a special meeting of the executive committee at Lord's on Monday afternoon, two days before the full spring Board meeting. I did not know it then, but the original meeting was scheduled for the Tuesday, but I was not told the reason for bringing it forward, even when the meeting started under the chairmanship of the Board chairman, Dennis Silk.

Members of the committee included David Acfield, Duncan Fearnley, both of whom were on the working party which recommended me for the chair 12 months earlier, Tony Baker, Doug Insole, Sir Lawrence Byford, Mike Murray and Brian Downing. Also there was Alan Smith as chief executive and Mike Smith as the tour manager. We were both invited to have our say about the tour, and of course the management reports had been filed.

Mike spoke up for Keith, and made the fair point that so many injuries had disrupted things, and no blame could therefore be attached to him. I had my say, and it seemed that other people shared my view, including the chairman. I still had no idea of what action they were thinking of taking, and had to leave the meeting around 6 p.m. to appear on the ITV programme *Sport in Question*.

I have since read a lot of twaddle about how I kept a straight face when Keith's future was discussed on the programme, and it was even claimed that I knew I would be taking over when I dead-batted the question. Nothing could be further from the truth, because I only learned later that the meeting at Lord's went on for hours after I left, and no decision was reached until nearly midnight.

The real heat in the meeting was apparently not turned up until after Illingworth had left. Then, it seems that Mike Smith made a pretty strong attack on the chairman of selectors, with particular reference to his public utterances, before and during his three-week trip to Melbourne and Sydney. Having known 'M.J.K.' for nearly 40 years, I know how stubborn he can be when he makes his mind up, and his diffident appearance is a misleading one.

He said nothing that he had not said before to Illingworth in Australia, but it was surprising that he mounted his attack after Illingworth had left the meeting. As it happened, his was, more or less, a lone voice, with the majority of those present now leaning towards the replacement of Fletcher.

Once that bullet was bitten, the rest was straightforward, because more than one member of the executive shared the view that, if they wanted to get the best out of the Illingworth influence, he should be offered the chance to run the team during the second year of his contract. The point was made that changes at the top in soccer usually meant the new man installing his own team, whereas Illingworth's appointment was hamstrung from the start because Fletcher was less than halfway through a five-year contract.

Illingworth
The first I heard about the proposed changes was when I got back to the Regent's Park Hilton around midnight and Dennis Silk rang me. I met him downstairs, and he outlined the provisional decision to offer me a widening of my duties, to include coaching and the managership of the next winter tour to South Africa. Funny really. Here I was being offered the same sort of responsibility and accountability I was refused nine years earlier.

I quickly accepted, because I saw it as the best chance of making the most of the second year of my contract. There were a lot of things I wanted to change, and could not because of the other tiers of management on tour, and the Fletcher position at home. I repeat that the offer to me came unsolicited, and at no time following my return from Australia had anyone at Lord's discussed such a possibility with me.

The Board chairman told me the clubs did not know

155

anything about the change, and I suppose I was a bit surprised that none of the newspapers got a whiff of the story on the Tuesday. In fact, so well was the secret kept by the executive that the Wednesday morning newspapers forecast that Fletcher would stay.

Both Mike Smith and I attended the full Board meeting, and Dennis Silk had persuaded me not to read out a two-page statement I had prepared to correct various statements made about me by other people, including Mike Smith. Even though the statement was a factual one, Silk convinced me there was little to be gained by putting my side. As he said, what I said might be right, but it would not achieve much.

I had to bite my lip when Smith had another go at me in the meeting. He said that things had not been done in the right way, and he regretted the replacement of Fletcher. Things could have got very heated, but I refused to join in. I simply told the county representatives that I had not come there to argue with 'M.J.K.', and the only other thing I said was to ask Tim Lamb to confirm that Fraser was the only player the captain was refused when the Ashes touring party was picked. Lamb was at the selection meeting to take notes, and confirmed what I said.

That was that. The item did not take long, although the press conference afterwards did. Alan Smith made a lengthy statement, and I replied this way to a question about what areas I would be concentrating on to improve England's world standing.

'Team spirit, motivation and confidence. We have to get players consistently playing to their abilities. At the end of last summer, against South Africa, I would have fancied us to give anyone a good game. What we haven't done is to take that on. I can really help with team spirit, confidence and motivation. I have never seen a team with an unhappy dressing-room that has been successful. It's not all about ability. It's a game you have to play in the head.

'I won't be dictating tactics to the captain. He must be in total charge, but if he asks my opinion about anything, I will make suggestions if I think he has missed a trick. That is different. I must emphasise that it will not be a matter of "do this" or "do that". I want absolute pride in playing for England. Just as Basil D'Oliveira always did. He might have been born in South Africa, but it meant so much to him to wear the lion and three crowns.'

As for Fletcher, I told the press that I liked him and felt sorry for him. The same thing could happen to me after 12 months – that is the way the game is nowadays.

Alan Smith made it clear that the executive committee had also considered earlier defeats by India, Australia and West Indies during Fletcher's reign. 'Keith has carried out his duties conscientiously and has contributed to the development of many members of the team with his professional expertise in coaching. But his lack of success has led to a loss of confidence in his abilities, and there has been little progress in the development of the England team.'

A curious twin use of the word 'development' by Smith, one in a positive context, the other less so.

Smith also said, 'We believe we have to look elsewhere for a man to rekindle the pride and passion in playing cricket for England – a motivator who is also an expert cricketer, somebody who will raise team spirit and get the best out of the individual players and the team as a whole. Our choice is Raymond Illingworth.

'Raymond will continue as chairman of selectors, take on full responsibility for the England team and be accountable for its performance. This appointment is for this summer against the West Indies and next winter in South Africa and for the World Cup in India and Pakistan. At the end of this period his performance will be reviewed.'

And so the TCCB took the biggest gamble in its 28-year history. No longer would the buck be passed around a selection committee and the Board who appointed them. Illingworth was now in the hottest part of the kitchen, and would remain there for 12 months. Would his fingers get singed? His first job was to meet Atherton and agree guidelines for the next 12 months which would vary considerably from those of the previous year.

Hardened cricket correspondents were either for or against Illingworth. Predictably, the *Mail on Sunday*'s Peter Hayter, whose interview with Atherton in the middle of the Australian tour created considerable mischief, went in head first on 12 March 1995.

Opinion. 'In securing for himself the role of English cricket's omnipotent being, Ray Illingworth has pulled off an astonishing feat of escapology.'

Fact. Illingworth sought nothing. The offer was made to him by the Board's executive.

Opinion. Hayter: 'A close look at the timetable of events might be helpful. Prior to the executive committee review of the reports on

Monday, it was widely believed that Fletcher would survive. It was also known that Bolus was almost certain to make way for Graveney. Illingworth's power base was about to be pulled from under him.'

Fact. The so-called power base – presumably comprising a majority of Illingworth, Bolus and Titmus, numerically stronger than the captain and manager – was non-existent, because Illingworth's original 1994 contract gave him power of veto over any player, except the captain.

Illingworth
It is a veto I never used. I could have done twice – Crawley v. Thorpe, and the omission of Salisbury at Old Trafford against New Zealand – but I did not. Nor was the omission of Fraser down to my veto. It was a straight majority decision.

Paul Newman wrote in similar vein in the same day's *Sunday Telegraph*.

Opinion. Newman: 'By the time Illingworth made an appearance on Carlton Television's *Sport in Question* on Monday night, during which he told the assembled gathering that Fletcher should not be totally blamed for everything that went wrong in Australia, the chairman of selectors had already sat in the TCCB committee room at Lord's while Fletcher's fate was sealed.'

Fact. As already explained, the discussion about sacking Fletcher and widening Illingworth's brief took place *after* he left the meeting.

A more balanced view appeared on the same *Sunday Telegraph* page from Scyld Berry. 'Fletcher would still be England's team manager, and a good one, if on the international stage he had been anything like his Essex persona – stimulating, proactive and venturesome. Instead he was the opposite as an England batsman, captain and manager – reactive and cautious.' Fletcher's overall managerial record supports this view – played 26, won five, drawn six, lost 15.

Alan Lee of *The Times* was nearest to the mark, a month before the March Board meeting.

When Illingworth was appointed, it was perfectly obvious that he would want to run the England team in his own way, which seemed to ask serious questions about the roles of Atherton and, particularly, Keith Fletcher, the team manager. Captain and chairman have managed to co-exist. It has not always been a close and cordial relationship – how could it be when

Illingworth has carped from afar as he did in such untimely fashion just before the Ashes series? – but there is a mutual regard which will see them through.

Chairman and team manager have rather less in common. The situation became ludicrous one day in Sydney when Illingworth announced that Neil Fairbrother would be joining the party and Fletcher, a few minutes later, irritably responded that nothing had been decided. Fletcher was angry because protocol had been breached and because his own duties had been undermined. Illingworth was bemused because he was simply being his usual, autocratic self. On that day, it became clear that this team is not big enough for both of them.

It is scarcely likely that Illingworth's portfolio will be withdrawn after 12 months. Fletcher is midway through his five-year contract. This winter, he has become an ever-more nondescript figure, and although he has not lost the affection of the players, he can no longer relate to the majority, nor they to him. The TCCB now has to take a difficult decision, for a change, and pay up the remainder of his contract.

Which, four weeks later, they did.

Lee again. 'The solution is to put Illingworth in overall charge, obliging him to manage overseas tours and be fully accountable. The priority is to identify precisely who is working with the captain at the helm.'

A prescient analysis with which the Board's executive committee was to agree, word for word.

The TCCB's executive committee was rarely influenced by the press, even by a journalist such as Martin Johnson, then of the *Independent* before he moved to the *Daily Telegraph*. Never a man afraid to stick a pin into the balloon of pomposity, he also has the ability to reach the analytical crux of an argument quicker than most. For instance, his review of the tour of Australia included these two paragraphs.

It is an education to watch the way Australia and England prepare for a Test match. Australia come close to organising commando drills, while England's practice sessions would not cause a sumo wrestler any discomfort in the wind and limb department. This has been apparent in two areas: Australia's batsmen turn singles into twos, while England turn twos into singles; and Australia's fielders save about 30 runs per day while England's leak the same amount.

England have a bowling coach (Geoff Arnold) whose most obvious contribution is to wander around with a baseball glove on, and to hit balls high into the air for people to catch. They have a team manager who organises practice sessions about as intense as a game of hopscotch, a tour manager who organises the baggage, a chairman of selectors who watched most of the series at home on satellite TV, and a physiotherapist who believes that non-stop county cricket is the reason he has spent most of this tour administering potions and plasters.

Johnson's summation of the tour ended thus:

Atherton's ambition now is to be able to captain a team as competitive as Taylor's, and that he believes will take more than changing the county system and kicking out a few grey hairs. He spoke about a 'lack of empathy and unity' in the squad, which was Gooch's lament on the previous Ashes tour in 1991.

Australia keep on winning because they are proud to represent their country. Sadly, some of our lot play for their country because they get paid for it. Until that attitude changes, whatever the authorities do – revamp the county championship, disqualify everyone old enough to need a shave or zip around the field on roller skates – won't matter a hoot.

All of which went straight to the heart of most of Illingworth's grumbles and grouses which emanated during and after his short visit to Australia. Never a half-a-loaf man, he had fretted his way through the first year of his contract, because he soon realised that, with his powerful selection brief ending in the committee room, he was denied the chance to follow through in the way he wanted. A clash with people such as Keith Fletcher and M.J.K. Smith was inevitable, as it would have been with other men in the same posts, because of the nature of the beast.

As a player, captain, manager and television pundit, Illingworth was never in danger of suffering from self-doubt. The view of critics who complained that he was always right he would regard as a compliment, and that is one reason why he received the backing of the TCCB. When the offer came to run the whole show on his terms, he jumped at the chance. Genghis Khan, Margaret Thatcher and Brian Clough always thought they were right. Raymond *knew* he was.

He already had the right of veto over selection – now it would extend beyond the committee room. The press greeted his appointment with as much enthusiasm as Europe in the 1930s welcomed the increasing power and influence of Adolf Hitler. The Mail group of newspapers led the anti lobby.

Brian Scovell said that the lack of unequivocal support from Illingworth for Atherton's reappointment as captain meant that 'Alec Stewart cannot be discounted as a rival for the job'.

Peter Hayter went much further, suggesting that not only had Illingworth conned the Board into giving him powers that he would manipulate in order to take credit for victory and shift the blame to others in defeat, but that if Atherton did not agree to 'clean chin, sharp creases, tidy hair, a substantially better performance with the media – namely whatever Raymond says is spot-on – then it would be a case of "or else".' By which Hayter meant 'or someone else'.

Illingworth

At the press conference, I made it clear the sort of things I would not do. Such as hitting catches and giving batsmen throw-downs. I would be involved in pre-match preparation, and I wanted to use a squad of specialist coaches. They would be entirely my choices, because it was essential that I used two or three blokes I knew, and who would get on with the players. It would have been useless to bring in someone who the players felt uncomfortable with. They had to respect the coach and his suggestions, otherwise everyone would have been wasting their time.

Before that, I needed to meet Mike to sort out the past and, much more important, the future. Things had not gone well in Australia. Certainly not on the field, otherwise there would not have been the upheaval, followed by a new system in which one man would run the show. The first problem was to settle whatever differences we had off the field in Australia, which mainly concerned things we were both quoted in the press as saying.

I had already spoken to Mike about the lunch in London just before the first Test in Brisbane, and there was no real problem about that. I wasn't happy about him sounding off about the side he'd got in Australia. Even if he hadn't gone along with all of them except McCague for Fraser, he still should not have gone public so often. I knew from my own experience how easy it is to be drawn by the travelling press on tour, so I wanted all that out of the way so we could concentrate on the future.

I met him privately a few days after the Board meeting just off the M62, and we had a good couple of hours. We agreed to disagree on a couple of things, but Mike said the same as me – namely that he had been done a couple of times. As far as I was concerned, there was no good reason to change the captaincy, but I didn't feel I could commit myself until the first meeting of the selectors which I'd arranged for the first day of the Champion County v. England 'A' match at Edgbaston. It started on Tuesday, 18 April, and was the first time the new committee met.

The counties reappointed Fred Titmus but not Brian Bolus, who was replaced by David Graveney. I was sorry to lose Brian, because he was a conscientious selector, a sound judge and also good with the players. I thought he deserved to stay on, but I had no problem with David joining us, as long as there was no clash with his new duties as the first full-time secretary of the Cricketers' Association.

The national press turned out in force, mainly because they wanted to know about the captaincy appointment. Originally, I told them we would probably announce it during the four-day game, probably on the Thursday, but that was before David joined Fred and me. The only way that Mike would not keep the job was if he jibbed at the way I wanted to run things, but I never thought he would do that.

Fred was quite strong about some of the captain's quotes in Australia, particularly when he questioned the fact that we were all over 60. I might have looked at a change if we had been unanimous, but David was very firm about keeping Mike. He also made a good point – that before we announced it, I should meet Mike again and spell out in full detail the things I wanted to do, and how I thought it best we worked together.

It was also thought it would be a good idea if either or both of David and Fred were there with me so there could not be any misunderstandings, so I had to tell the press that we were delaying the announcement for 10 days – until the Sunday of the one-day friendly between Yorkshire and Lancashire at Headingley. I tried to hint that there was nothing sinister in the deal, but in they went, head first, next morning. I was accused of dangling Mike. Of humiliating him by keeping him waiting to show him who was boss and so on.

All rubbish, because all we wanted to do was to clear the

decks for what was bound to be a tough series against the West Indies. I also needed a bit more time to work out on what basis we would make the appointment. My first thoughts were, assuming it was Mike, to give it to him for the three Texaco games and the first Test, but a lot depended on our meeting.

We arranged it for the Benson and Hedges match at Old Trafford between Lancashire and Leicestershire, but we had to wait for most of the day, because Lancashire fielded first and then Mike scored 71, which took us close to the tea interval.

David Graveney was a little surprised at the strength of feeling about the press hangover from the winter.

It started off with one saying that you said that, and then the other would say the same, and we weren't getting very far. I honestly wondered for a while where we were going, but that side of things suddenly subsided, when the question was asked, 'Do you both think you can work together?' After both agreed they could, there was no real problem left. Raymond laid down the guidelines he wanted following. Things like not turning up to press conferences unshaven or sloppily dressed. I suppose I had some sympathy with Mike, in that he saw little wrong in that, and my own final years in county cricket showed me how times change. The modern cricketer does not see that an untidy appearance means he is rebelling against authority, but Mike took on board the suggestion that a captain of his country should make an effort.

That said, Mike was agreeable to making the change, and that was more or less that.

Illingworth
I told Mike that I wanted him to open the batting and captain the side. I didn't want him involved in the politics that invariably go with the job. That was my responsibility. I also did not want him making public statements, other than at the press conferences before and after each Test. I outlined how I thought the get-togethers would go before each Test. The players report Monday evenings after their county games. I saw the Tuesday as the hard practice and training day, with Wednesday just a loosener. We both agreed that the bowlers should not be worked too much, particularly if they had just had a hard five days with their counties.

He took everything on board, and he left the room while we made our minds up. It didn't take long because, as I have already said, I was never of a mind to change – not unless Mike did not see eye to eye with what I thought were common-sense suggestions. It was never a matter of telling him it would be done my way or not at all. Simply that we would have a clear demarcation line about duties. He was the captain and I was the manager. Once the games started, it was all his. If he wanted to talk to me, or if I'd got a particular point to make, then we'd discuss the issue, but decisions were still his. I'm not so forgetful that I can't remember my own time as captain of England. If a captain allows himself to be overruled against his own better judgement, then he's not doing his job. But Mike knew enough about me from the 1994 summer when he'd asked me to spend a lot of time in the dressing-room.

I just believed that a new start would bring the best out of everyone. We had a good dressing-room spirit in my first year against New Zealand and South Africa. That went sideways in Australia, although again I recognise that, sometimes, it is more difficult to sustain that spirit on tour than at home when the players only play and live together for one week at a time. It can work the other way of course, but in the end it comes down to the character of the players you pick.

I rang Dennis Silk to tell him of our decision because, as chairman of the Board, he is the only man who has the right of veto about the captaincy. It used to be with the chairman of cricket who sat on the England committee. It was with Ossie Wheatley, but the first time he used it against Mike Gatting in 1989, the clubs insisted that the veto go to the chairman of the Board.

The press came to Headingley on the Sunday morning, and we messed the announcement up a bit. I didn't know that Mike was playing golf and was not at the match so at midday, when he wasn't there, I went ahead with the announcement. There was nothing wrong in that, although I suppose that it would have been better all round if a proper press conference had been arranged by the Board's media man, Richard Little, with both of us there to answer questions.

As it was, I dealt with it on my own and then left the ground, not knowing that the press found Mike and asked him the same questions as I'd answered. I accept that that was not right, because he could easily have contradicted me on a matter of fundamental importance, but he didn't so we managed to avoid getting off on the wrong foot.

Richard Little's defence was that he did not see any necessity to arrange a formal, full-blown press conference. He was surely wrong, if only because of the potentially damaging situation which arose. He was a step behind the needs of the press, rather than anticipating them. The two previous press liaison officers, the late Peter Smith and Ken Lawrence, were hard-nosed journalists who appreciated the necessity to humour the sometimes excessive demands of the press. Love them or, mostly, hate them, they still have to be lived with and sensible pre-planning often avoids confrontation.

It led to the most vitriolic attack on Illingworth yet. It came from Patrick Collins of the *Mail on Sunday*, who prophesied that 'one more calculated insult, one more gratuitous humiliation from the chairman of selectors is all it would take for Atherton to decide that the game is no longer worth the candle. And given Raymond Illingworth's track record, the insults and humiliations may not be long delayed.'

Collins was upset that Illingworth announced the reappointment of Atherton without the captain being present.

'There are those who believe that Atherton has already taken a great deal too much from a man whose ability is dwarfed by his self-esteem. Illingworth's brief, arrogant and wholly shambolic stewardship of English cricket has been notable chiefly for the testy rejection of opposing points of view, and the systematic under-mining of his captain's position.'

This was penned on 7 May 1995, and the piece included the forecast that the coaches would be John Lever and Geoffrey Boycott, if he could agree terms. And so it did not come to pass that the right Lever was pulled. Either Collins blasted away in this piece with his own gun, or he had been supplied with what he clearly believed to be live ammunition. By the end of the summer, he knew the bullets were duds.

Illingworth
We hadn't got much time before we picked the Texaco squad, so I divided the games up between the three of us, plus Brian Bolus and Alan Knott as observers, as best I could. I watched Yorkshire play Derbyshire at Chesterfield, and Lancashire play Durham at Old Trafford, and had plenty of players to watch in those two games. Lancashire got off to a terrific start, and half

their side was in contention, while I was keen to see how Darren Gough and Craig White were after their injuries in Australia, and also Richard Stemp to see how he was progressing. Also Devon Malcolm and Phil DeFreitas were in our thoughts, and I wanted to see what form and frame of mind they were in.

By then I had told Fred and David what I wanted from them, both in terms of the county matches they watched and also the Tests. I've heard it said that it is a waste of time the selectors watching the Tests, because they would be better off watching county games to keep their eye on fringe players. I don't agree with that, and I told them they must watch at least the first three days of each Test to see how the players they had helped to pick reacted to the big-match atmosphere.

I know there's been a lot of 'gin and tonic' jokes from the likes of Ian Botham, but that is just cheap humour. Anyone who knows me understands that I always want to be involved once a game has started, and I rarely miss a ball. Because of that, I often spot things other people miss, and I wanted the other selectors to watch with the same level of concentration.

I had the coaches to sort out, and eventually decided on John Edrich for the batting and Peter Lever for the bowlers. Everyone assumed that John was only second choice because I couldn't reach agreement with Geoffrey Boycott. That wasn't true, because I was always going to use John for our left-handers. I really do believe that even the best batting coaches are not quite so good with batsmen who play the other way around. Geoffrey has a great analytical ability – no one better technically for the right-handers – but I remember he used to struggle a bit against the left-arm over-the-wicket quicks.

Anyway, it was not just purely for technique that I wanted the coaches. If a cricketer is that much in need of technical advice, then we shouldn't be picking him, but I wanted the coaches to be able to talk to batsmen and bowlers on their approach to the game. To develop the mental toughness that is vital in Test cricket. To talk players into making the most of what they'd got.

My problem with Geoffrey was that he saw it as much more of a full-time post than I did. I wanted the coaches to attend for a couple of days before each Test – namely 12 days for a fee of £8000. I saw Geoffrey at my house on one occasion and spoke to him on the telephone later. He wanted more involvement, and that would lead to a lot more cash. It's funny with Geoff. He doesn't need the money now, but regards it as an affront if he doesn't get what he sees as his market price. I can understand that, but with all his media involvement, there were too many problems to resolve.

I was happy with John and Peter, both of whom played a lot of their Test cricket with me, and I knew they were tough as well as knowing the game through and through. It was often said of John that he was no talker, but I knew he set so much store on the right attitude, and I reckoned there was nobody better to help and push players into a better approach to their game. Geoff is technically flawless, but he can be destructive.

As for Peter, he is a strong character, and I told him that I wanted the players to enjoy their cricket. He was good on technique because, like John, he had to work on his own game. Once a player can do that, he shows he understands the different strands of technique which he can then pull together.

The next problem, although I only saw it as a slight one, was how best to ease John and Peter into the dressing-room. I knew they should do it gradually, because neither was really known to the players. It was a matter of softly, softly, and then once the players knew they could trust them, they could get to work. I had asked them to be involved just for the summer to see how things worked out, so Peter came to the first Texaco match at Trent Bridge, and John came to The Oval and Lord's.

The Texaco squad was picked at the Hilton opposite Lord's. It didn't take much over an hour, because the batting more or less picked itself. We didn't think that Robin Smith was throwing well enough after his shoulder operation to be picked in one-day cricket, so it came down to John Crawley or Alan Wells. Mike was not surprised when Wells was mentioned, because he impressed everyone at Edgbaston when he captained England 'A'. Not only with his hundred, but also in the debriefing from the 'A' tour of India.

We went for Wells, and then concentrated on the bowlers. I knew White was not bowling well enough, so Dominic Cork was picked with Gough, DeFreitas, Udal and Fraser. Glen Chapple came back from the 'A' tour with good reports, but the captain said he wasn't bowling that well, and had a slight injury niggle. Mike said that if it was a straight choice between Chapple and Peter Martin, he would rather stay out of it, so the rest of us settled for Martin. Phil Newport and Peter Hartley also got a mention, but we went for the younger man, even though his selection came as a big surprise to everyone.

Part 5
WEST INDIES, 1995

15

THE DAWN: THE ONE-DAY INTERNATIONALS

The world awaited the launch of HMS *Illingworth*, which came at Trent Bridge with the first of the three Texaco one-day internationals. Wells and Martin were omitted from a game that West Indies won more easily than was suggested by the final margin of six wickets.

Illingworth
We were always on a shoestring after we scored 199. They gambled by bowling their main four bowlers to get us into trouble, so we could never have a dart at the fifth. Even then, we might have pushed them, but we bowled too many four-balls. Campbell and Lara settled it with 114 for the second wicket, but at least we stuck at it well and picked up three wickets at the end. That was the first one-day international we lost in England to the West Indies since 1984, but I still reckoned we could win the other two games.

Illingworth was proved right in glorious fashion at The Oval – the first time the teams had played each other in limited-overs cricket at that venue since 1973. It was also the 1000th official one-day international. Atherton and Hick both passed 50 in rapid time – off 66 and 63 balls respectively – and with Fairbrother sprinting to 50 off 44 deliveries, Curtly Ambrose lost his control and England totalled 306 for five, the highest score ever conceded by the West Indies in one-day cricket.

Umpire 'Dickie' Bird had an eccentric match regarding the referral of run-outs to third umpire George Sharp. Hick was thrown out by Hooper and went without waiting for the verdict, out by several feet.

Bird called for that, but not for one when Ambrose side-footed the ball into the stumps to beat Fairbrother home. The replay showed that the Lancashire man was out, but Bird hung himself out to dry with the press and public by not referring the decision. Not only unbelievable in the world of modern technology, but inexcusable.

Illingworth

We made one change, Martin for Fraser. I was keener than the captain, but I felt Martin should play and I wanted to see how he bowled to their left-handers. I also felt we might have fielded first because The Oval is so difficult to set a target on because of the even bounce and the large playing area. Mike wanted to bat first, so he was proved right when we lost the toss and were put in. I thought 270 was minimum, so the rest was a bonus.

They got off to a good start – 50 in the first nine overs – but Martin settled the match with three wickets in his first four overs. I think he's got a reasonable action and he does swing it away from the right-handers and into the lefties. He did Campbell by opening him up and then got Adams and Lara with good deliveries back into them. Murray and Arthurton got them back on to the fringe for a while, but we would have to have bowled rubbish for them to win.

For Lord's we brought back Fraser for DeFreitas and gave Wells his debut. Mike was keen to play Fraser on his home ground, and DeFreitas had proved expensive at The Oval, although I personally thought he was bowled for too long and I had a word with Mike about it. I know that 'Daffy' felt he'd drawn a short straw there.

I heard it said that we picked Wells to keep Atherton on his toes, but that is untrue and unfair to Wells. He had been on the fringe of selection for a year or two and had conducted himself brilliantly on two 'A' tours. Also he could play fast bowling, so he was a live contender for the five-day series. He played instead of Fairbrother who had a hamstring niggle. He could have played at a pinch, but I told Mike to make sure with the wet ground, otherwise play Thorpe, because we were always going to pick Wells.

It's hard to say we were lucky when we won by 73 runs, but we were. It was a dry pitch but rain had juiced it and we badly wanted to bowl first. Mike lost his third straight toss, and Ambrose bowled so well, for the first time in the series, that we could have been anything after 20 overs. He made it bounce and move all over the place, and all the batsmen could do was to concentrate on survival and hope for things to become easier.

Mike scored his first run off his 27th ball, but he then played as well as I've ever seen him. He was in good nick anyway with Lancashire, and as soon as Ambrose was off, he climbed into the other bowlers so well that his last 50 runs came off only 48 balls. I was pleased for him, especially at Lord's after all the pocket fuss the previous year. It makes such a difference to a captain if he is in good form, and also to the side under him.

We had appointed him for the three one-day games and the first three Tests, and I thought that was as far as we could go. Naturally we hoped that he would do the whole summer and then South Africa, but what if we had lost the first three Tests? He might not have wanted to continue, or even if he did, we might have wanted to make a change before the winter. Confidence plays such a big part in success, which is why I was delighted to see him bursting with the stuff. It was the best I'd ever seen him play and I thought it augured well for the rest of the summer.

The 270 he helped us to achieve at Lord's was a better score than the 306 at The Oval, but I was less happy about our bowling. Part of the problem was that everyone wanted the Pavilion end so Udal had the nearly impossible task of bowling to right- and left-handers from the Nursery end, bowling his off-spin against the slope.

You can't afford to read too much into one-day results, but we won the Texaco Trophy from behind, and that did the dressing-room a lot of good. Ambrose only had one good game out of three, but I knew he would be a problem, as would Walsh and Bishop as well. His selection was a bit of a surprise, but if he came good we would find life more difficult than if it was only Ambrose plus Walsh, with support from the Benjamins and Gibson.

A four-man pace attack depends upon unrelenting pressure coming from all corners, just as West Indies had done for the last 15 years, but I still fancied our chances in the six Tests because they had one or two weak areas we could work on. For instance, Richardson didn't look himself, either batting or mentally, and although Lara, Hooper and Arthurton were dangerous, attacking batsmen, I still thought we could contain and frustrate to force errors.

As for Mike and the captaincy, I thought he'd done well in

the three games. He was certainly thinking deeply about it, and I've always said he has a good cricket brain.

Illingworth had used the word 'decent' before to describe the Atherton brain, only to be scolded by Patrick Collins just as though he had said 'indecent'. By the middle of May, Illingworth had received two *Mail on Sunday* barrels from Collins and cricket correspondent Hayter, and a third was fired off by Ian Botham. He said Illingworth was 'clueless about the demands of modern cricket. He would have been the right man 10, 15 or 20 years ago. But to be removed from the game for such a period of time, I don't see how he can have a conversation with the players. He hasn't got a clue what the players of today go through. It is a totally different ball game.'

Botham might have asked Atherton about that. Of the captain, he said, 'I'm not quite sure what the England captain's job is. His treatment has been disgraceful. I just hope Atherton is not being lined up as the next scapegoat. The way he's been treated is very shoddy. The captain should have the final say, not Raymond Illingworth, who has made a lot of rash statements and rash decisions. It should be a partnership, not a dictatorship' – views that were neither supported by the facts before he uttered them, nor the results since.

Illingworth was in trouble from another quarter. Whittingdale, the City of London company that had put £3 million into English cricket since 1990, announced in mid-May that the company would not continue its sponsorship after the end of the 1995 season. The general charge centred on Illingworth and his style of management, and was made by Patrick Whittingdale.

> Criticism of the players through the media is bad man management and simply does not get the best out of the players. Mike Atherton had a rotten job taking over the captaincy from Graham Gooch and was treated like a child by long-range criticism during the winter. The treatment of Angus Fraser, who works for me when he is not playing cricket, has not been acceptable either. I cannot continue to work with anybody who is going to deal with players in this way. While the management persist like this, there is no way they will be getting my money.

Ray Illingworth said when he became manager that his job was to instil confidence and 'make the most of the limited talent at my disposal'. I don't subscribe to the view that talent is limited, but we are not getting the best out of the talent.

That was certainly true of the side that was beaten in Australia, but as the rapidly unfolding events of February and March showed, this was because of too many managerial cooks. The appointment of a head chef was to contribute materially towards a more palatable offering later in the year.

Illingworth confined himself to: 'I don't want to get into a slanging match. All I'm prepared to say is that we've had a lot of good sponsors over the years who are still with us and don't try to run the game. Any sponsorship is welcome, but not at any cost. What I feel is most irritating is all the criticism we're having and we haven't started yet.'

Quite a gang of four: Whittingdale, Collins, Hayter and Botham, not to mention a generally hostile national press which, virtually uniformly, believed that the Illingworth regime was a doomed one, and overlooked no opportunity of sniping to that effect.

What they forgot was that like poles do not necessarily repel, and Atherton and Illingworth's slowly developing mutual respect was forged from shared characteristics such as stubbornness, pride in performance, and an intolerance of a lack of fight when the proverbial chips are down. Neither deal in verbal frills, nor is there any misunderstanding when they speak. Their relationship is a salty one – even peppery at times – but their common aim to produce a good, tough, competitive side is more than enough to keep them together.

Significantly, as the summer of 1995 evolved, the attitude of the media towards them changed – not the other way around, as their sharpest critics hoped for. The refusal to compromise can be a strength or a weakness, but at least everyone knows where they stand.

Atherton said this of Illingworth and their relationship before the start of the Lord's Test.

It might surprise some people to know that Raymond has a fine presence in the dressing-room, and all the lads enjoy his company and input. As for the public perception of our not seeing eye to eye, then I think we both take the blame for giving the media scope to promote it.

I told him I thought it was wrong of him to criticise us before the first Test in Brisbane, and I admitted I was wrong to have a

175

public dig at the selectors in the press. After Australia, we agreed to sort out any differences in private. Basically, Illy is in charge, although to be honest he often takes a back seat in selection rather than try to run the show himself. I'm more than happy with the extent of my input.

Occasionally, he gets into the 'in my day' syndrome, but that always leads to plenty of good-natured humour. There was a classic in the Headingley Test when they were rerunning some old footage and we all fell about laughing when Illy padded up to Gary Sobers and was LBW playing no stroke right in front of all three. Needless to say, he shot straight back with, 'What you lot might like to know is that I top-scored with 97.'

We often set him up but he always bounces back.

Hardly the words of a man who feels he has been constantly humiliated and belittled by his chairman.

16

DISASTER: HEADINGLEY

Illingworth

A vital factor in the coming Test series would be the pitches we played on. I have always believed that we are one of the few countries who do not play to their strengths by preparing the right sort of pitches. By that, I don't mean unfairly doctoring them, but rather varying the amount of grass dependent upon the opposition. For instance, do the West Indies ever play on a green top in India or Pakistan, and do those two countries ever find a shaved, bare pitch in the Caribbean which will suit the spinners?

Now that I was in charge, there was no objection to me meeting the six Test match groundsmen to talk to them about what I was after – which was even bounce with the grass taken off at both ends for the spinners. I was not asking for a dodgy surface, just a chance for the ball to start turning a bit towards the end of the second day.

We met on 1 May, together with Donald Carr and Harry Brind from the pitches sub-committee and Tim Lamb. I stressed that the pitches should be hard and firm, but when I spoke about less grass at the ends, I was asked who would carry the can if things went wrong? I told them that I was empowered to speak to individual groundsmen and, if they thought I was being unreasonable, they could refer back to Donald. I knew I would have problems at Old Trafford and The Oval, because neither pitch offers much for the spinners, no matter what they do.

There is much more to a Test match than just picking a team, with the pitch the most important factor. In most games, you could get three different results if three extremes of pitches were prepared. A big problem in England is that some grounds have so much cricket played on them that the square loses a lot of life, and nothing much can be done with it. Also, the groundsman is important. They vary a lot, and all have their own ideas. I just wish the Board would listen to me and centralise their employment. While they are employed by their county, they are often caught in a cross-fire of committee, captain and coach. If Lord's employed and paid them as their only employer, surely it would be easier to keep an eye on those pitches which are mostly prepared to suit the home side. I don't mind that, because that is what I am after for England, but it must be done within reason.

Starting the series at Headingley is a mixed blessing against a side like the West Indies. You know that any variability of bounce will be better exploited by their faster bowlers, but often the ball swings and seams because of cloudy overhead conditions. That makes selection even more difficult, because you can pack the side with seamers, only for the sun to shine and nothing happens.

The first Test was the most important for England since I took over, 11 games earlier. We had played badly in Australia and the new management system would be judged on results. Quite right too, because we were trying something radically different. I felt quite excited about it, as it was the ultimate challenge.

Regarding the fitness of the players, I had written to every county through the England physiotherapist, Dave Roberts, with a request for fitness reports about three times in the summer. I arranged for fees to be paid to the local physios for their help in what I saw to be an important part of our planning. I was not going to place the same emphasis on training as had happened in the past, but I was keen to maintain a high standard of general fitness. If I mention John Crawley, it is only to hold him up as an example of how to work hard. I reckon he was nearly two stone overweight when he came back from Australia, and for a specialist batsman, he was too moderate a fielder. He responded well and deserves praise for it.

Lancashire did not have a match the week before the Test, so we met at the Copthorne in Manchester on Saturday, 3 June. We started the meeting with the biggest problem facing us: who

kept wicket and, if it was Stewart, where was he going to bat?
The arguments are old ones. He averaged half as many again
without the gloves, and Jack Russell averaged about the same
as when Alec kept, so how were we bolstering the batting by
asking him to keep?

Figures can be made to prove most things, but he had kept
enough times for a valid trend to develop. If we won the toss,
then there was no problem about him opening, and that was
where we wanted him, with the captain. They had a good
record together, and contrasted in style nicely. But we couldn't
pick a side based on winning the toss, so we had to resolve
three things.

1. Should we pick Stewart to keep?
2. If so, where in the middle order would he bat?
3. And who would open the innings?

Whichever way we went would be a fudge, particularly if we
did not pick a specialist opener. It is no good saying that a
number three is virtually an opener, just because he can be in
after one ball. What about the other times when he has to wait
for long periods before he goes in? That calls for a different level
of concentration, and also he should be a batsman capable of
adapting to different situations. As a regular opener, you set
your own pace, and it is a different mental rhythm when you
always face the first ball of an innings.

What made it a difficult problem to solve was the fact that we
knew which batsmen we wanted to pick. We needed the best
against fast bowling, which meant that Atherton, Stewart,
Thorpe and Robin Smith were automatic picks, and Graeme
Hick and Mark Ramprakash were nearly so. I thought Hick
was now a better Test batsman than before and we had to find
out once and for all if he could stand up to the West Indies.
Ramprakash had played most of his cricket for England against
them, but he did well in Perth when he flew from India and he
was in prime form.

Assuming we would play six batsmen, and that Stewart
would bat in the middle order, it meant that Smith would either
open or not play. Mike didn't mind him opening, nor did David
Graveney, but I wasn't so sure. Yes, he was a player who liked
to take them on, but he was too firm-footed and hard-handed
for my liking against the new ball.

You need to ride and roll with it sometimes, especially against Ambrose and Walsh, and I was not convinced that Smith could do that first up. In the end I went with the decision, and we picked 12, including Devon Malcolm, Martin, DeFreitas, Gough, Fraser and Richard Illingworth as the spinner. That caused a surprise, but we had watched him and he was a much better bowler than when he played two Tests against the West Indies in 1991. There was a touch more body in his action, and he was not afraid to vary a flight which used to be too flat.

On the first morning, I was not keen to pick Fraser. I know people think I have a block about him, but it wasn't that. He never swings it and the ball has to seam if he is to take wickets. Gough was always going to play, and once the captain settled for a spinner, it meant three out of the other four. I had seen Martin swing it and Malcolm was the loose cannon, so I went for him and Mike did not make a fuss, because Fraser's pace was like the others, so Malcolm gave us a different option.

At the team dinner the previous evening, the mood was reasonably positive. I stressed the importance of good running between the wickets, not just for the extra runs it brought, but also because it would rotate the strike more often, and that is important against the West Indies. I also told them that if the pitch was up and down, as seemed likely, they must try to square-cut with a cross-bat and not a straight one. Mike does that, which is why he is a bit vulnerable in the gully area.

The game was a disaster after Mike's 81 got us to 142 for two after being put in. I didn't mind that, because the ball was likely to go up and down more as the game went on. Bishop bowled well, but we should never have lost our last eight wickets for 57. I know we went out to be positive, but three catches in the covers and one at long leg showed that we weren't selective.

The West Indies also had a batting game plan – to get after Malcolm and hit him out of the attack. Lara whacked 53 off 55 balls, and with three of the other top four batting well, we were always on the wrong end of the match, even though we bowled better on the third morning to keep their lead down to 83.

Our second innings was no different from the first. Smith holed out in the covers, and Hick was suckered into trying to pull from too far outside off stump. Again, there was no balance between aggression and common sense, and only Thorpe fought it out, although Ramprakash got a good one which left him off the pitch.

I was not impressed with the attitude of Hick or Ramprakash while they were waiting to go in. They are intense, too much so for my liking. But what I really did not like was that they sat in the dressing-room, which is under the football stand and a bit like a dungeon. You can't see the cricket, so you can't know what the bowlers are doing, even though there is a television on there. It's not the same. Neither is the light. How can you prepare properly when you suddenly walk out into a different light?

Ramprakash just sat staring into his bag, and I tried to talk to him, but it was no good. I know that players psych themselves up in different ways, but it struck me then that Ramprakash in particular was too intense for his own good. John Edrich agreed with me, although he didn't say anything because it was his first Test with the players, as with Peter Lever.

They won by nine wickets, scoring 129 in 19 overs, which is ridiculous. I know Lara played well, although his innings was more of a slog than anything else. The bowlers did not do what we planned, which was to bowl at his off stump if it swung, and straight at leg stump if it didn't.

We were well beaten. No excuses, although the only time we bowled in a morning session, when more happened each day than later on, we got five wickets. It was a bad start to the series, not only because the West Indies are the hardest side to peg back, but also because it showed us that Smith must not open, and Stewart failed twice again. Only the captain and Thorpe batted anything like, and we were also going to have to think about the bowling. I knew we hadn't got a lot of firepower unless Malcolm clicked, but somehow we had to maintain control and avoid being rushed out of a game in a couple of sessions. We had a lot of thinking to do.

I would have minded less if we had competed in the areas we had talked about, but we didn't. You can argue until you are blue in the face about the balance of the side, but it doesn't matter one bit if you bat and bowl like we did. We tossed wickets away, and rarely bowled to plan.

What disappointed me more than anything else was that the West Indies came into the game short of confidence. Their batting was suspect. Their captain was short of confidence, and their bowling had a big query against it. They were there to be taken and we blew it.

17

TRIUMPH: LORD'S

Illingworth

In a six-match series, there is hardly time to blink once it starts. Between the end of the Headingley Test and the beginning of the second at Lord's, we had the Benson & Hedges Cup semi-finals and one full round of County Championship matches. The way we lost the first Test meant we had to have a close look at most players, especially the bowlers, but we had two other problems.

Mike has got a recurring back problem and it flared up at Worcester so badly that he did not bat in the second innings and missed the Sunday match. There was a real chance he might not be fit, although he reckoned that he would make it. Peter Martin was the other injury – he'd developed a thigh injury in the one-day series, and he missed the Championship match at Worcester, but he did play on the Sunday. As a proper fitness test, eight overs in a period of two and a half hours in the field proves nothing except he did not rule himself out of the Lord's match.

I know that only the bowler knows whether he can stand up to a five-day game. Some bowlers have a higher pain tolerance than others and, for a young bowler like Martin who had just got into the side, there is a great temptation to say he is fit when he isn't. I normally would not consider anyone who was not fit enough to play in a four-day game, not unless the injury was such that a week off would clear it, or the player concerned was important to our game plan.

We met on the Saturday evening in the Diglis Hotel in Worcester, and again we started the meeting with a talk about

Stewart. I had been at the Worcestershire v. Lancashire match for a couple of days and had said to Mike that one of us ought to talk to Stewart to see if he would open and keep, because his answer was crucial to the balance of the side. If he wouldn't, then we would have to decide whether he batted in the middle and kept, or did he open with Mike and we would bring in another wicket-keeper?

It was a real Catch 22 situation, because if we did that, we were back to four main bowlers plus fill-ins, assuming that the new 'keeper would bat no higher than seven. Mike said he would ring him, and told us on the Saturday evening that Alec did not want to keep and open.

If we kept the same six batsmen – and we wanted to do that – then Alec had to open, because Smith showed that he would be much better off down the order. That part of the meeting did not take long, but the 'keeper and the bowling did. It was between Steve Rhodes and Jack Russell. Rhodes had a poor tour with the bat in Australia, which was disappointing after his performances the previous year against New Zealand and South Africa. David Graveney naturally made a case for Russell, because of the runs he had scored as captain of Gloucestershire, but Mike has always been keen on Rhodes, so we picked him.

Fraser was an obvious pick on his home ground, and if we were down to four bowlers, Malcolm would be an even bigger gamble. We spent a lot of time discussing DeFreitas before we put him in the XIII. We needed a bit of bite from somewhere, and I couldn't see where it was coming from. We discussed a few bowlers, but Dominic Cork had pushed hard for some time. A lot of people only saw him as a one-day cricketer, but his bowling had plenty about it. I know that David was impressed with his method and thought he was a wicket-taker, so we settled for him. We had to pick a cover opener for Mike, and we settled on Jason Gallian who was having a good season and had impressed everyone with his approach. Nick Knight was also mentioned.

It wasn't the side I wanted, not with only four bowlers, but there was nothing else we could do. When I announced the side on Sunday morning, I explained our thinking and said it was totally governed by Stewart's unwillingness to open the innings and keep.

It turned out to be the best thing I could have said, because as soon as the player heard me at Horsham before Surrey's match against Sussex, he contacted John Edrich and denied he had said anything of the sort. As soon as I heard that I thought of nothing other than the arguments for and against altering the selection.

Had it been any other player than the wicket-keeper, we might have got round it on the morning of the match, but Alec held the key to everything. The more I thought about it the more I knew I was going to change everything by leaving Rhodes out and letting Alec keep and open. I also knew I was letting myself in for the biggest press reaction to anything I'd done in my first 15 months as chairman. Almost to a man, they were against Alec keeping and batting anywhere, never mind opening.

His batting figures supported them, but I was still convinced that in a tight series like this one against the West Indies, we had so many more options if he became the all-rounder of the side. Firstly, I needed to confirm with him that he would do both jobs and then work out a plan if he was caught in the field for the best part of two days. Other than that, I thought we could get away with it. If we batted first, that was all right, and if we fielded first, he could still open the innings for at least half of the second day because he would have had a night's sleep.

He told me on Tuesday that he was willing to do both jobs, so now it was down to me. I suppose it taught me a lesson. If you want a question asked, put it yourself. Not that Alec told Mike anything that was much different – I think it was a case of Mike asking him his preference rather than making a direct request.

I spoke to Mike first and said we should change. It surprised him, and he made the point that it would cause a lot of fuss and lead to all sorts of adverse comment in the press. I reckon that the easy thing would have been to say nothing and do nothing, but that is not my style. I always want to go into a cricket match knowing that my side has done everything to ensure it has the best possible chance of winning the match.

Mike didn't dig his toes in, because he knew that the Saturday selection meeting centred entirely on the fact that we did not think Alec would open and keep. I rang Fred and David to tell them what I wanted to do, and there was no disagreement from either, even though they were surprised. David asked me what the captain thought, but raised no objection in our telephone call.

* * *

The new selector had a change of mind overnight. Graveney said:

> I did not sleep much, thinking of the implications of leaving out our chosen wicket-keeper. It had probably never been done before, and I wondered if it was the right thing to do. I had felt my way gradually into the position of selector – for instance, I watched all three Texaco games but made sure I only went into the dressing-room when we were fielding. I remember hearing from Australia that our dressing-room seemed to be littered with ex-England captains, and I thought it only right that the new system of an overall manager and the captain should be left to get on with it by themselves.
>
> I knew Raymond had the final say, but I wanted to make sure that the captain was not being forced into something he didn't want. My normal routine was to travel to the Test match in time to arrive for the team dinner on Wednesday evening, but this time I left Bristol early enough to arrive at Lord's at 9.30 a.m.
>
> As I walked into the Long Room from one end, Mike and Ray were walking in from the other, on their way over to the Nursery for practice. I told them that I was worried about public reaction to the switch and also said I hadn't slept very well thinking about it. Ray said he'd slept very well, and his mind was made up. I asked Mike what he thought, and he shrugged and said he would leave it to us, and then went to practise.
>
> It was the first time in what was now our fifth game against the West Indies that I had any misgivings about selection. I always tried to make my input constructive, and I think it was accepted as such, even though it was always clear that the chairman would have the final word on anything he felt strongly about.
>
> But this was something very different. I had to admire his refusal to back off, and it says a lot about the man that he was prepared to back his judgement in a situation in which his neck was on the block.

I doubt if there has ever been a more controversial volte-face in the history of selection, but Illingworth had no qualms regarding doing whatever was necessary to put what he thought was the best side into the field. It would have been a bold move on any other ground, but to do it at Lord's called for even more nerve. The ground was, historically, England's least successful venue against the major cricket-playing countries. They had won only three and lost eight of their previous 17 Tests there, and had not beaten West Indies at Headquarters since 1957.

No other English ground would have such a concentration of top brass, and the infamous Atherton pocket incident had happened barely 12 months previously.

Illingworth

Once my mind was made up, there was no turning back. The first and worst thing was to tell Rhodes, and he was shocked. I explained all the circumstances and, being the good pro he is, he accepted what I said, but I knew he was really brassed off. Richard Little suggested a press conference for Steve to attend, but I squashed that. I couldn't see what purpose it would serve, because even if we kept a close watch on the questions, the press would have made the most of his obvious disappointment.

Mike announced it at the normal eve of Test briefing of the press, and they were incredulous. I could have made a fortune guessing the Thursday morning headlines, and they hung me out to dry. I was a dictator, a man with no consideration for the captain or Rhodes. I rode rough-shod over the other selectors, etc. They mostly crucified me for overturning the original selection, but one or two also had a go because they did not agree with Stewart keeping wicket. I was expecting heavy flak, but I have to say it was more than I thought.

It was certainly the most controversial decision I have ever made in cricket, but at least it showed that I was not afraid to back my judgement, even in the face of criticism and ridicule. The only thing that upset me was the statement in most papers that I had belittled Mike. It was the same section of the press that persisted in saying that there was trouble between us. They could not accept at face value my reasons for the change, and I knew I was in for a very rough ride if things went wrong in the match.

The Thursday morning headlines included 'Silly Illy' and 'U-turn fiasco'. The *Daily Mail* trumpeted, 'It is a high-risk policy. If it works, it could strengthen Illingworth's authority by proving his cricketing wisdom. If it does not, his credibility – already challenged by the first Test selection blunders – will never be the same again. It is an extraordinary about-turn which, at best, reeks of indecision and, at worst, panic.'

The *Daily Telegraph* echoed the thoughts on Illingworth's credibility, but their former cricket correspondent, E.W. 'Jim' Swanton, took exception to an article in the leader column of *The Times*. 'Entitled "No ball Illy", it was stuffed with amateur opinion dressed as fact and extravagant prognosis, falsified by events, and it took the biscuit.'

Illingworth had one point to make. 'The trouble with you buggers is that you've moaned for years about nobody being accountable. Now I'm prepared to stand up and say that the buck stops with me, you call me a dictator. You want it both ways.'

Illingworth
Before the start of the match, I went over everything again, starting with the selection meeting at the Diglis in Worcester. Each time, I came to the same conclusion. We got it wrong at the meeting, simply because we did not clarify things properly with Stewart. Therefore we did the right thing in the end and, win or lose, that was all that mattered. If it went wrong, it was down to me – nobody else. That is the point the press missed when they said I had made a fool out of the captain and the other selectors.

When I asked for the right of veto in my contract, I never imagined it would be used in such circumstances, but what's the use of asking for and getting complete accountability if you shirk it when it matters? I have never dodged big issues, so it wasn't all that big an effort for me to do what I did.

With Rhodes gone, we were down to 12, and it was just a case of whether we went in with all seam or picked Richard Illingworth and left DeFreitas out. Martin declared himself fit, and I wanted to see more of him. Gough had a moderate game at Headingley, but he had to play, and we went for Cork for the final place. I thought he had a bit more to offer with the bat than 'Daffy', and we could afford to gamble a bit with him because we had five bowlers, including Illingworth if we got stuck. I think Richard surprised a few critics in the first Test, because he got us a bit of control back in their first innings, when Lara was running away from us.

He got him out by tossing it up and generally bowled well. Mike always tells the players who are left out and, although we have been criticised a few times because players hear their selection or otherwise on the radio first, we always try to let the player concerned know first. It isn't always possible, but

Wicket-keeper Steve Rhodes (standing) being told of his surprise omission from the England team to play the West Indies at Lord's in June 1995. He left the ground to play for Worcestershire the next day. Illingworth took full responsibility for the shock move. (*Graham Morris*)

Illingworth's decision to give the gloves to Alec Stewart paid off with this match-turning catch on the final morning to dismiss Brian Lara off Darren Gough. (*Patrick Eagar*)

(From top left) The worst pitch of the series handed the match to the West Indies fast bowlers. Robin Smith batted for five hours despite being peppered with short bowling. Darren Gough is attacked from round the wicket, and Graham Thorpe got a lifter from a good length on the first day. (*Patrick Eagar*)

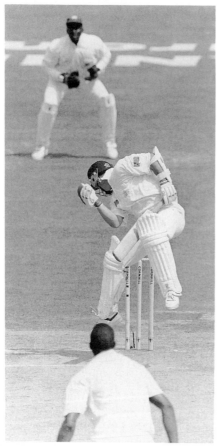

Dominic Cork's hat-trick against the West Indies at Old Trafford in July 1995. He bowled Richie Richardson (top), and had Junior Murray (centre) and Carl Hooper LBW (bottom). It was the first hat-trick for England since Peter Loader's at Headingley in 1957, also against the West Indies. (*Patrick Eagar*)

Graeme Hick acknowledging applause for his brilliant hundred in the first Test against South Africa, November 1995. (*Patrick Eagar*)

Dominic Cork's theatrical style of appealing, which attracted much criticism during England's tour of South Africa in 1995–96. (*Graham Morris*)

(Left) Michael Atherton and Jack Russell celebrate a miraculous draw in the Johannesburg Test. Atherton batted for 643 minutes and Russell for 277. (Right) A dejected Hansie Cronje congratulates Michael Atherton on his magnificent unbeaten 185 which saved the match. (*Graham Morris*)

South Africa's Craig Matthews shown on Sky Television with his fingernails working on the seam during the third Test at Durban. (*Graham Morris*)

The strange action of young spin prodigy, South African Paul Adams. Apart from the head facing the wrong way, note the unusual grip for a back-of-the-hand bowler of one finger and the thumb. (*Patrick Eagar*)

Jack Russell celebrating a new world record of 11 victims in the second Test v South Africa at The Wanderers in November 1995. (*Patrick Eagar*)

Graham Thorpe out of his ground, but given not out without referral to the third umpire by Dave Orchard in the Cape Town Test, January 1996. Hansie Cronje objected and Orchard compounded his first error with the second one of bowing to the Cronje pressure, despite a Code of Conduct rule which says that a fielder may not request a replay. (*Patrick Eagar*)

Robin Smith, controversially given out caught behind off Paul Adams by umpire Dave Orchard in the fifth Test at Newlands. Replays showed that Smith did not hit the ball, leaving his bat well behind the front pad. (*Allsport/Clive Mason*)

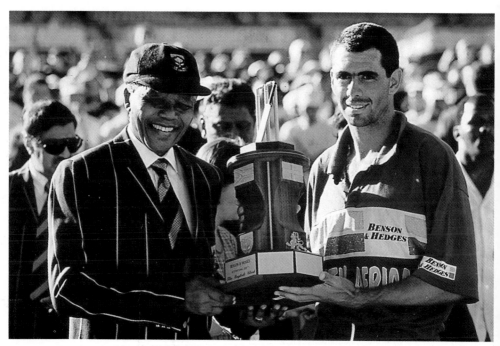

State President Nelson Mandela presenting Hansie Cronje with the spoils at the end of the seven-match one-day series against England at Port Elizabeth in January 1996. (*Allsport/Mike Hewitt*)

I always made a point when I was playing of not only telling the player myself as captain, but of explaining the reasons to him.

We needed a bit of luck with the toss and we got it. Mike won his first toss of the summer against Richardson, and we batted first on what was a dry pitch. I know a bit about pitches, but you can never be completely sure. I thought it would do more as the game went on, but it did most on the second and third days and then got a bit easier.

It started cracked, but the cracks mostly held because they were dry. If a cracked pitch is damp at the start, the cracks usually crust and then crumble a bit so, although it was never going to be a bad pitch to bat on, we wanted a good total. I had a word with Robin Smith, because if he settled into the series, it would make a big difference.

I told him that we couldn't promise him five Tests, but he'd already played 50 Tests and there shouldn't be a confidence problem. He was a senior batsman who had got a good record, so there was no point in worrying himself silly about failing. He agreed and I felt we were getting somewhere. That left Hick and Ramprakash to sort out – or rather to sort themselves out, because that is half the battle of Test cricket. You can't wet-nurse anyone. I know that the first few games are nerve-racking, but successful Test cricketers soon get rid of tension and produce the talent that earned selection.

We struggled at first until Thorpe and Smith put on 111 for the fourth wicket, but another collapse saw us 203 for seven before Cork and Martin batted with a lot of guts and common sense. They provided what I want most, the lower order chipping in with 20s and 30s, and that makes a big difference to the side. We squeezed 78 from the last three wickets and we won the match by 72 runs, so the importance of those tail-end runs is obvious.

We bowled well on the second day with Fraser attacking the crease much more. Our main problem was that the wind blew mostly from the Nursery end, so we couldn't attack as much as usual from the Pavilion end. Gough had a mixed match, taking five good wickets, but he seemed to have lost his swing. The ball did not come out of his hand in the right way, and he will have to work hard to get it back.

He is at his best when he pitches it up and gets the reverse swing going, but if it doesn't happen, then batsmen like the

West Indians just hit through the line. I didn't think that Richardson helped their confidence much. Fraser made the odd one bounce, but the way their captain took his hand away when he was caught by Stewart in the first innings suggested the pitch was much worse than it was.

Team coach Andy Roberts criticised the pitch at the end of the day and was reprimanded by referee John Reid for suggesting it had been improperly prepared to favour England. The number of runs scored in the match – 1146 from 389.2 overs – suggests otherwise. As did the West Indies' first-innings total of 324 after being 23 for two and 169 for five. Keith Arthurton's 75 from number six held the innings together in the same way that Smith did with his 61 and magnificent 90 in the second innings.

Thanks to him, England won the match after trailing by 41, and leading only by 114 with their first four wickets gone in the second innings.

Illingworth

Without Smith in the second innings, we would probably have lost the match, but he played one of his best innings. He took everything that was going from Ambrose, Walsh and Bishop, and Hick played very positively. The better spirit in the team was shown when Thorpe came back from hospital after losing sight of a high full toss from Walsh and fought it out for well over two hours for 42. I watched everyone closely in the dressing-room, and I was privately thrilled to bits at the general attitude.

Without it we would have lost, because the West Indies are relentless when they get their teeth into a side. They had us going two or three times, but we kept fighting back. There was a lot of talk about why we didn't declare on the fourth evening, but we weren't 300 ahead, and Lara could win that sort of game on his own.

He didn't, because of one of the best wicket-keeping catches I have ever seen from Stewart. He'd had a reasonable match before that – 34 and 36 with the bat and kept well – but they were going well at 99 for 1. Gough bowled one across Lara which went a bit more and the low edge was taken diving and one-handed to his left only inches above the ground. It was his wrong hand, but he produced one of the best reflex bits of 'keeping I have ever seen.

I knew then we would win if we kept our heads, because the quicks were bowling much better than at Headingley. Especially Cork, who bowled brilliantly. Things went for him, but he makes most of them happen with his method and sparky approach.

We won a game that we would have lost more times than not in recent years. Of course I was pleased with some of the performances – Smith, Hick and Thorpe with the bat and Cork, Fraser and, to a lesser degree, Gough with the ball – but the biggest bonus of all was the fighting spirit the side showed when the game was going against them. Also, we didn't bowl a no-ball or a wide in the game. All in all, I felt for the first time that we were making progress. I have been in the game too long to get carried away with one win, but that one was one of the sweetest I'd known.

I couldn't help but have one dig at the press after the match. I told them 'not bad for a bit of muddled thinking'. I know they've got a job to do. I was part of it for a few years when I wrote a regular column and was on television, and I know the pressures from editors and producers, but I just wish they would stop and think sometimes when they have a go. Why don't they try to put themselves in my shoes and ask 'now why has he done that?' Unless they think I am a complete idiot, there is always a reason, and I wouldn't mind the stick if they tried to explain what I was after. But they never do.

Atherton made this shrewd assessment of the England victory.

The press obviously had a field day after the strategy had been changed, but once we started practice on the day before the match, everyone knew where they stood. I was happy with the situation as I tried to point out at the pre-match press conference. Rumours started, including the one that I had had enough and was about to give up the captaincy in protest. I've simply no idea where this particular story came from – it smacked very much to me of Chinese whispers.

The fact is I'm more than satisfied with the extent of my input, and Ray is good to have in the dressing-room. The key to the win was on the final day when we discussed who should bowl from which end. I had a chat with Ray and we decided that Darren Gough should bowl from the Pavilion end. He might go for a few but the slope would help his swing against the left-handers.

* * *

Which it did, to dismiss Lara thanks to the brilliant catch by Stewart. Atherton's bigger problem was who should bowl at the Nursery end.

> As the bounce was uneven from that end in the first innings, we thought we should try our two tallest bowlers first. But the pitch had eased and Angus Fraser looked a bit innocuous. I tried Peter Martin but it didn't take too long to work out that he was struggling for rhythm.
>
> Whereas on the first morning of a Test match I might have given both bowlers a few more overs to get it right, there was no time to mess about. The time had come for Dominic Cork to have a go. He bowled magnificently, but we still had to make sure we kept it tight at the other end. That was where Fraser, in particular, and the others, including Richard Illingworth when I put him on to give Cork a breather, played their part to perfection.
>
> In terms of judging how things were progressing, it was very important for me to have Illy available at lunch and tea to bounce ideas off. The match was there for the taking but, at the same time, it was being played on a knife edge. Having Ray around, who is involved in everything but at the same time detached from the action, is vital.
>
> I might not agree with everything he says, but it is refreshing to have a different angle. Sometimes he will spot something I have missed because I'm too close to events to notice. *Ray's presence certainly helps me to get things right in my own mind.*

What the win did was to stop the anti-Illingworth bandwagon in its tracks. Virtually every national journalist pinned his colours to the flag of critical convenience. They had an obvious target when Illingworth became the first chairman of selectors to abandon a key original selection, of a wicket-keeper, and they fired away in blunderbuss fashion. It is always wise to leave an escape hatch, but none did. What the acid journalist has in his favour is the short memory of his readership. Wisely, they concentrated on the positive and good things to emerge from the England win and, for a few days, all was right with English cricket. But Edgbaston was only 10 days away . . . and Illingworth would be in the spotlights and the headlines yet again.

18

FIASCO: EDGBASTON

The lull in the battle between Illingworth and the press lasted from the final day of the Lord's Test until the start of the third Test at Edgbaston – all of 10 days. It was a different problem this time. Not one of selection – Jason Gallian for Mark Ramprakash was the only change from Lord's – but a rogue pitch which produced the shortest Test match in terms of overs (172.2) in England since 1912, and a frantic bout of buck-passing.

The Edgbaston pitch, prepared by Steve Rouse, offered an extravagance of bounce which the West Indies fast bowlers exploited to the full, with their extra pace and height. Especially from the Pavilion end, batting was not quite a lottery, but close to it. The first ball of the match – a loosener from Curtly Ambrose – sailed over the head of a dumb-struck Atherton, with the only debatable point being whether the distance the England captain's jaw dropped was greater than the width of Ambrose's surprised smile.

England lost by an innings and 64 runs, and also lost Stewart for the rest of the series with a broken finger. His injury was sustained while keeping wicket, but the broken fingers of Richard Illingworth and Jason Gallian came about while they were batting.

With Illingworth having the ear of the Test match groundsmen in terms of reasonable requests for even bounce and assistance for the spinners, how did things go so wrong? How did the Warwickshire club and the TCCB find themselves in the most embarrassing situation of modern times regarding pre-match sales of tickets for the third and fourth days, with the purchasers seeing 80 minutes' cricket only on the third morning?

Was the fault with Illingworth, Rouse or the Warwickshire club as the host for a third Test which, following the Lord's win, was a marketing man's dream?

Illingworth

I spoke to Steve Rouse about 10 days before the start of the Test, and he told me that the pitch would be hard and quick. I didn't mind that if the grass covering was even, and I was told it was, both then and when I checked two days later with Dennis Amiss. I asked for some of the grass to come off, especially at both ends in the hope it might take spin.

My third effort to ensure that we got the right sort of pitch involved ringing Fred Titmus and asking him to call in on his way up to Manchester to pick the team, and have a look. He said it was a funny-looking pitch, and the grass looked a bit tufty, but he didn't seem too alarmed.

At the selection meeting, I asked Mike about Devon Malcolm, but he wasn't in favour. He said that if it did go up and down, then Fraser and Martin were both well over six feet and they would exploit it better. If Malcolm was in the XIII, then Gough wouldn't be, so we stayed with the Lord's attack. The time had come to replace Ramprakash. I felt sorry for him, but he had to change his approach, otherwise he would never make the best of his talent. We had Gallian in mind for a while, although we talked around other batsmen, such as Nick Knight, David Byas, Alan Wells and John Crawley. We went for Gallian, partly because he was an opener, although Robin Smith told us he was prepared to stand in for Stewart if necessary.

I first saw the pitch on the Tuesday lunchtime and could hardly believe what I saw. The last thing I wanted against the West Indies was an up-and-down pitch. That would play right into their hands, which is why I always emphasised to the groundsmen that I wanted an even bounce more than anything else.

I suppose I should have gone and had a look myself when I first spoke to Rouse and Amiss. All the fuss about selection at Lord's was because I should have talked to Stewart before we picked the team and not afterwards. Now I'd done it again. Listened to people who believed what they were telling me, but that was no good to me when I saw how wrong they were.

I know that the Warwickshire club was pleased that Rouse had got so much pace into the square, and it suited them with

Allan Donald playing. But the mixture of loams they had used, and the amount of rolling the square got, meant that it was almost impossible to produce an even growth of grass. I believe that Rouse tried to reseed parts of the pitch in the early part of the season, but it was too late then. The tufts were thick and clumpy, and I asked Rouse and Amiss what would happen if he took them off.

I was told that the bounce would be even more inconsistent, but I got Rouse on his hands and knees brushing them up and then cutting the crowns off. He did everything he could, but I knew it was too little, too late, and just hoped that it would play a bit better than it looked. The worst areas were just outside off stump, and I asked our bowlers to go wide of the crease, but they are different in pace.

It was just right for Walsh, not to mention Bishop and Ambrose before his groin went after eight overs. Their fourth bowler, Kenny Benjamin, was hardly needed and only bowled 15 overs in the match. Mind you, we were bowled out in 44.2 overs and 30, so my worst fears were realised. The press went berserk, and I don't blame them, even though they all turned on me and said that was what you got for trying to interfere.

The Warwickshire authorities originally tried to defend the pitch. Michael Hurst, their chairman of the grounds committee, said: 'We were asked by the England selection committee through Ray Illingworth to induce as much pace and bounce as we could – hopefully even bounce.'

Illingworth would claim that the addendum – 'hopefully even bounce' – was his top-priority request because he wanted, within reasonable bounds, to deny the West Indies the sort of conditions that suit them best – a pitch from which the short-of-a-length delivery will occasionally rear head height.

Hurst insisted that 'the pitch is within current recommendations laid down by the TCCB. Ray Illingworth asked us to do it and we obliged. There isn't much bounce in the middle. It is a very hard pitch. Ray Illingworth confirmed this was the kind of pitch he wanted, shaven at both ends. We told him what kind of pitch we were preparing and he said, "Good. Keep it going."

'You are always searching for even bounce. Here the short ball is going high and the full-length ball is coming through at the right height. I think we are generally happy that the pitch has proved itself.'

That verdict was delivered at the end of the first day in which England were shot out for 147 with only Smith (46 in 144 minutes) and Stewart (37 in 114) managing to survive for more than 50 minutes. Thorpe was gloved from nowhere, which should never happen on a dry pitch on the first day of a Test match.

Rouse and Amiss followed the Hurst line. 'It has been quick here all season. We've got to get used to playing on this sort of pitch, and I did say it would be quick and bouncy. The England selection committee asked for a true pitch which might turn towards the end of the game.'

At least that last sentence from Rouse supports Illingworth's defence against what the press considered to be interference in the preparation of pitches.

Illingworth

The press tried their hardest to get me to talk at the end of that first day, but I didn't want to stuff Rouse. All I said was that it seemed to me that the mixture of loams was wrong, and that had led to an uneven covering of grass.

The second day was no better for us, mainly because, Cork apart, we didn't bowl well. Fraser particularly disappointed me, because I thought he would get something out of the pitch, but he didn't seem to run in and attack the crease. Martin also could have done a lot better. I know that Walsh and Bishop are quicker, but our seamers could not really have asked for something better to bowl on. They would be lucky to bowl on a pitch like that more than two or three times in their careers, yet the West Indies sealed the game by scoring 300. The difference in batting consistency was that three of our batsmen reached double figures, and only three of theirs did not.

We dropped Richardson when they were 227 for six. Had Mike caught him then we might have got away with arrears of about 100, and then we would probably have forced them to bowl somebody else other than Walsh and Bishop, who bowled us out between them in 30 overs. Ambrose was not on the field, so we just might have got back into the match. As it was, only Smith was able to cope – the rest were just blown away, and there was no point in risking Stewart's finger.

Smith was superb. His 41 in the second innings gave him a match aggregate of 87 out of England's 236, and he fought it out for exactly five hours in the match. His massive contribution is evidenced by the fact that the two England innings lasted only 384 minutes and, other than Stewart, who batted for 114 minutes in the first innings, no other home batsman managed 90 minutes in the match at the crease.

Smith never flinched, despite being treated as a human punch-bag by some fearsome fast bowling which was never in danger of being checked for intimidation by umpire Ian Robinson from Zimbabwe. This view was expressed by the then-current Hampshire captain, Mark Nicholas, writing in the *Daily Telegraph*.

'One umpire, Ian Robinson, from Zimbabwe, was culpable in his lack of directive authority, and this was not the first time either. It was Robinson who allowed Walsh to come around the wicket and intimidate Devon Malcolm, a defenceless case if ever there was one, in Jamaica 18 months ago.'

Robin Marlar made the same point. 'Whether the West Indians like it or not, their bowlers were guilty of intimidation, if that word has any meaning. Bishop was aiming to hit and hurt Smith and others. There were overs in which five deliveries were aimed at the rib-cage or above.'

Fred Trueman offered the opinion that 'Robin Smith won't be sleeping on his left side for a while', and Mike Brearley mused that 'to think that players in the 1970s used to face this type of stuff without helmets'.

Another former England player, Mike Selvey, widened the debate. 'A small fortune has been lost to the coffers of Warwickshire and the TCCB, but that is nothing to the damage, physical and mental, that has been perpetrated upon Atherton's side.'

Refunds and the offer of cut-price tickets for the Edgbaston Test against India in 1996 cost the authorities well over £250,000, although the now-extinct recalculation rule saved them from that cost being doubled. The only reason that Saturday's capacity crowd of nearly 20,000 saw 13 overs of play was because the first two days were reduced from 180 to 78.2 and 81 overs respectively.

Every spectator was robbed. Those on the first two days were denied over 10 per cent of the advertised number of overs, and the Saturday crowd was denied a refund as a result. The game should have been over within two days, but at long last the ICC, led by the nose by South Africa and England, have replaced the illogical rule with one which, poor light excepted, will give the spectators better value for money.

What the Edgbaston pitch proved was that, more than any other factor, a Test match is decided by the surface upon which it is played.

The England batsmen were booed off the field to complete the unhappiest couple of days in home international cricket for many years.

Illingworth
It was a complete fiasco. We had squared the series at Lord's, and the West Indies were in disarray. After we beat them in the second Test, they lost by an innings to Sussex – the first such defeat in over 50 years – and they had internal problems which led to Winston Benjamin being sent home. We could hardly have gone into the game on a bigger high, and we lost it under stupid circumstances. You can plan and plan, but a pitch like that ruins everything. Mike got himself into a bit of trouble with his comments. He said it was diabolical and the worst pitch he had ever batted on in Test cricket. He was right. As for Warwickshire, M.J.K. Smith apologised after the game, because he must have known that they had got it wrong.

He and Dennis Amiss were later called to Lord's to explain what went wrong, and Amiss wrote this in the club's winter magazine, which was circulated to all members.

You just cannot have a Test match finishing before lunch on the third day in beautiful sunshine with a 20,000 capacity gate, and to see the England team so humiliated. The wicket controversy will continue until we produce an easier batting pitch for the 1996 Test against India.

We have every confidence in Steve Rouse and his team. In hindsight, we should have slowed the pitch down, although it was prepared to TCCB recommendations. It was very quick with some variation in bounce, and when you have the quality of the West Indian bowlers on it, there is only one winner.

We have definitely learned from the experience and will in future produce good batting pitches for Test matches.

Distilled, those words confirm that the club did not meet the request of Illingworth for 'even bounce'. Only two words, but they cost a Test match.

19

ALL SQUARE: OLD TRAFFORD

Illingworth

Now we were in real trouble. The West Indies are just about the most difficult side in world cricket to peg back, and we had unwittingly played right into their hands by giving them their confidence back. Not only that but Stewart and Illingworth were out with broken fingers, as was Gallian. What a costly couple of days they were at Edgbaston.

Yet I knew we had the makings of the right sort of dressing-room spirit, and that is more important than the odd injury. If new players come into the right atmosphere, it helps them and everyone concerned. Just because Walsh and Bishop had smashed us in over-helpful conditions was no reason to assume the series had gone. I've seen the West Indies too many times – they can be anything or nothing if you pressure them in the right way. I still thought their batting was vulnerable, providing we could contain Lara to something reasonable, but we had to bowl better than at Edgbaston.

Our batting would take a bit of picking, because we had to have a specialist wicket-keeper, so the balance of the side was difficult to get right. I was not going to make the same mistake about the pitch again, so I went to see Peter Marron at Old Trafford, and he seemed confident the bounce would be even. He also said it would turn, which is why we needed to cover all options in the squad. We had a bit longer between Tests, 17 days instead of 10, but it didn't give us much more cricket because of the second round of the NatWest competition and the Benson and Hedges final at Lord's.

We still only had one round of Championship matches to see, so I was careful to cover the matches featuring players who might play in the fourth Test. I went to Cheltenham where Lancashire were playing, so I could watch Mike Watkinson and John Crawley, as well as Jack Russell. I sent David to watch Nick Knight for Warwickshire at Cardiff, and Fred to see Essex play Somerset, and look at Mark Ilott and Peter Such.

Richard Illingworth had done a good job and we would miss him, so we had to think long and hard about the best spinners for Old Trafford. We ended a long meeting with a squad which had six changes. Knight had deserved his chance, and Crawley was in good enough form to get another chance. The captain had never seen Knight, and I wanted to know what sort of lad he was, so I rang Phil Neale during the meeting and asked him if he would get up if they knocked him down. I got the right answer, so we picked him ahead of Byas, although it was only marginal, as the younger man.

With Russell the wicket-keeper and batting at seven, we had the old problem. Did we go in with a specialist batsman at six, or someone who could bowl and make a fifth bowler?

I have had a lot of stick in the press for believing that Craig White was good enough, but I think that he has ability in both departments. We also discussed David Capel, who was having a fine season with Northamptonshire, but it was felt that his bowling would not be good enough.

We picked White in the squad, which caused another uproar when we announced it would include Mike Watkinson and John Emburey. The row was not over Watkinson, because he had been mentioned several times in my time as chairman. He was an attacking off-spinner and, if Marron was right about his pitch, he would be effective against their left-handers.

I wanted the best spinner to support him, and to give the captain reliability if Watkinson did not come off. Emburey was having a good season and would give us a bit more with the bat at nine or 10, even against their quicks. It was a crucial game we had to win. If we lost, we would be dormy 3–1 down with two to play. So we picked 13 which included six specialist batsmen, a wicket-keeper, four specialist bowlers and two all-rounders in White and Watkinson.

As it turned out, our options were immediately reduced when Gough said that he was feeling his left foot again. I knew he had had problems at Harrogate, so I was not happy. Dave

Roberts gave him some ultrasonic treatment and he jumped – a sure sign that there was something wrong. We sent him for a scan and he was cleared. He had a long bowl on the Wednesday, but I could not see that it was worth the risk. I asked him 'yes or no?' and he said 'yes' but I was not prepared to accept that. If we went in with all the batsmen and only four bowlers, we would be taking an enormous gamble. Even if we picked five bowlers, he was never certain to play if fit, because he had lost his ability to swing the ball and he was nowhere near as effective a bowler as in Australia.

I ruled him out, which left us with 12. We were agreed that both spinners should play, but we couldn't afford to go in with Fraser and Cork as our only seamers. The batting order settled it for us. We had decided that Hick would not bat at three after Edgbaston, even though he got one unlucky decision there. Knight had to open the innings, which meant that Crawley was the obvious pick for number three.

Thorpe and Smith were settled at four and five which meant Hick or White at six. Everyone was agreed that Hick should be omitted, although I was a bit more for him than the others. John Edrich had been working with him and felt that he should play once more, otherwise it would be difficult to bring him back. He was very upset about being dropped, and when I went to have a word with him I decided against it because he was in tears. In a way, that pleased me, to see it meant so much to him, but I was still not quite convinced that he was hard enough, mentally, when it came to a crunch situation.

With White in, it meant six changes from Edgbaston, and a top six which included Knight, Crawley and White. The win at Lord's seemed ages ago, not just five weeks. We were able to pick only five of that winning side, and now we were one down again. Furthermore, we lost the toss and they got to 86 for two with Lara going like a train.

But the team spirit Mike and I had created helped us through. Fraser and Cork stuck at it and Watkinson picked up a couple of wickets as several of them got out with sloppy batting. Only Adams and Richardson got out to defensive strokes, which proved my point that they were vulnerable under pressure.

Thanks to the sort of batting from the lower middle order I think is vital, we got a lead of 221. They let fly as we thought they would, and I reckon they went over the limit with the short stuff. 'Dickie' Bird warned Walsh in a match which was a difficult one for the umpires. When we were 264 for five, we could easily have been bowled out for around 300, but Russell, Cork and Watkinson batted with common sense and guts. Thorpe was magnificent, but I thought Smith was getting too far inside the ball which therefore followed him.

Knight lost one from Walsh which came out of the background of a big red hoarding and we had it removed after the first day. When I went to the ground a couple of weeks before the Test, I also asked them to take away a blue board at the press box end but they didn't and that also caused problems. Before play started on the second day I asked the West Indies for permission to have it removed and they agreed.

On the third morning, Cork put the icing on the cake, although the West Indies reckon he must have been out, hit-wicket, when the bail was on the floor. All I know is that their wicket-keeper, Murray, saw nothing and he had come to the stumps while they ran four, and I believe that it wouldn't have been given out by the third umpire, had it been referred by Cyril Mitchley.

I was proud of what they all did and how they did it. You don't get a tougher Test than that one, yet we won it despite a second-innings scare after Smith suffered a fractured cheekbone. We only wanted 94, but at 48 for four, with Smith retired hurt, it could have gone wrong. Crawley stood up to it well, but only defensively, and we needed someone to push it around and take the pressure off. Russell was terrific with 31 off 39 balls and we had done it again – come back from one down to square the series.

While we were struggling, I got plenty of ice for Smith's eye and I wanted him there in case we wanted only a few runs at the end, but the medical view was that he must go to hospital, and I didn't argue. I rank it as an even better win than at Lord's, because of the six changes. Also, Lara played two big innings, yet we still won. He aggregated 232 runs in the match, but my one complaint is that he hit 32 fours. I know we attacked for much of the time, but we still didn't bowl as well to him as I wanted.

All our team talks had stressed the need to bowl straight and not give him width, but we didn't do it. What a game Cork had – that last-day hat-trick was marvellous. The LBWs he gets are mostly because of how close he gets to the stumps, although we still have to work on his fault of running down the pitch. What I like most is his attitude. He can bat and bowl well, but his self-belief enables him to try different things if the opposition look like getting on top. He is not a cricketer who drifts through a game. There will be matches when wickets and runs dry up, no matter what he tries, but it shows what a competitor he is to have helped win two of his first three Tests – and against the West Indies.

The only slight disappointments were White and Emburey. White looked uncomfortable on the front foot against the quicks, and didn't adapt very well, and Emburey knew that he could have bowled better. He did a good tight job, going for only two runs an over, but if Watkinson got five wickets in the match, he should not have finished wicketless.

Illingworth was entitled to feel proud of the England win. It was possible because of a non-stop exhibition of fight from a side thrown together by injuries to others. They stood up to an approach from the West Indies which, at times in the field, bordered on the bare-knuckled sort. Former fast bowler Michael Holding said, 'The official warning for Walsh was totally justified, and I was just hoping that the umpire at the other end would also dish one out. West Indies have batted and bowled like absolute rubbish.'

He was right. Some of the short-pitched stuff was ruthless, un-edifying and stupid. At one stage, during a television commentary stint, Holding actually grabbed a telephone to ask coach Andy Roberts if he could introduce some sanity into the bowling tactics.

John Woodcock in *The Times* wrote, 'Commentator Colin Croft described as a "perfect ball" one that had hit the England captain just above the heart. I am sorry, but I hate that. Test cricket is, and should be, a hard, unyielding game – but need it be malevolent as well?'

The win was England's first at Old Trafford since 1981 against Australia. As for Cork's hat-trick, it was the first for England for 38 years, and was watched by three other Test hat-tricksters – Wes Hall, Lance Gibbs and Courtney Walsh. Ambrose reached his 250th wicket in his 58th Test and Russell claimed his 100th victim in his 37th.

20

ANTICLIMAX: TRENT BRIDGE AND THE OVAL

The series was now alight. Bookings for Trent Bridge flooded in, and The Oval was mostly sold out before the start of the season. At 2–2 with two matches to play, it seemed as though the British public was set to watch a spectacular climax to a series that had yet to produce a draw. But, just as the first four matches were played on pitches more conducive to results than draws, so were the last two Tests played on more docile pitches.

That, together with the fact that both sets of players were close to being punched out, brought two draws, although England had to play heroically, albeit against an injury-ravaged West Indian attack, to save the Trent Bridge Test.

Illingworth
We wanted to play the same balance of side at Trent Bridge, although Smith was out for the rest of the season. I had a look at the pitch eight days before the game, and saw that there would be no problem with the bounce. There was a lot of grass on it, although when it was cut down, it looked a bit crusty, but on the day it seemed to have a bit of a gloss.

When we picked the squad, we named 13 including Wells and Ilott, but the captain's back injury flared up again, so we called up Byas as cover. He had had a good year and I knew he wouldn't let us down if he had to play. It would have meant an even more inexperienced line-up than at Old Trafford, but the West Indies had got problems too. Adams was out with a fractured cheekbone, and Hooper and Ambrose were unfit because of a finger injury and a muscle strain in the side respectively.

Richard Illingworth reckoned he was fit enough to play, although his finger was not quite healed, so he came back for Emburey. I knew Hick wanted to see me, because he told the press he wanted to sort things out, whatever that meant. He saw Mike and me and we told him that he was part of the squad, but was no more guaranteed selection than anyone else. I still don't know what he really wanted, because when I told him that I thought one of his problems was that he had a soft centre, he thought about it and then said, 'You might be right.'

What he did accomplish was to put extra pressure on himself, because the press gave it the full treatment. I personally thought he was silly to go public about his feelings after being dropped. I always try to tell players why they are left out, but when I approached him as he was leaving Old Trafford, he was so upset there was no point in talking to him.

We picked him on the morning of the match because Wells would have given us three beginners in the top five. He is a smashing type of bloke, and he took it well, although he was very disappointed. We won an important toss and got off to a good start, even though I was not entirely convinced about Knight's technique.

He has got a good attitude and he is as keen as they come. He is just the sort of batsman who should get most benefit from working with John Edrich. He stuck at it, and a combination of a flat pitch and the absence of Ambrose meant that things were easier for the batsmen than anywhere so far in the series.

We were going so well that I couldn't see us getting into trouble, but Mike's run-out came in the middle of a burst which cost us four wickets and another broken finger for Richard Illingworth, who went in as nightwatchman. Overnight, we were effectively 227 for five, with only Hick left of the specialist batsmen.

His hundred was a good one, and said more about his temperament than anything else. He has been an England player for a long time without ever convincing me that he could dominate except when conditions were easy. I am not knocking his hundred, because he had put himself under extra pressure by going public about sorting things out with me before the game.

He had a spinner to face for the first time in the series and he played him well. You can't do more than score runs, and without him I doubt if we would have topped 300 by much. In fact, considering the fight we had to draw the match on the last day, we could well have lost it but for him getting us to 440.

A couple of overs from Watkinson at the end of the second day convinced me that we would win the match and take a lead for the first time in the series. He made a couple turn and bounce, and I even thought then we could win by an innings. But Saturday was different, and a combination of poor seam bowling and indifferent handling of the bowlers by Mike gave Lara the opportunity he wanted to destroy us, and he did just that. But for Richard Illingworth bowling 51 overs for 96 runs, we would have been in deep trouble.

Fraser was poor. His action went to such a degree that the right arm was following through past the right side instead of the left side, which then gives him much more body action. It was nonsense for him to bowl his first six overs for nine runs and then 11 more for 68. He had six maidens in his 17.3 overs but still went for 77. Cork was better, but still bowled too many balls which went for four. I know he's still learning, but by then he knew enough about Lara to know where not to bowl. There comes a time when a bowler knows that, on a flat pitch, he can't continue to run in and try for a wicket with every ball.

That isn't being defensive, just realistic. If the ball isn't swinging much or hardly moving off the seam, you can't bowl the same line and length as if it was doing either or both. Bowlers have to be able to adjust to conditions in the same way as batsmen do. On some pitches, a batsman can hit through the line and bounce. On others, he has to be more watchful.

As for our third seamer, White, I thought the captain did him no favours at all. He didn't seem to want to put him on, no matter the trouble Lara was piling up for us, and he didn't bowl in the first 70 overs. That was silly, and when he came on he went for 30 in five overs. You might argue that's why he wasn't put on before, but whatever confidence he might have had was wiped out by not giving him a go earlier.

After all, we didn't take their third wicket until the score was 273, and they scored at such a pace that our total of 440 no longer looked safe. Lara hit 112 out of 152 in boundaries before we strangled him out down the leg-side to make it 323 for five. Watkinson was steady enough, and a split of seam and spin shows that our two spinners had combined figures of 86–33–180–7, while the three seamers were 58.3–15–217–3.

I know it was a flat pitch for the quicks, and I know that Lara batted brilliantly, but I maintain he was allowed to do so. With a day and a half left, only one side could win, and it wasn't us. We would never be able to declare and leave enough time to bowl them out, but we could get into trouble. Crawley was bowled playing no stroke, just as he did at Old Trafford, and that shows he has a lot to work on regarding knowing where his off stump is.

At the start of the last day we were 111 for two, 134 ahead and nearly safe, especially as their quicks were almost bust and the leg-spinner, Dhanraj, never threatened in either innings. But you have to admire their fast bowlers – they kept going, even if they overdid the short stuff against the tail when we were in real danger of being bowled out for under 200. We finally saved the game through sheer guts. Watkinson stuck it out, and made them pay for dropping him, while Richard Illingworth played just like a 'Yorkie' should, broken finger and all. If he'd got another blow on it, I dare not think what the consequences would have been, but he fought it out for a crucial hour and a half.

We all knew that the series was at stake, but those two showed just what a fighting unit we now have. It was the first draw of the series, and it came from a last-day situation which too many times in the past has brought defeat, simply because we seemed to have lost the knack of saving a game. The big thing with Watkinson is that he gives you what he's got, and that's what I am after with everyone.

We can now compete with any team. Despite all the injuries we won at Old Trafford and had now drawn at Trent Bridge with a patched-up side which included no more than about six automatic choices, had everyone been fit. The team now had pride, and I was proud of that.

The one disappointment about the fifth Test was the umpiring. I am not picking out Nigel Plews and Cyril Mitchley, because we all have days which are better than others, but there were too many not-out decisions given for no apparent reason. I am not talking about the marginals where a batsman or a bowler believes it might have gone the other way, but the stone-bonking sort about which there is no argument. They mostly concerned the left-handers, because we reckon Knight was out twice, and Thorpe and Lara once each at least, to LBW shouts.

The left-handers are the easiest to give when the ball, from over the wicket, comes back into the batsman. If it pitches on off stump – and only a seamer like Cork who bowls close to the stumps can pitch just outside and still hit if he brings it back – and beats the bat, it must hit the stumps. I am not talking about the doubts of height or perhaps a thin edge, because none of the decisions in question had that sort of doubt about them.

If a seamer like Cork pitches middle, then movement back can take it past leg stump. As for Richard Illingworth and other left-arm spinners bowling to left-handers from over the wicket, they hardly ever get a decision for LBW for no stroke played, simply because the umpires are conned when a batsman props forward but leaves his bat well behind the pad.

The series could not have been better set up for the final Test. All square and everything to play for. We were now getting the respect we deserved from the press, although some of them went overboard in telling us that we should go in with all guns blazing to try to win the game and the series. I didn't agree, because I didn't want a reckless approach. Not after all we had gone through to arrive there all square.

We still had to do without Stewart and Smith, and Knight and Illingworth were also injured from the side in the fifth Test. We dropped White, who never really shaped up with the bat and was not given much chance with the ball. Even after doing so well in the first five Tests, we faced the same problem at our selection meeting for the sixth Test as for the first – could we find someone to bat at six and bowl? Or, failing that, could we bat Russell at six to fit in a fifth bowler?

Gallian came back to open the innings instead of Knight, and we picked Wells again in the squad. The choice of a spinner was not straightforward. Phil Tufnell had never been discussed at length, because of problems of attitude, and he had not bowled that effectively in his last couple of Tests. But he was doing well enough with Middlesex and we all agreed that, if we did pick a spinner, he was the best available. I think the attitude towards him was a bit different in a home Test, because all he had to do was to turn up a couple of days before the game and play, if picked.

A tour, where a player who gets at odds with the management can be a big handicap, is different. Anyway, we picked him, and Devon Malcolm had to come back into the squad, even though the pitch was unlikely to be a normal fast one. I told them at The Oval that we would rather have one more like their county pitches, but I was happy to leave it to Harry Brind and his son.

On the Tuesday before the game, I was in favour of Tufnell playing, but when we had a final look at the pitch, I felt as I did the previous year against South Africa. It was not so much a case of thinking it would favour the fast bowlers, but I couldn't see the spinners getting anything from it in five days. The brave decision, once we decided on only one spinner, would have been to pick Tufnell and leave Watkinson out, but we were all happy about the final team.

I had a word with Tufnell on the ground on Thursday morning, and he took it very well although, like Wells at Trent Bridge, he was bitterly disappointed. He must have hoped that if he played and did well we would take him to South Africa, but with Malcolm in the side it would give us a tail with two easy knock-overs for their fast bowlers.

For instance, we got to 336 for six, thanks to Hick and Russell both getting to 90, Thorpe 74 and 50 from Crawley, and our last four wickets added another 118 and gave us a score which should have guaranteed we wouldn't lose. It is so vital for bowlers to get a few runs, and everybody got into double figures, except for Gallian and Wells.

Regarding Gallian, I'm sure we've got something to work on, although I'm not sure Mike is convinced yet. As for Wells, it was like a nightmare for him. He had waited for years for his chance and then – a first-baller. It's a cruel game sometimes, but you've got to take everything and still fight. He was philosophical about it, and I am sure he believes he might get another chance, even though we didn't pick him for the tour of South Africa.

He must pile up the runs in 1996 and hope that another chance comes, either through injury or loss of form by someone.

The only way we could get into trouble was if Lara went crazy again, because even if the others got runs, the time they would take would lead to a draw. But we fed him again. Malcolm bowled well in patches, but we conceded 90 fours and three sixes. We scored 192 out of 454 in boundaries – they scored 378 out of 692, and that's why, for the second Test running, a score of around 450 did not keep us out of trouble. Lara would have been run out at 30 if Watkinson had hit, but that was the last we saw of him. Again, it was a case of too much width making it easy for him.

I thought Ambrose bowled magnificently, especially on the last day when they pushed us hard enough to have put us in real trouble if Mike had not played so well for six hours. He is now a much better batsman against the quicks, and the more I see him, the more he strikes me as having a bit of Geoff Boycott about him. He is tough, and rarely gives his wicket away. I thought he developed as a captain as the series went on, and I was more than happy with how things worked out in the dressing-room between us.

When you think that we had to use 21 players, including 10 batsmen and six seam bowlers, it was a great performance to halve the series. Only Mike and Thorpe played in all six Tests, and only Hick, Cork and Fraser played in five. We had serious injuries to Smith, Stewart and Gough, and others to Illingworth, Gallian, Martin, and Knight. We went behind twice, and still we fought back, despite Lara having three wonderful Tests in the second half of the series.

Cork was the big find, but I was just as pleased that Watkinson and Illingworth did so well, and I knew we had a good nucleus for the winter, always providing we could sort out the injuries to Malcolm and Gough. Malcolm had a problem with his right knee at The Oval, and aggravated it in the county match against Essex in the same week.

I told him that we wanted Peter Lever to have a week with him before the tour, and he was happy about that. The Gough case annoyed me, because I reckon that Yorkshire should not have played him, even in important one-day matches, until he was fully fit. They kept insisting that he was fit enough for limited-overs cricket, yet they didn't pick him for the four-day matches. That proved they were bothered about it, and it also proved I was right not to pick him at Old Trafford.

We met at Lord's to pick the two squads, and the senior party did not take long. The only discussion about the batting was whether we should take a reserve opener, or pick the best seven batsmen. I was in favour of another opener, but I didn't feel strongly enough to overrule the others. Anyway, the 'A' tour of Pakistan would run at the same time, so we could whistle someone from there if necessary. Knight and Gallian were the front-runners, although I still think Moxon is one of the best three openers around. What was nagging at the back of my mind was that Stewart had not played for seven weeks, and it seemed that his finger had still not healed properly.

I had a small reservation about Ramprakash, but not enough to leave him out. After all, I had told him to go back to Middlesex and score runs, and he'd done that in marvellous fashion. Wells got a brief mention, but there was no room once we went with Ramprakash and Crawley.

The wicket-keeper and the two spinners were easy, which left six places for the fast bowlers. The first three pitches of the series looked like being quick, and that was where South Africa's bowling strength was. We had fitness doubts about three – Malcolm, Gough and Richard Johnson of Middlesex, who looked like just the sort of bowler to do well out there. He hadn't played for a while because of a back injury, but we picked him for the last spot, with Martin and then probably Tim Munton the next in line as replacements.

Munton had been pushed from a few quarters, and he had certainly come back well from a serious back injury. We still felt he was a bit short of pace at Test level, which is why, once we took fitness on trust, we chose Cork, Malcolm, Gough, Ilott, Fraser and Johnson.

That took us a bit over an hour, but the 'A' party took much longer. We didn't pick a captain until we had chosen the squad. Mike has always been keen on Nasser Hussain, and we agreed that he could be a good choice. If we had picked Wells to do the job again, it would have meant leaving out a young batsman and, with John Emburey in charge of the team, we were happy that the players would be in good hands. We could have nearly picked another squad from all the names mentioned, but I suppose the big surprise was the choice of young McGrath from Yorkshire.

I had seen enough of him to know he could be a very good player, so we took a bit of a flyer and named him. Warwickshire did a bit better this time, with Knight, Ostler and Piper included. I took some stick the previous year when I was misquoted about them being an ordinary side, but I can honestly say no candidates from any club did not get a fair shake in the meeting.

David and Fred had seen a lot of cricket in the summer, and the final party looked a good one for what was bound to be a difficult tour.

We also named three players to be on stand-by to join us in Port Elizabeth – Reeve, Neil Smith and Fairbrother. They were among the best one-day cricketers in the country, and we would probably use them in the seven one-day internationals in South Africa at the end of the tour, just before we had to finalise our World Cup squad.

Smith interested me, because he can bowl to a split field in one-day cricket – as he did in the NatWest final against Northamptonshire, a couple of days before we picked the two squads. That was important because the rules of the World Cup limited the leg-side fielders to five, whereas most English off-spinners use six or even seven. Reeve had another brilliant one-day season and Fairbrother is still one of the best batsmen in that sort of cricket.

Having picked our two squads, I then had to sit back and wait for the medical bulletins, and they weren't long in coming. Johnson was ruled out and Derbyshire suddenly and surprisingly told us that Malcolm had had a keyhole operation to the right knee. They insisted that he was fully fit, but it knocked on the head our plan for Peter Lever to have a week with him before we left England.

We brought in Martin for Johnson, and with Gough also declared fit and Stewart insisting he would be all right, that was the only change. The biggest fitness problem was my own, because I spent a few days in hospital having all sorts of tests, after I had passed some blood and they didn't know what my problem was. All they could do was say what it was not, and that elimination of the more serious possibilities was a great relief to me.

I had a few days in Spain at the beginning of October, and came back to prepare for what was bound to be a tough tour. All I wanted was a bit of luck with injuries, and for the players to continue with the same fighting spirit they developed against the West Indies. I was determined we would not miss anything regarding preparation, so we took both coaches, Edrich and Lever, for the first month, as well as a new physiotherapist, Yorkshire's Wayne Morton, who I knew well, and Dr Phillip Bell. Also, I broke tradition regarding the scorer.

The county scorers understandably saw the job as their property, and people like Peter Austin, Clem Driver and Alec Davies had done a good job in the previous 10 years. The thing was the job called for duties outside the scorebox, and the sort of extra administration concerning hotel bills and general book-keeping seemed a job for a younger man. I therefore went for

Malcolm Ashton, the BBC Television scorer, who I'd known for several years. The irony is that he had applied to Tim Lamb for three or four years and was told to reapply. He did, and I thought he was the best man for the job.

It was no slight on the county scorers, although they sounded off as though I had insulted all of them. As far as I was concerned, I reckon the party which flew out of Heathrow on 18 October was the best we'd got in every department, on and off the field. It was to be my one and only tour, and I was determined it would be a good one.

Part 6
THE TOUR TO SOUTH AFRICA, 1995–96

21

DOWN TO BUSINESS: VERWOERDBURG

The tour began and ended with problems surrounding Devon Malcolm, in whom Illingworth had invested a great amount of faith, bearing in mind that it was unlikely England would ever be able to include him in a four-man attack. When the touring party was selected at the beginning of September, Malcolm was one of four then unfit cricketers chosen; Darren Gough, Richard Johnson and Alec Stewart were the other three.

At least Gough had returned to first-class cricket before the end of the 1995 season, but Illingworth had to take the other three on trust. Johnson quickly withdrew, replaced by Peter Martin, who would have won any award for the most improved cricketer on tour. Gough and his medical advisers assured Illingworth before the end of September that he was 100 per cent fit, and Stewart also said that his finger had completely healed.

The Derbyshire chief executive, Reg Taylor, gave a similar assurance regarding Malcolm, backed up by the club's medical advisers. Despite that, Illingworth and his bowling coach Peter Lever were unable to implement the plans they had to try to make the fast bowler more repetitive and consistent in his action. They had hoped for Lever to have at least a week of one-to-one bowling flat out with Malcolm to address a problem affecting his lack of follow-through.

Watchers of sport, as opposed to players, might well ask how relevant any action is after the ball has been released or, as in football, rugby and golf, kicked or hit. The answer is that if there is no follow-through with arm or leg in those sports, the very fact that the limb virtually stops stone dead means that there has been a

217

considerable deceleration in the key area before the ball becomes airborne.

Malcolm has always been inconsistent, not just because of his extra pace, but because that pace is dependent upon a strong, complete body action. Lever and Illingworth will go to their graves swearing that, at no time in their dealings with the fast bowler, did they attempt to change his action to any radical degree. Neither manager nor coach is stupid enough to think they could re-model a 32-year-old fast bowler, but they did think they could improve what was still, after 182 first-class matches in 11 years including 34 Tests and four tours, a raw talent. The first clue from those figures is that he has played well under 150 games for his county, and 593 wickets at the end of the 1995 season gave him a wicket-ratio of fewer than seven every two matches.

For England, his ratio per match and overs bowled for wickets taken is little different from county colleague Phillip DeFreitas who, in contrast to Malcolm, has plenty to offer in the other two departments of the game, batting and fielding. Also, prior to the South African tour, Malcolm's 34 Tests had come in 14 different series, nine at home and five away. The split of matches is even, 17 home and away, which reveals that, no matter who were the selectors, manager and captain since his Test debut in 1989, only in 1990 and 1992 has he played more than twice in a home summer. He played once in 1989, twice in 1991, once in 1993, and twice each in 1994 and 1995.

Now, have Messrs Dexter and Illingworth, as chairmen of selectors, Stewart, Fletcher and Illingworth again, as team managers, and Gooch, Lamb, Gower and Atherton, as captains, all got him wrong? Or could it be that, in the last six and a half years, a touch of blame lies elsewhere?

Malcolm also received one bit of pertinent advice from a fellow Jamaican fast bowler, Michael Holding. As written by former England and Lancashire pace bowler, Paul Allott, in an appreciation in the 1995 *Wisden Cricketers' Almanack*, in his appraisal of the selection by editor Matthew Engel of Malcolm as one of the Five Cricketers of the Year: 'Michael Holding highlighted the one single factor that transformed Malcolm, more than any other bowler, from also-ran to danger man: "Follow through straight".'

Simple. Straightforward as far as any bowling coach or manager is concerned. Yet, as soon as Illingworth and Lever preached the same gospel, they ran into a brick wall.

* * *

Illingworth

The thing that annoyed me most about Malcolm's reaction at the end of the tour was that he never mentioned the fact that he was the one and only England cricketer I told at The Oval that he would be going on tour. I did that to try to settle and encourage him, because I knew what he had done once to the South Africans and they would not forget The Oval in 1994 in a hurry. Also, I was told that the first three Test pitches would be the quickest of the five, so I was desperate to get him right for the first Test at Centurion Park.

Remember he had bowled only a handful of overs after The Oval Test against West Indies, when he developed fluid in the right knee. I arranged a net session at the Headingley indoor school in late September and got Peter Lever there at short notice. He needn't have bothered. Devon was half an hour late and did a bit of skipping because he said he didn't want to bowl indoors on the hard surface. The Derbyshire physiotherapist was there and I asked her, 'Can he bowl?'

She replied that he could. We did manage to get him out of doors once and he bowled well. Peter didn't have the video with him, but he followed through properly, which was all we wanted. It was rubbish for Kim Barnett, and other people who should have known better, to say that we were trying to alter his action. What was the point of that?

What I wanted was for him to attack the crease properly, and let his natural body and arm action lead him down the pitch in a proper follow-through, instead of bowling off the left foot, taking one more pace with the right and then cutting off sharply in his next left stride towards cover. That made him purely an arm bowler with no pace, no aggression or hostility, and no chance of controlling where the ball was going.

The right arm cannot find direction, length and pace on its own. Those have got to be generated by the body with the left arm playing a big part. Devon has never been a classical sideways bowler, looking at the batsmen outside the left arm and elbow, but few bowlers are. Allan Donald does not use the left arm to wind up his body action, but at least he makes it lead him down the pitch. And just remember how Devon out-bowled Allan at The Oval, although I know he was struggling with a toe injury.

That was all I wanted from Devon. A recognition of a basic fault which we all wanted to cure. Anyone would think that no

219

Test cricketer had ever been told about a fault before. Devon either would not, or could not, work it out for himself, and we were soon in trouble when we got to South Africa.

I know that much of the first month was a political exercise in which we were thrilled to take part. I also know what an honour all our boys felt it was to meet President Nelson Mandela in our first four-day game in Soweto, so I can guess the extra pride and excitement Devon felt when he walked around the ground with the President.

I tried to make allowances for that but, in the next few days, it seemed to me that Devon had got carried away a bit, and it was difficult for him to focus on the job in hand. We had so little meaningful match practice available before the first Test, and all on slow pitches completely different from what we could expect in Pretoria, that I wanted to get as much hard practice into all the players, not just Devon.

During each day of the Soweto game, I organised with Peter Lever and John Edrich that the players not in the Soweto game would travel to Centurion Park for practice, because their net facilities are top class. That is why, when the home side had nine wickets down at the start of the third day, I reckoned that Devon would be better off having a hard net than staying with the team and spending most of that day doing nothing.

He was not picked out, but was told to go with the others which, after a few moans he did. I remember once in that first month telling him that his bowling arm and hand were not right. He told me that his arm was so explosive that I had no chance of knowing whether it was right or wrong. I told him straight. 'Even from 70 yards range, the all-important position of the palm of your hand is clear to anyone who knows what he is looking for.'

Graham Gooch once told me: 'If you want Devon to do something, tell him the opposite.' I was beginning to know what he meant. We spoke to him on his own twice. We spoke to him in nets, but we got no clear response. I was beginning to wonder if he was unfit, because he seemed so reluctant to run properly in matches, and would often try to bowl off a short run in the nets.

South African coach Bob Woolmer had this to say to me after the series was over: 'We reckon Devon was never fit during the tour. That is not just my opinion, nor that of our players who faced him, but the view of all our medical staff, including physiotherapist Craig Smith and our exercise expert, Paddy Upton. They said that he showed every clinical and physical sign of carrying his right knee. They watched how he trained, how he practised and how he ran and walked. They were in no doubt that he had a problem, even if it was only a subconscious one.

The storm clouds gathered quickly, and broke together with the arrival of the rain that washed out the final day of the game in Soweto. The travelling journalists were short of copy and were understandably keen to find some. Lever and Illingworth obliged them in a manner which took little embellishment to generate lively – even lurid – headlines in their newspapers.

The now-famous press conference was not called – it came about by chance, so much so that several of the national correspondents were not present when the manna started to fall into their laps. It was an open secret that all had not gone well between Malcolm, the manager and the bowling coach, but now the 'classified' tag was removed when questions were answered honestly as far as Lever, in particular, was concerned.

He and Illingworth were approached by no more than six of the media to comment on remarks it seems that Malcolm had made to them about the attempts to change his action. The first question put was about the claim of Malcolm that the management were trying to turn him into a medium pacer.

Illingworth
Peter's reply was that Devon couldn't bat, couldn't field, but he could bowl quick. He then asked why anyone would therefore try to take away his one attribute by asking him to bowl slower. *He never used the word 'nonentity'.* That was used by journalists when they wrote the articles. The point that needs emphasising is that we were responding to remarks Devon had already made. We did not instigate the press conference but, when asked questions, answered them honestly.

The criticism of the press conference came flooding back from writers in England, including Ian Wooldridge of the *Daily Mail*. A reason for the attitude of Lever and Illingworth was that their patience – and that of the captain – was now exhausted after the softly-softly approach of the previous few weeks. Public kicks up the backside have been known to work, but not this time.

* * *

Illingworth
It was even put to me that we should send Devon home during the tour, but I wasn't having that. I had picked him to do a job and still hoped he would see that what we were trying to do was the best for him and the side. Peter reckoned that if he had had him at the right time, he would have not missed a Test in the last two or three years. Yet here he was, at 32, still the same sort of hit-and-miss bowler he had always been.

As far as I am concerned, most players get into Test cricket on their natural ability, but those who are successful then work on technique to cut out faults and play to their strengths and within their limitations. Why should Devon consider himself to be any different?

If I have to point the finger, it would not be entirely in his direction, but at Derbyshire. It seems to me that he does not know what it is to have a good, hard net, and their rota system of resting him has definitely done him no favours. He is not the first strike bowler to be kept in cotton wool by his county, but he should therefore have a much better Test record. I hate getting into a slanging match with anyone, and I am not doing it with Devon. I just want the record set straight because, dammit, *I wanted to pick him for the Test matches*.

The fact that he seems unable to believe that is true pinpoints the problem he has always had in the England side. I am just the last of several men in charge who have tried everything to get him to fire more than once in a blue moon. If cricketers cannot be frank with themselves, they have no chance.

We played him in the Kimberley game against their 'A' side, but it was still the same. He had gone off the cut part of the pitch in two strides instead of at least six more after the delivery stride. Next time the reader watches a fast bowler on television, watch how many running strides down the pitch it takes him to go completely off the pitch after he has let the ball go. Then watch Devon.

Young Paul Adams diddled us so easily with nine wickets that I had to tell the batsmen that their performance was unacceptable. If Jack Russell could score 133 for once out in the match, why couldn't the frontline batsmen do better? It was application, or rather the lack of it, I had a go about, and they accepted the criticism as fair. It wasn't the perfect preparation for the first Test, but we had to forget the minus aspects of the first month and concentrate on the next 51 days, in which five

five-day Tests would be played in front of a band of British supporters that would increase throughout the series to a final figure of around 5,000 in Cape Town.

I was surprised and disappointed about the Centurion Park pitch. We had heard so much about it being quick and consistent in bounce but, as soon as I saw it on the first day of practice, two days before the start of the Test, I didn't trust what the groundsman told me. I only had to look at the rest of the square to know that, because of the uneven covering of grass, it would be variable in bounce and I thought it would take spin well before the end of the match.

When we picked the side, there was no way we could get five bowlers in, unless Jack Russell batted at six, and the captain preferred to go in with six batsmen. I agreed with that, because the first Test of a series is vital and, too many times in recent tours, we had lost that one and were always playing catch-up cricket.

The unlucky batsman was John Crawley, because we wanted Robin Smith to play, also Mark Ramprakash. I had a word with Mark and told him, if it would help him, that he would play in the first two Tests. After how he seemed to freeze against the West Indies, I wanted to relax him so that he could play as he does for Middlesex. I asked him if it would help and he said it would.

I then had a word with Crawley and told him he was unlucky, but to keep trying and his chance would come. The bowling caused some discussion, mostly around Devon. Richard Illingworth had to play, as did Dominic Cork and Darren Gough. We went for Angus Fraser instead of Devon, mainly because Devon still had not shown us much, and he would be a huge gamble as one of four bowlers.

I was surprised when they put us in, because we were always going to bat. Also, they went for five quicks and left the spinner out, so we had a situation in which both managers and captains had as big a difference of opinion as I can remember.

It turned out to be the only Test of the five in which we were in a strong position, although we only got there because of three batsmen, the captain, Graeme Hick and Robin Smith, plus a typical improvised knock from Jack Russell. Mike played the anchor role superbly and was unlucky to get a nasty one from

Shaun Pollock in indifferent light at the end of the first day. He got a real working over, and we knew then he would be targeted for the rest of the series.

He kept us out of trouble after Stewart, Ramprakash and Thorpe went before lunch. Alec played an airy stroke and Ramprakash went to a wide one, first ball after the drinks interval. Thorpe got a decent one from Pollock who had a good debut. He is sharp enough, and gets in so close to the stumps that his short one gets every batsman in trouble.

Hick played as well as I've ever seen him. He took them on, and pulled and drove with terrific power. It was his fourth hundred for England and easily his best. Robin Smith fought it out, but then got bowled on the outside from Brian McMillan by one which didn't do enough to beat half a bat.

On the second day, we could still have gone wrong, but Jack Russell's unbeaten 50 made sure we got close to 400. I honestly thought we could win from there, but a big electrical storm ended play after five sessions, and killed the game stone dead. It wasn't raining when they came off, and Jack wanted to stay, even though the light was awful. But umpire Cyril Mitchley insisted they came off because of the lightning. He told me: 'I've seen someone killed by lightning and I wasn't going to have a death on my conscience.' It was an unusual decision, but I couldn't argue.

I love a game of bridge, and we had plenty in the next three days, involving Mike, our scorer Malcolm Ashton and the doctor Phillip Bell. Centurion Park is a pretty ground, and I felt sorry for them to have their first-ever Test match ruined by the weather. As the rest of the series turned out, that was our one and only chance to put their batsmen under the pressure of having to score nearly 200 to save the follow-on.

Peter Pollock and Hansie Cronje said at the post-match press conference that they did not think they had read the pitch wrongly, even though England scored 391 for nine in 143 overs after being put in. They claimed that the game plan was not necessarily to bowl England out for 200, but to limit them to about 350; then score a rapid 500 and win the match that way.

A nice theory, but we shall never know. On the second day, the ball started to go up and down a bit, and the signs were that, if they had bowled well, England would have called most of the shots in the last three days. What was a surprise was that the much-vaunted back-up team of experts and consultants employed to support the home side, fell at the first hurdle.

Brett Schultz came into the game with a suspect leg injury, and was never given a proper fitness test. Dr Ali Bacher criticised the manager, Alan Jordaan, and coach Bob Woolmer and, not for the first time on the tour, showed he was prepared to act swiftly and openly when necessary. The British media were already impressed by his open-government approach, compared with the smokescreen approach often adopted by the Test and County Cricket Board.

22

THE GREAT ESCAPE:
JOHANNESBURG

The scheduled four-day game between the first and second Tests against Orange Free State was altered upon arrival in Bloemfontein. Journalist Ted Corbett heard the management regretting that they could not get more cricket into the entire party and suggested that they divide the four days into a three-day and a one-day game.

Illingworth
It made sense to Mike and me. That way, we could play everyone, and have another go at getting Devon right in time for The Wanderers Test. If ever he was going to play in a Test it was there, and we simply had to get him into some sort of form. The Springbok Park pitch looked slow and low, but that didn't matter, providing Devon ran in aggressively and, as Michael Holding had told him at Derby, followed through straight.

The switch from the four-day game took one telephone call to Ali Bacher. I had had dinner with him during our first month in Johannesburg, and he impressed me as someone who wanted to do the best for the game and had the personal clout to do it. We talked the same language about most topics of the game. He put to me an idea about using all three umpires in a day, because of the increasing pressure on them. The idea would be that they all do two sessions out of the three, which would give them a two-hour break which should make a difference to them, physically and mentally.

It needs thinking about, because that would mean one session in which the international umpire does not stand. Also the session off the field would be spent doing the third

227

umpire's job, and that is just as taxing on their concentration in a different way. The whole series was spoiled a bit by the standard of umpiring, and I was disappointed with some of the decisions.

Mistakes are made and I don't mind those. What I do object to is when LBWs are given to bowlers who bowl so wide out that they can't hit, except with near half volleys.

On my count of definite not-outs, not the 'probably nots' or the marginals, England lost out 4–2 in the five-match series. Part of the trouble nowadays is that, mathematically, more mistakes are made because the modern player now shouts for everything.

Dominic Cork is a case in point. He has a theatrical, beseeching appeal which suggests that the batsman must be out. As he bowls from so close to the stumps, he has a better chance than most, and certainly was not given a couple of LBW decisions in The Wanderers Test when it was difficult to see why not. He is especially dangerous to the left-hander, as his stock ball moves back in. If he pitches it outside off stump, it cannot possibly miss leg stump but, because he swings it away so much, he can miss off stump if he pitches on middle. That leaves him a channel of nearly a foot wide in which, assuming the length and height is right, the ball will hit the stumps. Against the right-hander, a couple of inches of lateral movement from leg to off is worth six inches the other way, yet few umpires appear to take that into account.

As the tour progressed, Cork's appealing was just as impassioned, but replays showed, more often than not, that the ball had gone from off to leg against the right handers and would have beaten leg stump. Yet such was the strength and conviction of his appeal that the first impression of the not out decision, given by his facial expression of incredulity, was 'there's another one I should have got'.

My point is that the modern player has contributed towards the moderate standard of umpiring, because he shouts for everything. In simple mathematics, if he only appeals for definite outs and close things, he will probably get six or seven out of ten. But, if he then lets rip ten appeals which have little validity, he might get one or two more making, say, eight or nine out of twenty. The two mistakes rankle with the batting side, who then take on the umpires when they field, and so the circle becomes more vicious.

A bowler like Angus Fraser puts another point of view. 'I know that most of our batsmen stand there for everything, when the fielders appeal, and they often get away with it. That upsets the bowler who wants an equaliser.' As I said, a vicious circle.

Illingworth

The three-day game in Bloemfontein died a death, but at least Stewart and Thorpe got hundreds, and Crawley and Ramprakash also got runs. I was beginning to get a bit worried about Alec, because his feet were going nowhere and I was afraid their quicks would find him out in the Tests. He has always been a hand-and-eye batsman, but the longer you play, the less you can rely purely on reflexes and timing. In all my time of playing and watching, I have seen a lot of batsmen who have succeeded in spite of their basic technique and not because of it. Then, when they get a bit older, the holes start to appear. I had a chat with him about it, and he knew he wasn't right and tried hard in the nets to put it right.

We got bogged down on the last morning – Smith batted for 42 minutes for nought – so we couldn't set them anything reasonable. Devon ran in a bit better, but was still nowhere near right. We didn't play him in the one-day game, but Donald played for them.

What interested me most about the set-up in South Africa is that their Board contract the Test players, and they decide on when and if they play between Test matches. For instance, neither Donald nor Pollock was allowed to play for Free State and Natal in between the second and third Tests.

I asked for the same control from the TCCB at their winter meeting in December 1995, but was knocked back by the clubs. I was told that the players were contracted to them and they would play them when they wanted. As a sop, I was told that, while they would not give me blanket control, they would consider any request I made. A fat lot of good that is. The difference between English cricket now, compared with a country like South Africa, is that they decide where their priorities lie and act accordingly. That is why as soon as a player plays in three Tests, he is contracted to their Board, who then control his season.

Obviously, our 18 county clubs have a different priority, but they mustn't have the penny and the bun by complaining when the England side is no longer as strong as it used to be. Too much of our county cricket is played in the comfort zone, which is why we don't produce youngsters of the same

229

quality as Jacques Kallis, Pollock and Paul Adams.

We won the one-day game easily, with Mike and Alec putting on 116 for the first wicket in 22 overs, including three from Donald which cost him 25. I found it interesting when, having been told to play in the game for match practice, he chose not to bowl again.

I enjoyed the week in Bloemfontein. A lot of South Africans reckon it is in the back of beyond, but we had a decent hotel with a lively restaurant and everyone made us welcome. Also the weather was hot, so we made up for those awful last three days in Pretoria. Now for Johannesburg and The Wanderers.

As soon as I saw The Wanderers pitch, I knew it was different from the three strips I had seen in the previous 18 months for the Tests against Australia, New Zealand and Pakistan. The first two started cracked, but this one looked a better surface. Also, it had been moved half a pitch sideways, because the usual pitch had too many cracks in it. I discussed it with groundsman Chris Scott and his assistant, the former Derbyshire player Ashley Harvey-Walker, as I have to do a daily pitch inspection for South African television, I try to get my cards marked by those who know, so I also talked to Jimmy Cook, now in charge of the Transvaal side. They all told me the same: it might have a bit in it on the first day – most Test pitches do – but win the toss, bat first and get a decent score. Raymond thought differently.

Illingworth
Mike and I had a look at it and decided that, if we bowled anything like, it was worth putting them in. We had decided to play Devon in place of Richard Illingworth and leave whatever spin was necessary to Hick. The pitch looked as though it would bounce, but it also looked as though it would last. Some of the press thought that, once we had picked a four-man pace attack including Devon, that we had to put them in.

It is rarely that simple, because you have to consider the possibilities if you don't bowl them out for under 300. A big factor this time was that I reckoned we would have a decent pitch to bat on during the last day or so. Even so, I believed that there was enough grass on, and enough moisture for us to bowl them out on the first day, always providing we put the ball in the right place often enough.

I listened to all the local experts, and I knew that South Africa had gone the other way. They brought in spinner Clive Eksteen for the injured Schultz, so it was a reversal of the first Test, with both managements again taking a different view.

Mike won the toss and we had a reasonable first session, thanks mainly to Cork. He was the one bowler to get it right, and he got Hudson and Cronje in the morning. Hudson may have been unlucky, because everyone thought he was caught in the gully, but Karl Liebenberg made it clear at the drinks break that he had given him out LBW.

The afternoon session was a nightmare. Kirsten and Cullinan hit 110 from 31 overs, and only a few economical overs from Hick prevented it being even worse. Again it was Cork up front, and the rest nowhere. Gough and Malcolm sprayed it, and even Fraser never got it right. Goughie had no luck, especially when Cullinan edged him for three fours and Jack dropped him when he was 55. That would have been 168 for three, but we didn't take another wicket until they were 211. Even so, Gough hardly swung a ball because his hand action was wrong.

At 211 for two, they looked as though they would get over 400, but at least we stuck at it, and Devon came back with two of the five wickets we got in the last session.

They were 278 for seven at the close, which looked all right, but it wasn't because of the number of four-balls we bowled. Kirsten and Cullinan scored 179 between them, and I know they played well. But they should not have scored 104 in boundaries – that was undisciplined bowling.

I asked Mike later where Devon was supposed to be bowling, and he said full and off stump. The long hops he bowled showed a lack of control, and I cannot emphasise enough how indifferently everyone bowled, except Cork and Hick. I reckon we could and should have bowled them out for 250, and then we would have had the best of the batting conditions on the second and third days.

I can't praise Cork enough. He was over-bowled because of the rest of the attack. Hick's 15 overs for 38 helped to keep us in the game, and limiting them to 332 should have ensured that we kept out of trouble for the rest of the match.

It didn't, because we batted poorly, except for Robin Smith who gutsed it out for 52 and was last man out. Once Mike was bowled by Donald, we looked vulnerable and we lost four key wickets to bad shots. We knew we had to bat well against their fast bowlers, but to lose three wickets to Eksteen was a killer. Thorpe was very unlucky to be given out by Liebenberg, caught at short leg, off one which was clearly nowhere near the bat.

But that sort of thing happens and you've got to put up with it. What was unacceptable was the way the others got out. Ramprakash was rolled over too easily by Donald, but Stewart, Hick and Russell really dropped us in the cart. After Thorpe went at 109 for three, Alec should have made sure we got through the few minutes left until tea. Instead, he flicked one to mid-wicket, and when Hick was caught and bowled by Eksteen straight after the break, I could hardly believe we'd gone from 109 for two to 125 for five in four overs, thanks to one poor decision and two bad shots.

Jack then holed out to mid-wicket, and only Smith's 52 got us to 200. To limit them to 332, but then give them a lead of 132 with three days to go was bad cricket, and left us with a big fight on our hands to save the game. We did it thanks to three factors.

We bowled a bit better, although Malcolm and Gough going for 113 off 25 overs placed a big load on Cork and Fraser. Their 60 overs for 162 helped, as did Hick again with 15 overs for 35.

The second factor was their unaccountable decision to take the light towards the end of the third day, when McMillan was smashing us everywhere and had just hit Malcolm for 16 in an over. They ignored the golden rule of cricket – always try to do what the opposition wants least, and they must have known how pleased we were to come off. It was a silly and stupid decision, and showed they were still frightened of us.

I still think we could have won the match but for McMillan. He is a fine cricketer and their best batsman, although I am not sure he is as good as claimed. The thing that struck me about both sides was that nobody knew where their off stump was. Jack caught some blinders and deserved his world record, but he was given the chance because so many played at balls they should have left alone.

The third factor was the biggest of all, because how often does a side bat out five sessions to save a game? I am on record as saying that Mike's innings was one of the greatest ever played, and I stand by that. To bat for nearly 11 hours was a monumental effort, and I have never seen a better or gutsier innings. The dressing-room was as tense as I have known, especially when Jack went in before lunch with only five wickets left, including the tail. He was also marvellous, because the captain needed someone like Jack to keep geeing him up in the last two sessions.

I have often said that there is a lot of Geoff Boycott in Mike, and he proved it that day. He just closed his mind to everything except the next ball, and I hoped that his example would rub off on some of the other batsmen. They can't all play the same, but all I ask is for the opposition bowlers to earn their wickets. We lost 15 wickets in the match, and I reckon at least 10 got themselves out, and we had two bad decisions. Doesn't leave much, does it? Not with three caught and bowled in one innings.

When Cronje shook hands with Mike, the dressing-room went mad. It was as though we'd won the game, not saved it, and I knew the psychological effect the result would have on both sides. We had done the impossible, and they must have known the game had got away from them.

The match was a statistician's dream. Atherton passed 4000 Test runs, and his 643-minute innings was the fourth longest for England, behind Len Hutton's 364 at The Oval in 1938, Ken Barrington's 256, also against Australia, at Old Trafford in 1964 and Clive Radley's 158 in 648 minutes against New Zealand in Auckland in 1978.

Atherton's 185 was his highest Test score and also the highest Test score at The Wanderers. Russell's 11 catches overtook the previous record of 10, held by Bob Taylor who watched the whole match. Donald took his 100th Test wicket in his 22nd Test, Pollock and Eksteen recorded their best Test figures, and Stewart played in his 50th Test.

All of which is trivia, compared with the innings which will never be forgotten. The Great Escape, engineered by one of the best captain's innings in the history of cricket.

23

STALEMATE: DURBAN AND PORT ELIZABETH

Nearly seven weeks after the start of the tour, the England party flew to the Cape for a scheduled four-day game in Paarl against Boland, skippered by Adrian Kuiper. For the second successive time, the four-day game was split into two, although under much more curious circumstances than in Bloemfontein. The decision there was taken before the start of the match, but in Paarl it was taken towards the end of the third day of the match.

In the view of Illingworth and the Boland players, the pitch was the villain of the piece, being so slow that both captains wrote off any prospect of a result after one innings each.

Illingworth

We took a long time over our 402 for eight declared, mainly because some more indifferent batting meant we were 233 for eight on the first day. Yet again, Jack Russell showed up the others with an unbeaten 129, and he and Richard Illingworth put on 169 in 62 overs before we declared. It was a great effort by Jack because he really shouldn't have played. He hadn't missed a match, and his wife flew in to Johannesburg at the end of the Test match on a surprise visit.

He deserved a break, but is such a real pro that he understood why I wanted him to play, once the captain decided to have a rest. After his heroics at The Wanderers, Mike had to miss the game, which meant that Alec would captain the side. As we hadn't got a reserve opener in the party, Alec had to open with Robin Smith, and that really settled it for Jack.

It would have been too much for Alec to captain the side,

235

open the batting *and* keep wicket, so I had to ask Jack to play. I can think of a few cricketers who would have taken it easy in the game, especially as he had batted well over four hours to help save the Test and had just set the new world record behind the stumps.

But he's not like that and, because we needed some graft from him, he batted for over five hours for a career-best 129. Once they avoided the follow-on, the game had nowhere to go, and I overheard their players say that the fourth day would turn into something of a one-day slog. So, I asked them if they wanted a proper one-day game instead, and they agreed. No one was enjoying playing on that pitch and, again, we could play most of the party in the two games.

Dr Bacher was contacted and gave permission, although such a precedent is a dangerous one. It seems that the England captain was not best pleased when he learned of the re-arrangement, and few touring sides can have played as fast and loose with their admittedly limited programme of first-class matches outside the Test series. A mitigating factor is that it was a weak itinerary, which excluded England from playing any top provincial side, or on pitches with the sort of pace and bounce which they had to combat in the first three Tests.

Bacher says that he wanted to spread England around the country to enable the smaller cricket centres to see the tourists, but it was a poor decision by the TCCB to accept an itinerary which prevented any experience of the five Test match grounds prior to the start of the series. Tours of yesteryear used to give the visitors a game against Transvaal before The Wanderers Test, Natal before the Durban Test, and so on.

Touring sides to England are treated much better, and the TCCB must avoid handicapping England sides in this manner. Mark Ramprakash wrote a tour diary for the *Independent on Sunday*, and made this comment: 'Up to the first Test we'd been playing on slow pitches. It was clearly a deliberate ploy by the United Cricket Board of South Africa.'

Illingworth
We won the one-day game easily enough to round off a very pleasant few days in the Cape. The captain enjoyed his few days off, and made his fishing debut with Johnny Barclay. I had a drive around Stellenbosch and it was beautiful, and those

players who didn't play in the three-day game relaxed on the beaches and at the waterfront in Cape Town.

On the flight to Durban, I was happy with our position in the series, especially after the second Test. I knew the South Africans would be a bit down, and I wanted to put them under further pressure in what was likely to be the last pitch in the series which would favour pace ahead of spin.

I had a chat with the Kingsmead groundsman, Phil Russell, and Mike and I had a long talk about the bowlers. We both reckoned it might swing more than seam, so there were immediate queries about Malcolm and Fraser. Also, Gough had gone bust in Paarl, so it looked like a new attack. The batting virtually picked itself, with Crawley coming in for Ramprakash.

Cork had swung the ball well in the first two Tests, so we wanted someone to support him with swing, more than seam. Mark Ilott was the obvious first choice, and we both agreed that Richard Illingworth had to play, both for variety and control. That left three quicks for one place. Devon did take six wickets in Johannesburg, but he only bowled a couple of decent spells in the match.

Gus bowled better later on in that game, but he doesn't swing it and relies on movement off the seam. I kept quiet while Mike thought it through, because I was interested to see what he would come up with on his own. When he told me he wanted Peter Martin ahead of Gus, I was pleased for two reasons. I also wanted him, but I wanted him to say it first and not be led by me.

I told him for the first time that I thought he was now becoming a good captain, because he had just made a cricketing decision above friendship, and he thanked me for that. If Mike has a problem, it is that he's the same age as most of the players. He wants to be one of the boys, and I can understand that from a relaxing point of view, but you can't always do that. Sometimes, you've got to stand back and be apart from them.

Saying that, I can only repeat that I can't imagine myself ever having been able to do what he has done at the same age. I try to think back to my late twenties and I don't see how I could have handled it as he does. He's got some special qualities and I like to think I am helping to bring them out.

We made four changes, Crawley, Martin, Illingworth and Ilott for Ramprakash, Fraser, Malcolm and Gough, and they brought in Jacques Kallis and Craig Matthews for Pringle and Eksteen. Again, for the third successive Test, we differed about spin, but Richard soon proved his point with what I rate as his best spell yet for England.

Once we'd split their openers and Martin got rid of a couple of early rusty and expensive overs, he switched ends and shared the first five wickets with Richard, who deserves high praise for creating the pressure which got wickets at the other end.

He got Hudson and Cronje in a long spell of more than 20 overs at not much more than a run per over. He used the wind from the Umgeni end for drift, and nobody played him well. Martin swung it, and when Ilott nipped in with three for one in six balls, we had them down and nearly out at 153 for nine. Pollock and Donald played well for their tenth-wicket stand of 72 in 23 overs, and we got caught about what to do with the second new ball. I can understand Mike delaying taking it, because when two tail-enders are in, the ball flies all over the place. I suppose Richard might have come back a bit quicker after the new ball didn't work, but that's no criticism of Mike who handled things well.

Anyway, we would have bought their final score of 223, but I knew that they now had something to bowl at, and stressed the need for our batsmen to get their heads down. Unluckily for him and the team, Crawley tore a hamstring in the middle of that last-wicket partnership, so we had to re-jig the order by pushing Thorpe and Smith up one, but letting Hick stay at five.

Donald dismissed the captain and Thorpe in his first three overs, but Stewart and Smith put on 70 before we had another off-side collapse. They caught their catches well, especially Rhodes, but we gave Matthews three wickets in seven overs and, from 83 for two, we were 109 for five. Alec's feet were again stuck in concrete, and he will suffer until he gets them moving again.

We could have been rushed right out of it, but Hick and Cork played sensibly and positively and their 44 runs put us on equal terms, when the rain came and stayed. I suppose it was because there was no play that we had all the fuss about the television pictures showing Matthews and Pollock apparently tampering with the ball. The curious thing was that the footage was from Sky's pictures on the Friday, yet their unit in South Africa did not file a story.

It was picked up back in England and not shown back in South Africa until early Sunday morning. Match referee Clive Lloyd had a look at the film and decided that he would take no action after listening to the players' explanation. I fully understood that with Matthews, who said that he was not picking the seam, but cleaning it and wetting down little scuff marks on the leather immediately adjoining the seam.

Pollock looked different to me, because it seemed to me from the pictures that he might be trying to pull the seam apart. Apparently, he said he was trying to close it, but I've got no complaints either way. What I will say is that, still, England are the only side to punish a player for doing something with the ball he should not. Ironic isn't it that, with all the fuss about ball tampering in the last four years, Mike Atherton is still the only cricketer to be fined?

Illingworth makes a valid point. The other aspect of the Matthews-Pollock incident was that Dr Bacher learned of the television evidence at 6 a.m. that morning. By 7.30 a.m. he had called the players together and asked them for the truth. Another instance of swift action to prevent a so-called story festering behind a smokescreen of 'no comment'. A light-hearted aside to the story is that when he asked Matthews if he had tampered with the ball, the Western Province man indignantly denied doing so. Upon which, another player suggested that Matthews should be fined heavily for admitting that he never picked the seam.

The grisliest statistic of the tour concerned the rain. In 106 years of Test cricket in South Africa, only 11 complete days had been lost in 112 Tests – five days in the previous five weeks. And of the other six, two were washed out in the 1939 Timeless Test, also at Kingsmead. What made the Durban Test even more gloomy than the first at Centurion Park was that the first few hundred of British tourists had now arrived.

Imagine Blackpool, Scarborough or Bournemouth on a rain-lashed day in the peak holiday period. Then add the extra frustration of a washed-out Test match, followed by another rain-ruined game the same week in nearby Pietermaritzberg, and the feelings of the Brits can only be imagined. Former players like John Edrich and Peter Walker were at their wits' end trying to relieve the boredom of their clients, because the touring delights of Natal are the same as anywhere else when the rain gods refuse to relent.

* * *

Illingworth

The players' wives and families had now arrived, and I could see we had a problem. Throughout the tour in the first nine weeks, we had a good spirit going and it was generally a happy tour. I know that the modern cricketer finds the tours more intensive than when I played, and I can understand his wish to bring his family out for a part of the tour. He might argue that he then feels happier and more relaxed, but the fact remains that important parts of team get-togethers disappear.

To show you how out of hand I reckon it got, our transport liaison man, Doug Russell, suddenly found himself with a travelling party of 64 to account for whenever we moved from one hotel to another. What with cricket coffins, suitcases, travelling bags, golf clubs and now push chairs, he achieved miracles to keep tabs on everything.

You can argue until you're blue in the face, but the plain fact is that it is impossible for a cricketer to be as focused on the tour with his wife there, as much as when she is at home. It is understandable and natural that he wants to make arrangements for her during the day when he is at nets, and at the ground when the Test starts.

It all helps to distract or, to put it the other way around, it cannot help the cricketing side of the tour in any way.

The following story illustrates the point. I sat next to Gus Fraser on the flight from Port Elizabeth to Cape Town. On the other side of the aisle sat Dr Bacher and his wife Shira. I mentioned to them that the England party had now increased from 22 to 64, and Ali asked his wife to tell me about the clause in his contract on the tour of England in 1965.

'Believe it or not, no wives, girlfriends or families were allowed within 5000 miles of the players in England.'

Fraser heard this and, bemoaning an interrupted night's sleep said: 'About three o'clock this morning, I wished we had the same clause in our contracts.'

Naturally, among the former England players on tour as media men, there was general derision when Illingworth's reservations about the family factor appeared in print, but he must have a point, or was it just coincidence that the playing side of the tour became fragmented from the end of the Durban Test onwards?

With three drawn Tests, the pressure on the tourists increased, particularly as more supporters were flocking in each day. How would the stalemate be broken and by whom? Paul Adams had finally been drafted into the home squad and was sure to play.

Jason Gallian had flown in from the 'A' tour of India to leapfrog Ramprakash for the last batting place, with Crawley's tour now effectively over. He would bat at three, because Illingworth and Atherton agreed that they would be better off if the top of the order was in the hands of three openers.

Gallian was to be the 20th batsman in 111 Tests and 198 innings to bat at three for England since August 1985. The pivotal position in any batting order had produced just ten hundreds – four by David Gower, two by Mike Gatting and one each by Graeme Hick, Alec Stewart, Graham Gooch and Bill Athey.

Ramprakash's diary note on the seconding of Gallian was this: 'I had high hopes of getting a game until they told me they were flying out Jason as replacement for Creepy. That was the killer blow. Someone who hadn't originally been selected was now playing in front of me.

Illingworth
We had a full net practice at St George's on Christmas morning. After that, the arrangements were that the players and families would have a barbecue around the hotel swimming pool in the afternoon. I wanted the nets to be organised properly, and that meant putting our bowlers on rota, because I wanted all the batsmen to have a good net against the best bowlers.

I wanted Devon to bowl at Alec, who would be one of the last to bat, so I asked him to stand out until I wanted him. I was standing at the bowlers' stump in the middle net, when I suddenly spotted Devon bowling. I repeated to him that I wanted to save him until later, and forgot all about him until, a few minutes later, I saw he had come back in the nets and was chattering away to Darren Gough at the end of his run.

I accept that Devon says he was trying to help a local black bowler to bowl straight, but even so he was becoming a distraction. I was trying to set targets of line and length for Gough, and I didn't want anyone talking to him. It was then that I went up to Malcolm for the third time in 15 minutes and told him 'to piss off (not F-off) until I'm ready for you'.

That was it. Nothing more, nor less. He wasn't picked out. He wasn't held up to ridicule, but it took three talkings to from me to get him to do what I wanted. He then bowled when it was his turn, and there was no problem. That is why I was so disappointed about what he wrote when he got back to England.

The pitch looked the best batting one of the series, and we made only the one change, Gallian for Crawley. They brought in Adams for Kallis and batted first after winning the toss. They batted solidly for their 428, but we bowled tightly enough to keep their run rate to under three per over. We stuck at it, although Richard Illingworth had three catches put down in one over at the end of the innings, one by himself which caused a muscular side strain that kept him out for nearly three weeks.

We seem to find ways of getting into trouble, and we did it again. Alec got himself out and we lost another couple before Mike and Hick seemed to have repaired the damage. We were 163 for three when the captain got a bad decision from Cyril Mitchley, who gave him out caught off Adams down the leg side.

That started the collapse, with Hick getting another LBW decision from wide out which I found hard to understand. After those two questionable dismissals, we could even have fallen short of the follow-on target of 229, although I doubt if Cronje would have enforced it. Jack and Richard used up 28 overs before Donald wound up the innings.

Atherton's reaction to his dismissal was, initially, one of sheer disbelieving disappointment which carried him dangerously close to the area of dissent. His slow walk off featured constant head-shaking, and he smashed his bat into a chair outside the sanctity of the dressing-room. Clive Lloyd took no action, deciding that the England captain's reaction was just about acceptable.

Illingworth
It looked much worse on television, because the cameras never left him until he was in the dressing-room. I don't agree with that. I remember telling the BBC senior producer Keith Mackenzie that they should not do that. Show one shot but then cut away. It is not right to go in close and feature an expression that the public on the ground can't see. Chris Broad was a victim of that at Lord's, and I think it should stop. I'm not condoning dissent, but the criterion should be actions that are clearly visible to the spectators.

For example, Graeme Hick got a string of dodgy decisions,

culminating with one for a catch behind off Paul Adams in the sixth one-day international in East London. He marched off, grinning in sheer disbelief. That was shown on television, but nobody on the ground would have seen it.

Going back to Mike in the fourth Test, his concentration was wound up so tightly to steer England out of trouble – that is why he reacted as he did. I know their players reckon he was out before – also caught down the leg side, but two wrongs have never made a right.

Another thing about television. I believe it is in the Sky contract that they should cut the stump mike as soon as the ball hits the 'keeper's gloves. But they never do. You always hear the comments of the 'keeper and one day, the viewers will get a mouthful of language. There is nothing to be gained by not switching the mike off at the key moment – other than the sensational element. I reckon that what they are doing is in danger of bringing the game into disrepute, and it is about time the authorities got a grip of television. They try to run the game for their own benefit, and I can understand some of what they do, because I had ten years at it. But enough is enough.

After being on the wrong end of the game for over three days, we got into a position from which we could have won it, thanks to a magnificent piece of bowling from Cork.

He'd gone off the boil a bit after Johannesburg, but that was understandable considering his workload. He probably bowled more overs in a short space of time than ever before, and with the extra demands on concentration, he did a great job for us. To appreciate fully what he did, he was the only bowler to play in all five Tests, and only Fraser and Illingworth played in three. His figures were almost the same as those of Donald – 19 wickets at around 26 apiece, although Cork bowled 23 overs more. To counter that, he was usually holding things together, while Donald was bowling as a strike bowler in shorter spells.

Peter Martin started it off by getting rid of Hudson and Cronje in the 75 minutes' play before lunch. At that time, we were so far behind that all we could do was plug away and hope to make them bat as long as possible in order to shorten the time we needed to bat to save the match. I was glad he picked up a couple of wickets, because he had tried hard on the tour, and was prepared to listen and work on his game.

Kirsten and Cullinan pulled them around, but at least we had stopped them crashing on. The pitch helped, because you couldn't hit through the ball, so they had to graft for runs.

At 60 for two in the 26th over with an overall lead of 228 and a day and a half left, they were well in charge.

Because Ilott had an injured thigh, we were down to three bowlers, but Corky kept going in magnificent fashion. He got three of the next four wickets to fall while they went from 60 for two to 69 for six, and only Kirsten held things together. Pollock again played well to show what a good temperament he has, and that seventh-wicket partnership virtually doubled the score and put them back in charge.

Once England's faint chance of winning went with the seventh-wicket stand, Atherton orchestrated a leg theory tactic with Cork which offended, among others, umpire Cyril Mitchley. It even upset one Trevor Edward Bailey, doing duty on BBC radio, who condemned it, apparently forgetting he had adopted the same sterile approach to save the Headingley Test against Australia in 1953.

Mitchley spoke to Atherton and Cork about it, and when the ball was fired down leg-side again, he chose to make his point by signalling wide for a delivery which was certainly not too wide to be hit. He was criticised for it, but umpires are the sole judges of fair and unfair play.

Illingworth

It was a surprise to me when Mike did it. He had not spoken to me about it during the tea interval, and it was a tactic I never used in my career. He did it on his own initiative, which might surprise those people who think I pull his strings for him. I have an input during the intervals when we are fielding, but only when asked. Usually he will ask if I have seen anything, but that is when we are trying to bowl a side out. By tea on the fourth day, it was just a matter of whether we could stretch their innings towards the end of the day or not. I happen to think that sort of tactic does the game no good, but Mike will have to work that out for himself. I suppose he must ask himself what his reaction would be if he was the batsman when a bowler started to do that to him.

They left us to score 328 in a minimum of 99 overs and we were 20 overnight. We didn't dismiss the chance of winning, although it was long odds against because, even if we got off to a good start, they could drop fielders back. We decided to see how the first session went and if we could get 70 or 80 without losing wickets, we could have another look at it.

The first hour went well, with us scoring 42, but Mike and Alec dried up after drinks, and scored only 18 in the next hour. We were criticised for that, but what about South Africa? They hardly attacked, opening with Craig Matthews and young Adams didn't get a bowl until 20 minutes before lunch. He'd been on after five overs the previous night, so they weren't prepared to push for victory as hard as they might have. It made me even more certain that they were a bit scared of us – if only we could have got into a position to pressure them. We hadn't and we didn't on that last day. Alec had his longest knock of the series and wasn't out until the 86th over of the innings. I wouldn't say his feet moved properly, but at least his bat came down straighter and much nearer his body.

Jason Gallian did us a job, sticking around for 40 overs, and looks as though he has got chances. I was happy with the result because, again, it was a match which we could have lost and mostly did in the previous few years. It meant that the only Test we had lost in the last nine was on that freak pitch at Edgbaston against the West Indies. So to Cape Town and all to play for.

24
A CRAZY THIRTY MINUTES: CAPE TOWN

What a climax to the series! British supporters poured into Cape Town, among them TCCB and MCC officials, including Alan Smith on his second visit within a month, Dennis Silk, Doug Insole, David Acfield, Michael Melluish and Roger Knight.

Insole did a rough head count during the match and reckoned that at least 37 former England cricketers were watching the match, and close to 100 past and current county cricketers.

All tickets had been sold many weeks before, and daily capacity crowds of 20,000 would see South Africa try to double their number of victories over England at Newlands.

They would watch their own Paul Adams play in his second Test match, and change the course of the match in one glorious hour with the bat. The travelling media, some of whom were departing the tour at the end of the match to rest their lap-top and human batteries before the World Cup, seemed just as wound up as everyone else when the bell sounded for the last round.

Illingworth
Mike and I discussed the team the day before, and this time the roles were reversed. He said that he wanted five bowlers to have a full go at winning the match, and there was I, asking him if he was sure, because we had not batted well throughout the series. For me to say that was against all my principles of always wanting a fifth bowler, but I was glad he felt the way he did.

I was sorry Richard Illingworth was not fit, because that would have made a difference. As it was, our five included

Devon Malcolm and Mike Watkinson, which was all we could do because we could not possibly have included both in a four-man attack. I didn't speak to Malcolm about his selection because, all the way through the tour, I left it to the captain to tell the players who was and was not playing. That is how I think it should be.

So we made three changes – Illingworth and Ilott were unfit, and Gallian went out because we were changing the balance of the side, so we brought in Watkinson, Malcolm and Fraser. South Africa went the other way and brought back Kallis for Matthews so, for the third time in the series, both sides went in opposite directions. It is easy to say afterwards, but with hindsight we would have been better off with the sixth batsman, but to do that you would have had to have known that Devon would bowl as he did.

I know he hadn't had much bowling, but what he did have was not great. Only he knows how he felt deep down about his knee, but something stopped him from putting it in consistently. Anyway, he was the gamble which I didn't mind losing, providing he bust a gut even if he got it wrong.

It was a tense dressing-room when Mike won what we thought was bound to be a good toss. The pitch had only been relaid eight months previously, and there were cracks at the Wynberg end which you could shift with your finger. Groundsman Andy Atkinson insisted they would stand up to five days, but I wasn't sure.

Batting last was bound to be a problem, so we had to put a decent total in the book. We got off to a bad start, losing Mike in Donald's fourth over for a duck. Whether the captain was mentally tired or whether they bowled at him a bit differently as the series went on I don't know, but he did play at deliveries he had left alone earlier in the tour. This one bounced a bit, but it was far from an unplayable ball. Our first run didn't come until the eighth over, but then Robin Smith hit a couple of fours.

He batted at three where, probably, he should have gone in earlier in the series, because he is better than most at dealing with a tight situation. And that is what it soon was when Alec got out in an awful-looking way. His feet got nowhere again, and his bat came down from slip to mid-on to drag a straight ball onto leg stump.

With only five batsmen, we needed everyone to make the bowlers get them out, yet three of them contributed too much to their dismissals. At lunch we were 54 for two, and Smith and Thorpe had both hit three fours and were settling in. The last words I told them before they went out after the break were 'now make sure they get *you* out'.

I could hardly believe what happened first ball. Donald slanted one across Thorpe. It was wide and went wider, but he threw the bat at it and was caught by McMillan at second slip. It was poor cricket, but what can you say? You can't bat for anyone – just try to get them thinking in the right way. It is pointless saying anything when a batsman gets out like that, because he must know what he has done and the best thing is to leave him alone. What I find irritating, they often come back in and throw the bat down in annoyance. It's too late then, the damage is done, and what damage it was when Hick went three balls later.

Remembering how positively he started the series at Centurion Park, and how well he had played in Port Elizabeth, it was more than disappointing to see him slice another slip catch to McMillan off one to which he only offered half a defensive bat.

Within four balls of lunch, we had lost two wickets to indifferent shots and, at 60 for four and a batsman light, we were right down to the bone. Jack helped Smith to put on 43, but it was grim stuff, with the 100 coming up in the 52nd over. Somehow we had to top 200 to stay in the game, but then Jack played the sort of shot to Pollock he had avoided for most of the series. McMillan's third slip catch meant we were 103 for five and only Smith's 66 saved the day.

As it was, the score of 153 was at least 100 under par and gave us no chance unless we could keep them down to a lead of no more than 50. Cork again nipped two out, Hudson and Cronje, but we needed wickets badly on the second day. Incidentally, Devon bowled six overs on the first day, which makes his newspaper claim that he had bowled 16 overs before he had a go at the South African tenth-wicket pair after tea on the second day, very misleading. He had bowled 16, but only ten that day before he got hold of the second new ball.

We had to get wickets on the second day, but when they were 125 for three in the 56th over, I could see us being batted out of the game. Devon didn't fire, so it was down to the other three seamers and they nearly pulled off a miracle. Martin and Cork got two each, Fraser one, and Watkinson nipped in with the wickets of Kirsten and Pollock, with Jack taking three more catches.

Not only were we right back in the game with them at 171 for nine, I reckon we would have had the edge if we'd rolled the last wicket over for no more than another ten runs. The pitch was still playing all right, but we were only in the second day, and any score of 175 or more batting last would have taken some getting.

Also, the way they batted to get to 171 for nine convinced me they were nervy and I really thought we would nick the match and the series. We were that close. All we wanted was one more wicket.

When young Adams walked to the wicket as the youngest player in the match, he joined the oldest, David Richardson. He was playing in only his seventh first-class match and had got a duck in his debut Test the previous week. Richardson certainly did not forget. He walked down to reassure Adams: 'Come on. You must have played against bowlers as quick as Devon Malcolm before.'

'No' was the one-word answer from the boy from Mitchells Plain. That was one of two significant conversations that took place on the field within a minute.

The second one was between Atherton and Malcolm, with the captain asking his fast bowler to rough up the batsmen in the same way as Donald & Co had done throughout the series to the England tail. In simple words: 'Let him have one. And another. And another.'

Illingworth
I knew what Mike was saying to Devon and I thought that this was the exact situation we had brought him on tour for. What more could he ask for? A brand new second new ball against a number 11 with an open cheque to run in and knock him over. I couldn't believe what I saw.

He was unlucky when Adams inside-edged him past leg stump for four, and he was also unlucky when Cork stupidly got the lad off the mark with a five, thanks to a wild throw going for four overthrows. But as for the rest . . .

Even that inside edge for four was off a full half-volley when the captain had told him to bang it in short around off stump. Worse than the edged four were two sets of four leg-byes off full inswinging half-volleys. What did he think he was playing at?

I know that a number 11 batsman can upset a bowler,

particularly when he thinks that his team-mates are wondering why he can't get him out. I know that last-wicket partnerships start in fun, but often give the batsmen the confidence to play properly, and I know that Adams is no batting rabbit.

I also know that he got only one proper bouncer from Malcolm who had been ordered to pepper him and, worst of all, he didn't even seem to run in with any aggression. I wouldn't have minded if he'd bounced in like he did at The Oval and hadn't got the wicket we wanted so badly. But he was asked the big question, the one we'd been trying to answer for him all through the tour, and he sank without displaying any trace of the fight and spunk we were entitled to expect from a strike bowler.

The game went in 15 overs, with the main damage done by the time Mike took Malcolm off after four overs. Including those eight byes, which came off badly directed bowling of the wrong length, 26 of the 31 precious runs that came in seven overs off the new ball were wasted from his end, including Richardson hooking him for fours as though he was nothing more than a medium pacer.

Imagine the shattering effect on the rest of the team. The batsmen had started to prepare themselves mentally for their second innings, believing the arrears would be 30 or so. The South African dressing-room must have been low, knowing they had blown their big chance. They wouldn't be able to post attacking fields, and their nerves must have been in shreds.

I wouldn't even have minded if that last wicket partnership of 73 had come at the same run-rate as the rest of the match. Before Adams came in, both sides had scored 324 runs for 19 wickets in 154 overs, of which Malcolm had bowled 16 overs for 38. For those 73 runs to come off 15 overs turned the morale of both sides upside down, and I am struggling to think of another Test match in recent years in which a tenth-wicket partnership that lasted for only an hour settled the match.

That is the background for what happened in the next 24 hours. When Martin finally had Adams well caught by Hick at slip, we were 93 behind and had only seven overs to bat, instead of what we might reasonably have expected – a deficit of 30 with about 20 overs to bat.

Nothing was said in the dressing-room in the ten-minute break. I think I made a mistake by not suggesting to Mike that we open with someone else. I thought about it for two reasons.

I could guess how upset he was at the prospect of the entire tour going down the pan in one hour, especially after all he had done with the bat to get us to Cape Town all square. I also thought it was essential that we had him there next morning, so what was the point of risking him that evening?

I said nothing, and only told him next day. He assured me that, by the time he went out to bat, he was feeling OK, but the second reason was still valid, and I really should have said something. Therefore it seemed almost inevitable that he got out, caught behind to Donald. I sensed then that we needed a miracle to win the match.

It was a quiet, deflated dressing-room that night, but nothing was said. That came at the end of the match, after we were unlucky to lose Smith and Hick to poor decisions just when both batsmen were in. We know that they can both play a big innings and, once we got in front, a good score from one of them could still have given us at least 150 to bowl at.

Even Thorpe's run-out decision was a poor one, although he was out. Umpire Dave Orchard should have called for the replay in what was a fast and tight finish to a single, but he did not. Everything stemmed from that mistake, including the bigger one of allowing himself to be pressured into referring it, once Cronje and his team were told from the hospitality boxes and the home dressing-room that Thorpe was out.

I believe this is not the first time Cronje has done his and, as a captain myself, I can understand him pressing as hard as he could. But rules are rules, and the Code of Conduct specifies that players must not ask for the replay. Fines are useless, because I imagine that Cronje would have been happy to settle for the subsequent penalty of 50 per cent of his fee. Indeed, I don't suppose he would have blinked at 100 per cent because the wicket of Thorpe was crucial at 141 for six, when we were 59 ahead.

To put the financial aspect into perspective, the South Africans earned £90,000 as a match-winning bonus, so a suspension would be the only answer in such circumstances.

Starting with Hick, we lost our last six wickets for 19 in nine overs, and they won in mid-afternoon by 10 wickets. Because the game ended inside three days, leaving the ticket-holders for the last two days with nothing, I was asked by the local authorities if I would agree to play a one-day game under lights on the Saturday.

I checked with the seven players not playing that they were happy and negotiated a fee of 25,000 rand. That was while the presentations were done in the middle, so Mike and Alec knew nothing about it until they came off.

They weren't happy, but I explained that I had to make a quick decision and told them that I only needed four out of the full side. That, and the fee, made them a bit happier, but it all helped me to get really wound up. It was then that I let fly at Devon, but not in the way he claimed in his newspaper article.

He was sitting on the physiotherapist's bed, *not* in the corner of the dressing-room as he says. I spoke to him from a range of about a yard, *not* six inches as he says. I did say 'You bowled crap and probably cost us the Test match.'

He did not say a word, *nor did he whistle.* What he is trying to establish by saying that, I don't know and I don't care. He wasn't the first cricketer to be bollocked after a game, and he won't be the last.

As for some of the other things he said, let me put the record straight. He says that I did not congratulate him at The Oval after his nine wickets in August 1994. That is not true. In fact, I congratulated him twice. Once as he came off the field, and then I went looking for him in both dressing-rooms until I found him and I shook his hand and said 'well bowled'.

So much of what he has chosen to write is hardly worth bothering with. Like his version of the meeting in my bedroom in the East London hotel in the first month of the tour, when Peter Lever was also present. He hasn't even got it right who said what, including the remark attributed to me accusing him of telling the press that I wanted him to bowl slower.

What Peter said, and I agree with him, is that Devon can't bat or field, but he can bowl fast. Having picked him for the tour, and gone out of my way to make him the only player who was promised a touring place before we picked the squad, I could not understand why he thought we were trying to get him to slow down.

And if he was upset because it was said he couldn't bat and couldn't field, then he is not being honest with himself. We had fielding sessions most days of the tour, and he sometimes went through one almost without catching a ball or picking it up cleanly. Some cricketers are not natural in that department, and I am not picking him out. But if he thinks any comment about his fielding is unfair, then that attitude goes a long way towards explaining why he has had such an erratic career.

I picked him for the tour. I made sure he was promised a place in order to help him. I wanted him firing on all cylinders, even more so when Johnson withdrew and Gough did not threaten much in the run-up to the Tests. What we tried to do was *not* to change anything, but simply to revert to his Oval 1994 follow-through. Assuming that it was never a question of him not wanting to do that, the only explanation is not that he wouldn't do it, but rather that he couldn't.

To sum up, I think Devon tends to make too many excuses, and gives the impression (rightly or wrongly) that he doesn't care sufficiently about anything.

Mike Atherton's view on Malcolm, the tour and the final Test, given in an interview in the *Daily Telegraph*, might be more moderately worded, but is little different in substance:

As far as the tour is concerned, the way I see it is that we were half an hour from winning the series. A crazy 30 minutes in Cape Town turned the entire thing, but it was nothing like the humiliation it was portrayed as being. I never criticise players in those circumstances. I never said it was Devon's fault and people can infer what they like. You can argue we might have handled Devon a bit better, but there are two sides to most stories. Peter Lever came in for a lot of stick, but he worked superbly well with Peter Martin, who came on in leaps and bounds.

Not many lines left to read between, there.

25

THE ONE-DAY SERIES AND TOUR REVIEW

The seven-match one-day series in 12 days was an impossible load for two sides who had just battled their way through a full, five-match series in 51 days. What should have been an even series became an apparently one-sided mis-match, with South Africa winning 6–1. The longer the series went after the opening two games in Cape Town and Bloemfontein, the stronger South Africa became as the England batting fell apart.

Even allowing for what seemed to be the home side's greater concentration on winning the series rather than using it as an experimental sounding-board for the World Cup, the gulf between the two teams looked embarrassingly wide. History will show that the effect on morale of the loss of the Cape Town Test was incalulable. England could – no, should – have won the first game and they did win the second, so they returned to the High Veldt for the pivotal, back-to-back games in Johannesburg and Pretoria, in good heart.

The series was tied 1–1, and South Africa knew it could have been 2–0 against them. The England management might justify their team selection for the showpiece game of the seven in front of a 30,000 Wanderers crowd by saying that they needed to give all their 17 players some cricket, and they had several minor injuries to consider.

South Africa had only a 14-man squad, which precluded the juggling thought necessary by Illingworth and Atherton. Whatever the reasons, England miscalculated badly by making five changes and omitting Graham Thorpe and Dominic Cork. They lost by three wickets, and then by seven wickets the next day at Centurion Park, when an England total of 272 for eight should have been greater after a start of 138 for one in 28 overs.

The shortfall of at least 20 runs, together with some ring-rusty bowling by Richard Illingworth in his first game for 16 days – 9–0–65–1 – gave the home side a 3–1 lead. Again, priorities were different in the fifth game in Durban. England made changes, South Africa did not. They asked Allan Donald for one last effort to win the series and promised him the last two games off.

England went into the final two games, determined to save something from the wreckage, but the neighbouring Eastern Cape grounds of Buffalo Park and St George's produced two more home wins, to leave the players and travelling supporters feeling as though they had been mugged.

Hick suffered yet another poor decision in East London when, with England apparently cruising towards their target of 130 at 75 for three, he was given out caught at the wicket off Adams. The pitch was a low, slow seamer, but surely the England middle-lower order should not have subsided to 115 all out. Adams was a real handful, but the fact was that the tourists' batting now looked horribly vulnerable.

Adams has a marvellous approach to cricket. He is not overwhelmed by anything, and has taken to international cricket as though he had played 105 first-class games before his Test debut, not five. When he came on to bowl at Buffalo Park, the worst fears of Gary Kirsten were about to be realised.

Kirsten had never kept wicket before, but was given the gloves when David Richardson smashed his left index finger in trying for a leg-side take against the seam of Jacques Kallis. Full of apprehension when Hansie Cronje tossed the ball to Adams, Kirsten raced the length of the pitch to join in the conversation taking place about the field placings.

'You'll have to give me a sign. I haven't got a clue.'

The 18-year-old nodded understandingly and said: 'Don't worry. I'll keep it simple for you.' *Sang froid* of the iciest sort.

The tour ended with another defeat, this time by a South African side that was minus five regulars, including Donald, Rhodes, Cullinan and Richardson. The final game on Sunday, 21 January was graced by the presence of President Nelson Mandela who succeeded, in unlikely fashion, in surprising Dr Ali Bacher. The latter is one of the most forward-thinking officials in world cricket, and has a gimlet-eyed approach to publicity which allows few opportunities to be missed.

Let the chief executive of the UCB tell the story. 'I went to the back of the St George's pavilion to meet the President, who had flown from Johannesburg especially for the match. It was 2.30 p.m., and he had agreed to present the trophy at the end of the match. Remember, he had worn the national rugby shirt in the World Cup, and also the soccer shirt at the start of the African Nations Cup, so I hoped he would wear our blazer and cap.

'He got out of the car, and I just stared in astonishment. Without any prompting from me, he had thought it out for himself and was wearing brand new cricket flannels and a new pair of Reebok trainers. All I could think to say was, "Mr President, as usual, you are one step ahead of the rest of us." Brilliant!'

If England had to stand after the match and watch and listen to Hansie Cronje take all the plaudits, their consolation was in being presented to Mandela. He spoke to every player, taking most time with Alec Stewart and Jack Russell – perhaps exchanging views on the value of a safe pair of hands.

Illingworth
A fairer result of the one-day games would have been 5–2 or even 4–3. We should have won the first at Newlands; we should have defended the 272 at Centurion, and we should have won the low-scoring game in East London. I know that one-day games are full of ifs and buts, but those were three very good chances that we did not nail down. If we win one, it is 5–2, two and it is 4–3 and all three gives us the series.

That is why I was not too despondent at the end of the tour, even though it all seemed to go sideways from the tenth-wicket partnership on the second day of the final Test. It might have looked as though we were demob happy, but that wasn't true. All the 17 players were battling to get into the final 14 for the World Cup, and anything could have changed right up to the time when we announced the squad after the last game at St George's Park.

I was disappointed to hear some sniping from Dermot Reeve that he thought he hadn't had a fair shake. We played him twice at the start of the series, and I know he believes we should have taken into account that that was his first cricket for several months.

We always felt that there was only one place between him and Craig White. I thought White did better in the two games in which Reeve played, and his fielding was another big factor.

Dermot has not got a great throw and, with Robin Smith also struggling to field outside the ring, we could not afford another. I think that if we needed 30 against quality spin, Dermot is the more likely to work it about, but in the end it was his lack of pace with the ball which decided it for us. He mixes it up well, but I didn't think his bowling had enough.

Just a word about Craig White; I suppose he is a cricketer I have backed more than any other, purely on my judgement. He needs people to believe in him, but I am sure he can make it at the top level.

The batting picked itself, except for the last place between Smith and Ramprakash. The younger player is the better fielder by some way, but Smith's record is so good that we had to pick him.

Neil Smith was a bit unlucky only to get two games, especially as we decided to take him to Pakistan as the second spinner in front of Mike Watkinson. The problem was Richard Illingworth. He was unfit for the first three one-day games, and we wanted him to play at Centurion Park. He bowled there like he did in a five-day Test, which is why he went for 65. So we had to keep playing him to get him back into one-day style.

If we made one mistake in the one-day series, it was at The Wanderers. Looking back at it, it helped the seamers a lot, and we should have played one more. We had several injury niggles and we tried to juggle those around to avoid too many playing in four games in six days. That is a tremendous strain, mentally as well as physically, and I think it is too much.

The tour was a good one, which should not be written down because of the last three weeks. I thought it was brilliant up to then. The press agreed that it was one of the happiest tours they had been on, and I enjoyed the terrific spirit among all of us. And that includes Johnny Barclay, Malcolm Ashton and the Doc, Phillip Bell. They fitted in perfectly, and some of our team meetings were great fun. I reckon I got fined more than anyone else – for being the first one to take 100 wickets on the tour, and for wearing knitted shoes were two of the excuses they found.

I've been on enough tours as player and captain to be able to compare, and I have never been on a better one in respect of fun and team spirit. I have had my say about Devon as a bowler, so here's what I think about the rest.

I'll start with the captain. I think he has been great to work with. We have never had the slightest problem about our working relationship, and I couldn't have asked for any person in his role more suited to thinking about the game as I do. We have the same priorities, both for the team and when we are assessing individual players. I have had plenty of personal experience of working with a manager who had different ideas from mine, which has probably helped me with Mike.

My first concern is for the team and the players, and so is his. He is now a much better captain, and I like to think I have had something to do with that. I notice that the section of the press that seemed to be forecasting a bust-up between us have now shut up, because the regular cricket journalists know that we work well together. He is a solid batsman and a solid young man. He has a good cricket brain and could captain England for a long time.

Alec had a mixed tour, scoring plenty of runs between Tests on slower pitches, but managing only one fifty in the series in which he averaged 29. I think he suffers from playing his home cricket at The Oval, where a batsman can mostly trust the pitches. His footwork is limited and always has been, but that is no problem if he counters that by playing straight. Only he can work it out, because we have discussed it several times, and he knows he has got a problem. Again, like Mike, I couldn't ask for anyone better to captain the side on tour when Mike had a rest. He is a lively lad, runs the side well, and has a good professional attitude towards his cricket. What he has to think about now is that, for the first time in a long time, he went on tour purely as an opening batsman, without any wicket-keeping considerations. If he works hard on his main fault, he should play for England for the next few years.

I have no hesitation in naming Jack Russell as the star of the tour. He was magnificent. Not just his wicket-keeping, which was of a higher quality than I have seen from him. He has been a bit suspect with catches to his right, but he is now much more positive and he took some great catches. His batting speaks for itself, and he is a model professional in every way. His attitude is so good. He used to be withdrawn, but his year as captain of Gloucestershire has brought about a big change.

If I want to know about a player or an incident, I know I can trust Jack's judgement. He has no time for anything less than the full commitment he gives, and he didn't mind telling me when the odd player, in the odd game, was not honest. By that, he meant that he heard excuses about a dismissal or some bad bowling when the player concerned, as sometimes happened, batted or bowled badly. Nobody underperforms on purpose, but the player with the right attitude will not try to find an excuse why he did it.

I must bracket Graeme Hick with Jack as the success of the tour. I count him as one of the plusses in my two years in charge. Not just for the modification in his stance and technique, but in his attitude. He now looks more like the Hick who smashes county attacks all over the place, and I now believe he will go on to great things. I don't like using the word 'great' too much, but Hick is now close to being in that bracket as a world-class batsman. He is just 30, so in the next few years he could achieve anything.

Robin Smith did a good job on tour. He started off out of nick, but we always wanted to play him in the series. I was disappointed that he didn't turn a couple of his good innings into major ones, but he helped to hold things together at Centurion Park, The Wanderers and Newlands, and his 34 in Durban steadied the innings. He still lunges too much, too early, and he is now a limited fielder, but he's got plenty of guts and that quality makes up for a lot.

Graham Thorpe never really fired. Since we brought him back at Headingley in 1994 against South Africa, he has never missed a Test and has played several fine innings. We need a left-hander in the top four, but he should now be capable of playing major innings. He knows he had an ordinary tour, but it was not just that he didn't get a fifty until the final Test. That can happen, but he got out too many times in loose fashion. He got a poor decision in the second Test, but other scores of 13, 17, 2, 27 and 20 show that he got in four times, only to be caught in the slips three times, and at mid-wicket off an Adams long-hop.

Like Smith, he's determined and he is gutsy. He can play the quicks, but he never really got to grips with Adams. England want him, and he wants England, so the rest is up to him.

I think that Mark Ramprakash is now beginning to see the light. He seemed more relaxed towards the end of the tour. Maybe because he thought things could only get better, after the way he got out in his two Tests. He must be a better player than that, and I made sure I told him that at the end of the tour. He is only 26, so he's still got plenty of time to come back. At least there was a smile on his face in the last few weeks, even though he'd had such a miserable time. I don't think we've seen the last of him at Test level.

John Crawley was unlucky. He could have edged Ramprakash out at the start when he was in the runs. Then, when we picked him at Kingsmead, he tore his hamstring before he could bat. I think he has got the right attitude. He never grumbled, and I know how hard he's worked on his fitness and fielding since the tour of Australia. He could not have tried harder, and he is another one who is bound to get another chance.

Regarding the two spinners, Richard Illingworth was always going to be first choice, and he is now bowling better than he's ever done for England. His spell in the Durban Test was a perfect example. He gave Mike control and created pressure on their middle order which the seamers cashed in on. Mike Watkinson was the perfect tourist. He is a cricketer who I think needs to be playing regular first-class cricket to enable him to contribute in a Test match.

He did well enough against the West Indies, but he suffered from not getting enough cricket on tour, as is always likely to happen with a limited itinerary.

Dominic Cork was in a class of his own among our new-ball bowlers. He was always our main wicket-taker, and he never flagged or let his head go down. I'm a bit worried about the workload on him, but that's our problem, not his. He gives so much energy in a spell – he never coasts, because he is always trying to take wickets. That is why he is a much better Test match bowler than in one-day cricket – a bit ironic that, considering he had to wait quite a while for his debut because he was labelled a bits-and-pieces cricketer. There's nothing of him, physically, but he has such a big heart that he seems able to keep going. I just hope we can pick a couple of bowlers to help him out.

Peter Martin looks like being one. He was our most improved player on the tour. What he did shows what can be done if you work hard. He worked a lot with Peter Lever and he listened to me about the need for greater accuracy. He took it all in, and his attitude earned him everything he got. What a bowler we'd have if you could combine his attitude and approach to bowling with Malcolm's pace. You couldn't have two more contrasting approaches to a tour, which is why the bowler who was not originally selected, Martin, played three

Tests and topped the bowling averages.

Darren Gough came back a bit in the last week in the one-day games. I spoke to him about trying to bowl too fast. He will never be an out-and-out quick bowler and, if he tries to be that, he is bound to suffer more injuries. His strength is a good pace variation, with the occasional faster ball plus the yorker. He has had a rough year, but it still a cheerful lad and now knows what he has to do to be more consistent at Test level.

Gus Fraser tried his hardest, but things never worked for him. I have had doubts about his nip for a while, but his accuracy used to be his strength. Perhaps he is now at a stage of his career where he needs to be bowling regularly, but he bowled too many four balls in The Wanderers Test, especially in the first innings. He is such a trier that I hope he forces his way back, because he is the nearest thing we've got to an old-fashioned seamer.

Mark Ilott did not let us down. He is another super tourist, and he bowled steadily when he got his chance. His three wickets at Kingsmead turned their first innings around, and it was a pity he got injured in the next Test in Port Elizabeth.

Jason Gallian is another with the right attitude. He didn't look out of his depth in the fourth Test at St George's Park, and missed the final Test only because we went for the extra bowler.

Which leaves Malcolm. If I could go back and do something different when we met to pick the party to tour South Africa, knowing what I know now, I would not have picked him. I knew that we needed to work with him a lot, but his knee operation in mid-September scuppered our plans. That is why we had so much to catch up on at the start of the tour. Remember, this had gone right back to the start of the series against West Indies at Headingley, when he bowled 11.3 overs and took two for 60 in a match in which we bowled 109 overs.

We picked him, because we hoped he would work with us, but that did not happen.

CONCLUSION

Illingworth

Since I became chairman, we have picked 32 players for 22 full Tests in my first two years, including experienced campaigners like Graham Gooch, Mike Gatting and John Emburey. It is interesting to see which players have been picked more often – the following lists might surprise a few people:

BATSMEN:	Atherton 22, Hick 19, Thorpe 18, Stewart 16, Smith 12, Crawley 10, Gooch 9, Gatting 5, Ramprakash 5, Gallian 3, Knight 2, Wells 1.
ALL-ROUNDERS:	White 6, Watkinson 4.
WICKET-KEEPERS:	Rhodes 11, Russell 8.
BOWLERS:	Fraser 13, DeFreitas 11, Malcolm 10, Cork 10, Gough 9, Illingworth 7, Martin 6, Tufnell 5, Such 3, Lewis 2, Ilott 2, Emburey 1, Salisbury 1, Benjamin 1, Taylor 1, McCague 1.

I had no direct input to the selection of the Test sides for Australia, other than helping to pick the touring party and the various replacements. Otherwise, I have chaired the meetings which had picked the sides for the other 17 Tests – six each at home in 1994 and 1995 and the five Tests in South Africa.

Regarding the other players not on tour in South Africa, I think that Paul Taylor and Martin McCague seemed to suffer from stage-fright in their only games. The hardest thing to learn is how to relax in a big game. If you relax too much, you can be caught napping, and you do need some adrenalin to gee you up. It is really a matter of controlling tension.

Of the other players picked only once or twice, I am most interested in Chris Lewis. Because of injury, I have not been able to work much with him, so I have not got a firm opinion either way. I have seen most of his home Test matches and believe he has under-achieved, but until I find out for myself, I shan't know whether or not he can respond to advice, or even instruction.

Phil Tufnell is a case of a good bowler who finds it difficult to fit into a team plan. Again, I have not closed the door, as shown by his inclusion in the party for the final Test at The Oval against the West Indies. He has burned a few bridges in recent years, but he is young enough to show he is capable of starting again.

Ian Salisbury is a different sort of man and a different sort of bowler. A shoulder injury held him back, but the fact we picked him for the 'A' tour of India should tell him he has not been written off. Alan Wells is another who has just got to keep battling away. Where he was unlucky was in not playing in a Test in 1995 before the final one at The Oval. Had we been able to get him in at Trent Bridge, he would have probably been given two games – as it was, it was just one ball in one innings. Cruel, but that is cricket. He is fit and has a great attitude towards the game.

Peter Such and Shaun Udal are two more with the right attitude. Udal has not yet played in a Test, but at 27 has oceans of time. Such has never let England down but, until we get pitches on which we can play two spinners, it will be hard work for him to compete for one place. Again, a good attitude with a pride in his cricket.

Phil DeFreitas was not picked for the tour, but impressed us so much when he played for Boland against us at Paarl in early December that we decided to bring him in for the one-day games, and he did well enough for us to take him to the World Cup.

THE FIRST TWO YEARS I got some criticism from several quarters about how our preparation for the tour compared with that of South Africa. The former Middlesex and Durham seamer, Simon Hughes, weighed in quite heavily in the *Daily*

Telegraph, just before we went to the World Cup at the beginning of February.

He never set foot in South Africa during the tour, but he seemed to have complete confidence in his sources. He said our net practices were less well organised; our fielding sessions did not compare; they had backroom staff which catered for every aspect of preparation, including expert dieticians; while we were sitting back in England in the last nine days of January, other World Cup squads were at training camps; and we did not use video footage to plan about the opposition.

To deal with his points in order, I organised nets so that all our batsmen could have proper bowlers at them. They were not haphazard, because if a batsman wanted two pace bowlers and a spinner, that's what he got. The reason I finally let fly at Malcolm on Christmas morning was because he had been told when he was required, but didn't comply. If the nets lacked organisation his behaviour would not have annoyed me so much.

In the fielding department, South Africa are blessed with two fast bowlers, Allan Donald and Shaun Pollock, who are natural athletes. Fanie de Villiers is not, and neither is their off spinner, Pat Symcox, but they didn't play in a Test. For us, Gus Fraser and Peter Martin will never be naturally athletic – it is just the way they are. If Hughes will excuse a dip back into the past, Fred Trueman and Brian Statham were also natural athletes and that makes such a difference to a side. We devised fielding programmes based on what we had to work with. They are intensive and hard work.

As for food, Dr Phillip Bell and Wayne Morton supervised the food and the preparation of it necessary on every ground we played on.

Yes, we chose to have a short break back in England after the tour. Some of the players, like Cork, were absolutely shattered, but why didn't Hughes point out that, in order to compensate, England went to Pakistan a full week before any other side?

As for use of the video, we got plenty of footage about the opposition from Sky, and often they would let our players watch film in their van at the end of the day. Our own video went bust, and we had trouble with the replacement, but that did not stop us using film to make a point with or about a player.

I wish Hughes had spoken to me to get the other side of

things, but that might have spoiled his story.

I spent my week at home writing my tour reports. I did a full one about the itinerary, the grounds, the hotels and everything to do with the tour. I also did individual reports on the players for the Board to consider during the World Cup.

Looking back on my two years, there are plus and minus factors. I believe I have brought about an improvement in several departments. We no longer lose Tests we should save, and that means a good dressing-room spirit. In turn, that has come about because we have tried to pick players who will fight and keep fighting. I am sure we have now got a harder team, mentally, although it is in spite of our county system, and not because of it.

We need two things to happen. We must have pitches on which we can play two spinners. Only then will we get a more balanced side and one which should be able to compete with anyone. The other thing is more control over what happens to players between Tests. The December 1995 Board meeting turned down my request for control in this area, particularly with bowlers.

I didn't overplay my request, because I believe that players should be proud to appear for their counties. But I want to be able to rest a player if he is shattered after a Test, like Cork was between Lord's and Old Trafford in 1995. I know that Derbyshire did the right thing by him and left him out of the next four-day game, but there are a few counties who would not do the same.

It is easier for other countries because they play less first-class cricket, but I would love to be able to copy South Africa who contract all their top players to the UCB, not the provinces. Pipe-dream? Maybe, but the county clubs have got to have another look at the principle.

MISTAKES It is difficult to imagine Illingworth admitting to mistakes. It is not in the nature of the man to own to a misjudgement, mainly because he makes few snap decisions. Whether the reasoning is sound or faulty is not the point; what is relevant is that there is always a reason.

So, what does he consider, with the caveat of hindsight, to be his errors in his first two years?

* * *

Illingworth

There are three main ones. I should have pushed harder for three openers for the South Africa tour. By being persuaded to take the best seven batsmen, I think we handicapped ourselves.

The second one was to go for the extra bowler at Cape Town. In defence of that, we were trying to win the series, and I thought that the first five, plus Jack Russell, would battle away to get us enough runs. The idea was that the top five would knuckle down even more than usual, knowing they had not got the safety net of a sixth batsman. It didn't work out with three of them getting themselves out, but we might have got away with it had Jack batted as he did earlier in the series. Sod's Law really, that he got out twice in ways he had not done before.

The third one? There were two of them in the Headingley Test against the West Indies. I was not sold on Robin Smith as an opener, and we should probably have played another batsman instead of five bowlers.

There have been other things I have been criticised for, but I can live with those. I could have pushed harder on those three issues but, as I hope everyone now knows, although I have the sole right of veto on any selection except for the captain, I have fought shy of using it because I still remember my playing days as captain.

PRESS It may surprise a lot of people to know that I have no real problem with the cricketing press. During my two first years as chairman, I have been open and honest with them, and have answered any questions they put to me. I don't mind them ringing me for an off-the-record briefing, and I have always tried to help them to do their job.

A couple of the tabloid journalists, Mike Beale of the *Daily Star* and Graham Otway of *Today*, lost their jobs in 1995, and I know what editorial pressure is exerted at times. That is another reason why I try to help them. At times, I am accused of being too ready to be quoted, particularly when I have discussed a player in public. I don't agree that I should not do this, because I have nothing to hide about how I have treated any player in my two years in the chair.

While I am in charge, the old days of a wall of silence have gone, and I think the public benefit by being able to read facts, instead of opinion. I was criticised when I answered questions at the Tetley lunch in November 1994, yet the captain did not moan, once I explained the context of the lunch and why my answers were given in the way they were.

I was criticised about the so-called poolside press conference about Devon Malcolm, when Peter Lever and I were shot down in flames back home because we were supposed to have said that he was a 'cricketing nonentity'. That, too, was not a conference as such, but just our answers to questions put to us about remarks Devon was said to have made to the press about Peter and me. Writers back home in England made us an easy target for poor man-management without bothering to find out the other side of the story, as they should have done in the interests of balance.

Does any journalist seriously think that I am such an idiot that I would antagonise a player, or players, by thoughtless remarks? My job is effectively in the players' hands, just as it was when I was captain, and all I have ever tried to do was to get the best out of everyone.

I admit failure with Malcolm, but so has every man in the England set-up over the last seven years. I tried everything from talking quietly, to coaxing and then the odd bollocking. His great insult was not just to me, but to the other players and to all the administrators of the TCCB; what on earth possessed him to say that, had he been a white bowler, he might have been treated differently? He withdrew it next day, but only after it was pointed out by everyone, including Derbyshire, that he was out of order.

As Peter Lever said: 'If only I'd had him in his early days, he would never have missed a Test match in the last two or three years.' He has wasted his time by having only half an England career. He didn't want to listen, and he'll have to live with that, not me. I honestly don't think I could have done any more.

I was also criticised first by Devon, when he broke his touring contract by writing without clearance, and then by all those media who were not in South Africa but back home in England. The common thread among those three cases of the wrong sort of headlines, for which I was blamed, is that they were all caused by non-cricketing journalists.

There is not one of the regular cricketing correspondents who is afraid to approach me on any subject on a friendly basis. I know I have to be a bit more careful with one or two, but that is only because of the type of sports desk they work for. I would be amazed if any one of them said that their job was harder, not easier, since I took over.

To prove the point, I was thanked by journalists from both countries after the final press conference on the last day of the tour in Port Elizabeth at the end of the seventh one-day international. They made a point of coming to me to say how much they appreciated my co-operation throughout the tour.

Also, when I got home, John Thicknesse of the *Evening Standard* went out of his way to telephone me to say the same thing. He has been on over 20 tours, and told me that I had been more helpful to the press than any other manager he had toured with. I am not putting it forward as anything special to be popular with the press, but I am pleased that they appreciated that I did my job with them to the best of my ability, and that by doing so had helped them.

It might be argued that I should be more careful when speaking to other press men, either the cricket number twos or feature writers who are always looking for a different angle. That was certainly the point put to me about that pre-Ashes tour lunch in London. All I know, I was asked questions and I answered them. Surely, it is unreasonable to say that I should have known that my answers would have been slanted in the most sensational way.

I have never dodged an answer, and I am not going to start now. The journalists I deal with regularly know one thing: the first time they stuff me, either by putting me on the record when I am not, or by mis-reporting facts, will be the last.

I think everyone learned a lesson in the Lord's Test against the West Indies, when they went overboard about changing the wicket-keeper. I didn't mind that, because they were the ones who had to back-track more than they should have, had they analysed the sequence of events better. I did object to the story floated that Mike was so fed up about the issue that he was ready to resign as captain.

We've all got a job to do. I do mine to the best of my ability, and have honestly tried to help them do the same.

THE FUTURE I have had my say about English cricket, and where we might improve things. I have always been a supporter of a split county championship with promotion and relegation. The two advantages are obvious ones. The public would see more games later in the season of vital importance to one side or the other, or perhaps both.

As it is, by the end of July, only a handful of sides can win the championship. The players would also benefit, because they would not be playing in so many 'dead games'. I understand the reluctance of the counties to give up some traditional fixtures, as would happen, but if the two leagues of nine had at least three up and down, I am sure the incentive and opportunity to get into the first division would benefit everyone, players and spectators alike.

If I have one big moan, it is about the Sunday League. I don't think you should have a match within a match, so the sooner the 40-over competition is shifted, the better. It is asking too much of players, which is why so many clubs rest key players as soon as they are out of contention for the title. That is not fair on the sponsors or the public.

The other thing we must look at is the uncovering of pitches. It is no argument to say that we must cover them because we don't play Tests on uncovered pitches. I played most of my cricket on uncovered pitches, and I know that they produce better batsmen and bowlers. People think they are impossible to bat on. Untrue. You can get a pudding, slow in pace and not dangerous. Then the sun gets on it and for an hour or two, bowlers have to cash in, *if they are good enough*. And that means being able to bowl the right line and length all the time. Also, that length might alter from one pitch to another, so a bowler must be able to adapt accurately. If bowlers cannot exploit the conditions, they are punished. Once they learn that lesson, they become better bowlers. In turn, that will bring an improvement in batting technique, otherwise batsmen cannot survive.

Uncovered pitches will definitely produce better cricketers and, if the run-ups are uncovered also, the spinners are bound to be used more. We did it all wrong in the one season of experimenting a few years ago, when we uncovered the pitches, but covered the run-ups. As for the fact that the public see more cricket now as soon as it stops raining, they might see a bit less with uncovered pitches, but what they do watch will be a lot more interesting.

The same with batsmen. They have to learn to cope with a greater variety of conditions, which means that when they get on a good pitch, they have a better, all-round technique. The biggest difference between the modern batsman and players like John Edrich, Colin Cowdrey, Tom Graveney, and Dennis Amiss, Graham Gooch and Keith Fletcher of the more modern era, is that they could play in so many different ways, while the player of today knows only one way.

I have already said that Hick is not far off being a great player, but his method is one-dimensional. It is not his fault, but it is the fault of the system.

ENGLAND SET-UP There is not much to alter. I like to think that we have got the preparation for a Test mostly right. Under our present county and Board system, we can't expect much more than we get, until I, or whoever follows me, is given the authority to pull the odd player out of a county match. I have mentioned the case of Cork, but also there was Gough. Yorkshire said he was fit, even though they knew I was not convinced. They proved the point to me by not playing him in four-day cricket for over a month in 1995, although they risked him in the one-day competitions. He came through all right but either he was fit to bowl or he wasn't. You can't be partly pregnant, and it was the same with him.

Unless we go down the same road as South Africa and Australia and contract our Test players to the Board, we are always going to struggle. And we can't do that unless we knock down the amount of domestic cricket we play, and I don't think I would be in favour of that. Chicken and egg, really, which is why I think we have to make do and mend.

What has happened in the last few years is that the rest of the major Test playing countries have caught us up. We didn't send a full side to tour Pakistan or India until the late 1970s, but now they are as hard to beat as anyone.

Until we produce more flair players, and county cricket is not geared for that, we are always going to have to work hard to make the most of what we have got. I am full of hope, because we now have a captain who is tough enough to build on the foundation he has helped me to put down in the last couple of years. My cricket philosophy has always been to make as few unforced mistakes as possible. England are now definitely harder to beat than they were before I took over.

The winning habit is the next step.

AFTERWORD ON THE WORLD CUP

The England World Cup campaign got off to a stuttering start with the narrow defeat by New Zealand, and only the unnecessarily elongated format of the competition enabled the side to progress to the last eight. Defeats against the three major countries played, New Zealand, South Africa and Pakistan, gave England a quarter-final tie against Sri Lanka instead of India but, in the light of the spectacular batting exploits of Arjuna Ranatunga's team, that particular straw was too short to grasp successfully. As a result, the England players and management watched the two dramatic semi-finals and final from the comfort of their own homes, with the inevitable inquests filling all the available column inches in the English press.

Illingworth
I know we got a lot of stick for our results, and I can't argue with that. I do take issue with those who said our preparation was lacking in thoroughness, because we had decent practice facilities only twice. The Gymkhana ground in Karachi was a pleasure to practise on for three days after the poor facilities in Peshawar and Rawalpindi, and the other good facilities were in Faisalabad, where we got some flak because we didn't use the match ground.

That was because we had arranged for a lot of bowlers for a ground that adjoined the hotel, and they gave us a pitch in the middle. Also, the game was not under lights, so we went for the best batting conditions.

Our main problem was the one we had in the last three weeks of the tour of South Africa – we never once batted as a

273

unit. I don't go along with criticism of the batting order, because I think there is room for a pinch hitter at the top, providing the tactic is used flexibly. The 15-over rule has changed one-day cricket completely, as Sri Lanka showed with their normal openers. But that is the only way they play, whereas other sides don't all have a couple of such class dashers to open.

That said, I don't think we were flexible enough at times with our batting order once the game had started. I'm not pointing the finger at Mike, because he is still learning the job, and one of the last things to complete a captain's education is how best to respond more quickly to the ebb and flow situations of one-day cricket.

I'm not shifting responsibility but, once we'd picked the side and chatted about the starting line-up, I don't believe that part of my job is to be heavy-handed about chopping and changing the order.

Where we struggled was that hardly any of our batsmen came to terms with the fact that, for most of the time, they had to put the pace on the ball. Jack Russell, Neil Fairbrother and Alec Stewart are three cases in point, which strengthened the case for letting Alec keep, I suppose. Rightly or wrongly, I paid more attention to the fact that Jack now has the most level-headed approach of anyone and I hoped that would get him through with the bat.

Even so, if any of our top four had just once played the sort of dominant major innings I know they're capable of, at least two matches would have had different results. I acknowledge that our bowling was limited and shown up on those pitches, but they were hardly ever given a chance to defend proper totals.

The only time we got a good start was against Pakistan, and then Mike and Robin Smith both got out in quick succession to poor strokes. If one goes, then the other has to tick things over while the next batsman settles in. That didn't happen and we wasted a good position and lost the match.

In the match against South Africa, the crucial factor was that we bowled for 45 minutes with a wet ball and then, during the interval, the pitch dried into a tacky surface. Pat Symcox agreed that more happened off it when they bowled, purely because of the changed surface.

As for New Zealand, they would have been 10 for two had we caught two slip catches. You can't cater for those sort of errors, and I am not putting this forward as an excuse. We got what we deserved, and I am very disappointed that my second year, and my only one as manager, ended on such a flat note.

The biggest disappointment of all is that for most of the South African trip I thought we had pulled the touring side of things around. I have made a lot of the awful hour on the second day of the Cape Town Test, but Test cricketers should have the mental steel to come back from even that sort of gut-wrenching blow.

I said when I was appointed that the buck would stop with me, because I had asked for and been given total accountability. Having seen the players I picked at close quarters for nearly six months, I now know that it is a tougher job than I thought. You can talk to players, but you can't think and play for them.

I was disappointed to hear that I'd been challenged for the chair, with Warwickshire and Surrey nominating David Graveney. As it turned out, he withdrew because of possible areas of conflict with his position as general secretary of the Cricketers' Association. I would have thought that, anyway, the counties would have listened in the first place to their own executive committee, and Dennis Silk, who spent a lot of time last winter on tour with us. Quite rightly, he emphasised the disadvantage we were under, compared with other countries, because of the selfish attitude of most of our county clubs. Nothing much will change until the players are contracted to the Board.

It may, on the fact of it, ill behove the wearer of two hats – co-author and president of the body (the Cricketers' Association) that employs David Graveney – to deny him the wearing of the extra hat of chairman of selectors.

Graveney was advised – the word 'instruction' was at his request – of the various potential clashes of interest. Warwickshire officials – notably chief executive Dennis Amiss – were even more forcibly advised over a much longer period of time prior to the announcement of Graveney's nomination, but chose to ignore it. They thought that serving two masters, as an employee of the TCCB and of the Cricketers' Association would not lead to conflict.

The TCCB, soon to become the English Cricket Board, resisted a misguided attempt to remove Illingworth. They were right because there have been many more plus factors than minus ones in his two years in charge. Or, rather, one year in total charge, with the real disappointment the poor performances from Cape Town onwards. Of course he made mistakes – Warwickshire people will never believe he got the best out of Dermot Reeve and Neil Smith – but his year as manager highlighted several crucial faults in the England set-up. A few days after he had been confirmed as chairman of selectors, he announced that he was no longer to continue as team manager, his one-year contract for that role now at an end.

Illingworth
I have stepped down as manager for two reasons: first, the public perception of the tour to South Africa and of the World Cup campaign was that they were not as successful as should be expected. Second, I felt that it was time to allow a younger man to be in charge of all aspects of coaching, which I hope will be of benefit to everyone, especially the players, who always have been, and will remain, my priority.

Although he was blasted for the heretic suggestion that the 45 wives and family who descended on Durhan, Port Elizabeth and Cape Town did not actually improve the party's chance of success, the fact is that team spirit off the field was inevitably fragmented. When Australia and South Africa allow it, then the England authorities might have a case.

What the Illingworth two years have shown, is what the TCCB missed 10 years ago when they should have given him the same powers then. Too little too late must be the verdict, but that was not the responsibility of Raymond Illingworth, who has never changed in outlook in the 40 years I have known him. And I hope he never will.

England have one consolation. There are not reported cases of any supporters committing suicide (India and Pakistan had several). No television owner blasted the screen out with a shot-gun (India). The TCCB did not sack Michael Atherton and the management during the tournament. Richie Richardson jumped before he was pushed, and the West Indies' management did it the other way around. Atherton has still to have his effigy burned in public, or have a police squad guarding his house. But then, as a section of the British media would have it; we do not take our cricket seriously enough.

INDEX

Index